CHRISTIANS AND MUSLIMS IN THE COMMONWEALTH
A Dynamic Role in the Future

CHRISTIANS AND MUSLIMS IN THE COMMONWEALTH
A Dynamic Role in the Future

edited by
Anthony O'Mahony and Ataullah Siddiqui

ALTAJIR WORLD OF ISLAM TRUST

Firrst published 2001
by
Altajir World of Islam Trust
11 Elvaston Place London SW7 5QG
Tel: 020 7581 3522
Fax: 020 7584 1977

ISBN 1 901435 08 3

The Bismillah *on the cover is reproduced by kind permission*
of the calligrapher, Dr Ahmed Moustafa.

Edited by Leonard Harrow
Produced by Fox Communication and Publication,
London, E18 2PW
Printed in England by the St Edmundsbury Press

CONTENTS

Participants at the Cumberland Lodge Conference, Windsor, July 2000.

ST. JAMES'S PALACE

This conference brings together two particular concerns of mine; to create better understanding between people of different faiths and to use more effectively the Commonwealth's unique position as a hospitable meeting-place for different cultures. So I am delighted that the King George VI and Queen Elizabeth Foundation of St Catharine's should be joining the Altajir World of Islam Trust and the Commonwealth Foundation to look again at interfaith understanding and co-operation within the Commonwealth.

Sadly, I cannot join you in this. But I much look forward to receiving the report on your conference proceedings and reading your thoughts on what we can all do to improve understanding between our two communities. I also wanted to send my very best wishes to all of you taking part. Your assessment of the roles of Commonwealth Christians and Muslims in the preservation and development of traditional values at the beginning of this new century is of real importance, and I wish you the most fruitful of discussions.

FOREWORD

Just over a year ago a gathering of international academics and other concerned experts came together to discuss possible options and scenarios for developing ways by which Commonwealth Christians and Muslims could develop their mutual interests and concerns within a global context.

The conference was hosted and organised by the King George VI and Queen Elizabeth Foundation of St Catharine's, sometimes referred to, by way of shorthand, as 'Cumberland Lodge', its home in the Great Park, Windsor. It did so in association with the Altajir World of Islam Trust.

What was considered by the conference is set out in the following pages. Sufficient here to say that the organisers were as broad-minded as we had hoped and optimistic as to what was likely to be achieved by the participants, many of whom were meeting each other for the first time! But readers will judge our collective efforts for themselves.

Our gratitude goes out to all our organisers, contributors and participants and our greetings to old and new friends who will follow in our footsteps.

Alistair Charteris Duncan
Director, Altajir World of Islam Trust
London, September 2001

CONTRIBUTORS

The Rt Revd and Rt Hon Richard Chartres, Bishop of London

HRH Prince El-Hassan bin Talal of Jordan

Revd Professor Michael Taylor, Selly Oak Colleges, University of Birmingham

Anthony O'Mahony, Director of Research, Centre for Christianity and Interreligious Dialogue, Heythrop College, University of London.

Ataullah Siddiqui, The Islamic Foundation, Markfield, Leicestershire.

Revd Phillip Lewis, Interfaith Advisor to the Anglican Bishop of Bradford

Peter Riddell, Director, Centre for Islamic Studies, London Bible College

Dato' Ismail Bin Haji Ibrahim, Director-General, the Institute of Islamic Understanding, Malaysia.

Anthony Johns, Emeritus Professor, Australian National University, Canberra

Revd Matthew Hassan Kukah, Secretary-General, Catholic Secretariat of Nigeria

Rt Revd Kenneth Cragg, Retired Honorary Assistant Bishop, Oxford

Revd Christopher Lamb, Rector in South Warwickshire and Canon Theologian of Coventry Cathedral.

Revd Canon John Ovenden, Canon of Windsor, Chaplain to the Great Park and to St Catharine's

INTRODUCTION

Today, contemporary society and culture are in search of a spiritual soul and religious identity, which will satisfy its longing. To date it would seem that the political world, has not readily understood this changing reality. One observer has recently commented: 'The Western culture of modernity and the institutions of international society embedded in it are being challenged by the global resurgence of religion and cultural pluralism in international relations. As a result of this large-scale religious change international society is becoming a genuinely multicultural international society for the first time. A new approach to international order is required which overcomes the 'Westphalian presumption' in international relations. This is the notion that religious and cultural pluralism can be accommodated in international society, but must be privatised, marginalised, or even overcome—by an ethic of cosmopolitianism—if there is to be international 'order'.[1] These observations find an echo in the thought of the Irish-American writer and political scientist David Walsh, 'Even the discovery of God does not lift us out of this world. For as long as he wills it we must remain in this life to work out as best we can the meaning and direction we must follow within it. The light of transcendent illumination is a piercing beam from beyond, but it does not illuminate the surrounding area. The mystery of the whole remains. The difficulty of articulating the consequences of revelation for the

---

[1] Scott M Thomas, 'Taking Religious and Cultural Pluralism Seriously: The Global Resurgence of Religion and the Transformation of International Society', *Millennium: Journal of International Relations*, Vol. 29, no.3 (2000), pp. 815-841, p. 815. See also by the same author: 'Religious resurgence, postmodernism and world politics', *Religion and Global Order*, (ed) John L Esposito and Michael Watson, University of Wales Press, Cardiff, 2000, pp. 38-65.

modern secular world is evident in the confusion concerning the relationship between religion and politics.'[2]

One crucial and important contour of our contemporary situation is the relationship between Christianity and Islam as religious traditions and between individual Muslims and Christians. A sense of crisis and opportunity seems to characterise the relationship between these two Abrahamic faiths, for the engagement is both difficult and problematic one the one hand, and expressive of new hope and creative possibility on the other. The essays in this volume, which are in turn based upon the St Catharine's Conference, 6-9 July 2000, Cumberland Lodge, Windsor Great Park, 'Christians and Muslims in the Commonwealth: a Dynamic Role in the Future', give expression and support to these two tendencies.

A vital component of our contemporary situation is the growth of a certain awareness among the world's religious communities of the Other. The engagement between the religions has been characterised by two points of orientation, one of fear and one of hope, both elements poised between, on the one hand, by conflict and on the other, a deepening realization of the necessity and possibility of dialogue. The re-discovery of compassion was one of the main themes of the Conference and one participant, Anthony H Johns, noted 'How can one re-discover what has never yet been fully realized ... such a compassion, in its fullness, is at best, something only dreamt of; or like the lost chord, is heard but once, and then vanishes into silence. Yet the memory of its haunting beauty has such power that it compels all who have ever heard it, to search to recover it, without ceasing.' One might say that the history of ecumenism and interreligious dialogue will be the history of growth and development of this awareness and of actions inspired by it, and of changes brought about in the direct relation to this creative virtue of engagement. However, this does allow for some sought of neutral position *vis-à-vis* ones own religious identity and the Other. Those who adopt a theoretical, privileged position outside any specific faith community, and elaborate a general structure of religious 'truth' that can provide a space for every religious tradition, but which nobody believes in, will not satisfy.

---

[2] David Walsh, *Guarded by Mystery. Meaning in a Postmodern Age*, The Catholic University of America Press, Washington, DC, 1999, p. 99.

The Christian and Muslim communities combined represent a third of humanity and an understanding of their historical and theological relationship is of the utmost contemporary importance. The papers presented here stand as testament to the multiple dimensions of how the relations between Muslims and Christians operate today within the context of the Commonwealth. Individual papers deal with the situation in Australia, Britain, India, Malaysia and Nigeria, whilst others try to grapple with the historical, political and theological dimensions of Muslim-Christian relations. However, what they have to say is relevant to other contexts as the engagement between these two Arabhamic traditions—Christianity and Islam— takes on a global reality. All the contributors give expression to this relationship in a number of committed essays presented here and which represent both up-to-date scholarly analysis of situations and or expressions of a deep personal and spiritual reflection. The Conference showed that a spirit and endeavour is now beginning to animate encounters between Christians and Muslims in the Commonwealth and beyond, 'looking ahead together to a world in the future'.

*THE ROLE OF RELIGION
IN SOCIETY*

FAITH IN THE 21ST CENTURY
A REFLECTION
Rt Revd and Rt Hon Richard Chartres,
Bishop of London

The *Discourses* of Rumi begin with this reflection, 'The Prophet, on whom be peace, said: The worst of scholars is he who visits Princes, and the best of Princes is he who visits scholars.' The great mystic's meditation on this dictum is instructive, but suffice it to say that it is a great privilege to be sharing this gathering with HRH Prince Hassan who is also an internationally acknowledged scholar. We think not only of his own publications but of the way he has inspired the Royal Academy for Islamic Civilisation Research and institutes like the Arab Thought Club. More than that, his own visits, I think especially of his compassionate meeting with Leah Rabin, have made a courageous contribution to peace-building in today's world.

It is an honour to be here as someone who is neither a prince nor a profound scholar but merely a bishop. Bishops must always remember the saying of St Ignatius of Antioch that 'A bishop never resembles Jesus Christ more, than when he has his mouth shut.'

I take courage, however, from the boldness of St Catherine, patron of this conference, who embodied the dynamic power of faith. It seems to me that the ancient world attempted to control women, principally by denying them higher education and by early marriage. Catherine who confuted the philosophers of Alexandria and refused the bridegroom chosen for her by Caesar stands for new possibilities opened out by faith.

I am also a trustee of another St Catherine's Foundation which, under the direction of the Holy Community, seeks to assist the work of the monastery in the Sinai where the remains of the St Catherine are preserved. This place, where Moses was granted his vision of God and which is sacred to all three Abrahamic religions, is one of the great symbols of hope for the 21st century. In the monastic enclosure you will find a mosque for the Muslims, the Jebeliyya, who have protected the community throughout the centuries. In the library, you will find copies of the letter from the Prophet himself, which guaranteed the monks safe passage in their journeys throughout the Islamic world.

> 'O men, behold we have created you all out of a male
> and a female, and have made you into nations and tribes
> so that you might come to know one another.'
> (The Holy Qur'an, Surah 49)

I rejoice in this conference and in the Commonwealth which draws us together so that we might know one another.

One of the most obvious features of the century into which we are moving, as we consider together faith in the 21st century, is the growing interconnectedness of a wired-up world with its developing global economy. Once homogeneous societies are becoming plural and once geographically concentrated faith communities are becoming dispersed around the world.

There are obvious challenges and possibilities in this development. Within faith communities there is now the possibility for co-religionists, living in different parts of the world, to communicate more easily and to learn from one another. As Christians in Britain experience growing religious pluralism in their own country, there are clearly resources in the Indian Christian experience of centuries of pluralism which have great value for us.

At the same time, it is already possible for relations between faith communities in one part of the world to be modelled in a way that is useful on a wider canvas. I am thinking particularly of initiatives like the visit made by the Bishop of Bradford and Muslim leaders from that city to Pakistan in 1998—an example of one of the fruits of the new dispersal of faith communities.

One major challenge confronting all people of faith together, however, is the belligerent McUtopianism of what the late Ernest Gellner named 'Consumer Unbeliever International'.

No less an authority than George Soros said of money, 'What used to be a medium of exchange has usurped the place of fundamental values, reversing the relationship postulated by economic theory. The cult of success has replaced a belief in principles. Society has lost its anchor.' A situation in which the 40 richest individuals in the world dispose of more wealth than the poorest 40 percent of the world's population is clearly unsustainable and contrary to the teaching of the Abrahamic religions as the Jubilee 2000 campaign on international debt has insisted.

At the same time faith communities all face the consequences of a new world disorder in which there is more than a risk that religion will be manipulated for godless ends.

The dissolution of the Soviet Union brought to a close a period in which inter-state contacts were the dominant threat to international order before the fall of the Berlin Wall. Instead we have seen intra-state conflicts, ethnic conflicts often fortified by religious rhetoric and symbols, and secession struggles become the norm. The war continues, albeit at a lower level of intensity in Chechnya, while in Africa the agony of the people of Angola seems to have no end. About 28 million people have been killed in 150 major armed conflicts fought mainly in the 'two-thirds world' since 1945. According to UNICEF figures, whereas only 5 percent of the casualties in World War I were civilians, now as our century ends the proportion has risen to at least 80 percent civilians, most of them women and children.

The task of managing the conflicts that cause such suffering is still largely the province of international institutions, which are constructed on the system of state sovereignty and the doctrine of non-interference which the new generation of conflicts undermine. The events in former Yugoslavia find the international community struggling to respond to internal conflicts which only tangentially affect the national interests of states with the capacity to intervene but which seem to present humanitarian imperatives to 'do something' nevertheless.

The question arises at this point as to whether the faith communities may have a contribution to make in this field. It is a question that is arousing some academic interest in Britain as many of the participants in the conference can attest. Westminster, one of the new universities in London, recently organised a symposium under the title of 'Diplomacy and Divinity: Religion in International Relations'. The same theme was the subject of a debate in Parliament last autumn initiated by the Archbishop of Canterbury. A number of participants stressed the religious dimension of some contemporary violent conflicts.

Their anxiety is widely shared at varying levels of sophistication. It is the orthodoxy of the lounge bar of 'The Pig and Whistle' in England that 'the most terrible wars in history have been wars of religion.' It is difficult to understand why this phrase is still so widely repeated, after the 20th century's evidence of the homicidal character of the secular messianic state, but it is undoubtedly part of the folk wisdom.

At a different level, in the Anglo-American world, the book by Professor Samuel Huntingdon published in 1996 and called *The Clash of Civilizations and the Remaking of World Order* has been influential. As you know, the thesis is that the post-Cold War world is being reconfigured along cultural lines.

Professor Huntingdon argues that the hot spots in world politics are now to be found on the fault lines between civilisations and he cites Bosnia, the Sudan, and the Middle East among other examples.

One ingredient in these confrontations, he alleges, is a pattern of conflict between Muslims and Christians. Huntingdon asserts that the causes of this conflict lie not in 'transitory phenomena' but they flow from 'the nature of the two religions and the civilisations based on them.' His apprehensions have proved influential.

It is evident that many of the violent conflicts in the modern world are rooted in threats to identity and they are misunderstood if analysed in merely Marxist terms. We only have to look across the Irish Sea to acknowledge the truth of this proposition. Religion in many parts of the world is crucial to social cohesion and is therefore likely to be co-opted in any struggle which centres on the identity of any particular group or people.

Folk wisdom understands how the highest ideals are bent to the most malign purposes. As Jonathan Swift, an Irish dean and the author of *Gulliver's Travels*, lamented, 'how is it that we have just enough religion to hate one another but not enough to love one another?'

There is of course another view given pithy expression in Professor David Martin's sparkling recent book *Does Christianity Cause*

War? His answer is 'no' but he imagines an eloquent opponent arguing that 'religion is the singular virus which more than anything else undermines the red corpuscles of reason and persuades us to evil courses: too many offspring, burning books in Bradford, patriarchy, fundamentalist insurgency in Algeria, sexual repression.'

As a believer, I can very easily see the perils of religion and I can sympathise with the position adopted by a great 18th century clergyman of the Church of England, Bishop Warburton. The bishop was said to occupy a small corner of reasonableness within the Ark 'as much disgusted by the stink within, as by the tempest without'. A fair degree of humility is required, I think, by members of all faith communities.

The trouble seems to be that if we do not exercise our faculty for worship in a worthy tradition then the vacuum is filled by something unworthy. In this century that vacuum has been occupied by the *Ersatz* liturgies of the messianic state according to Stalin or Hitler.

Is it possible, however, to move beyond the idea that reasonable religion serves to occupy the space where cults of unreason may otherwise flourish? Are there in our faith traditions positive spiritual resources within the traditions and institutions of the world's faith communities, especially in Islam and Christianity, capable of making a contribution to peacemaking in the 21st century? Is it possible that 'Religion' is *The Missing Dimension of Statecraft*, as the title of an influential book,[1] published in 1994, suggests? Obviously in what follows I am referring to a 'dimension' of a multi-track approach to preventing and transforming violent conflict and not a substitute for other approaches.

There is certainly great resistance to the idea that religion has any positive contribution to make in the Anglo-American world. Religion has often been edited out of grown-up Anglo-American discourse and relegated to the realm of private taste. This attitude can have serious consequences. It seems obvious now that US monitoring of Iranian politics ought always to have included the religious dimension but as a report from the Washington-based Center

---

[1]   Douglas Johnston and Cynthia Sampson (eds.), *Religion, the Missing Dimension of Statecraft*, Oxford University Press, 1994.

for Strategic and International Studies has revealed, 'the one recorded attempt to do just that within the CIA, before the revolution, was vetoed on the grounds that it would amount to mere sociology, a term used in intelligence circles to mean the time-wasting study of factors deemed politically irrelevant.'

The proposition that the role of religion in society would inevitably decline in the process of third world modernisation, just as it had in 18th- and 19th-century Europe, now appears more questionable.

It is true that there continues to be a crisis in the faith tradition of the West, rather than in Christianity as a worldwide phenomenon. Here, there are a large number of people, still in retreat from compulsory chapel at school, who cling to the old orthodoxy that modernisation and secularisation go hand in hand. They expect to see the pattern, enacted in our history since the 17th century, replicated throughout the rest of the world.

The ideas and the spiritual posture of this secular West European culture are still a potent missionary force in the world. It is a culture that emerged partly out of a struggle which expelled religion from public, though not from social life. It has given rise to the first truly global culture, Consumer Unbeliever International. The achievements of this culture are undeniable. It has brought an unprecedented standard of healthcare prosperity to hundreds of millions in the world today.

Consumer Unbeliever International continues to be inspired by the idea of growth without limits, with no other end in view beyond the process itself. This idea, dominant for the past half century, is still exerting a potent influence on the whole world. So engagement with this culture must constitute an imperative for Muslims and Christians in the century to come.

This modem project of growth without limits and with no end in view beyond the process itself arises from a particular way of seeing and thinking which has arisen in Europe and via America has been exported throughout the globe. It is a tradition which has hardened into a spiritual disposition with implications for the whole world. If there are to be centuries of faith to come, which will be a blessing to the world community, then we have to recognise the seriousness of the spiritual challenge that faces us.

We must not only recognise the challenge but be able to point to possible ways forward.

At the heart of West European experience there has been a contest between two figures, Christ and Prometheus, 'the Forethinker'. The 16th-century French philosopher Charles de Bouvelles compared the emancipated human being with Prometheus. He presented the Titan's theft of fire, his seizure of power from the Olympians, as a decisive, creative act. It was an act which allowed human beings to change their nature.

In his book *De Sapiente* written in 1509 de Bouvelles pictures a human being as 'no longer part of the universe but as its eye and mirror; and indeed as a mirror that does not receive the images of things from outside but that rather forms and shapes them in itself.' It is a small example of the potential of our Muslim-Christian dialogue that I am glad to acknowledge my indebtedness to Professor Seyyed Hossein Nasr for directing my attention to this text.

As such a being looks out on the world around, he sees not an animated nature in which he is a participant but simply matter to be exploited. Dominance has been substituted for connectedness in the relation between the Forethinker and the universe around him. Later, Descartes frankly confessed that the motive behind his method of reasoning, which followed the psychological shift prefigured in de Bouvelles, was to make man *maître* and *possesseur de la terre*—'maker and possessor of the earth'. So it has proved.

The cost has been very great. Prometheus was punished. An ancient vase painting shows him with a pillar driven through his middle, being attacked by an eagle. It seems to me that the bird represents the mental world of the Forethinker. It is significant that every day the eagle comes to devour his liver, the seat of the intuitive life. It is true that all that is consumed by day, grows back under the cover of darkness. This is yet further testimony, however, like Jung's discernment of the archetypes in the Collective Unconsciousness, of the inability of the great symbols and intuitive wisdom in our own time to influence the Western daylight world.

In consequence, the ambitions of Prometheus have become literally inordinate. The development of the rational calculating faculty at the expense of other ways of knowing and seeing has entailed great distress both in the landscape of the world around and in the inner life.

Contemplative attention enables one to participate in the universe. The avid manipulative gaze can identify only a world of objects to be exploited. The capacity to be aware of the sacred and animated character of the cosmos has been diminished.

Finally, as we read back the evidence of the world we dominate into ourselves, we can only see ourselves as objects, all surface and no depth. Under the rhetoric, which suggests a high doctrine of human dignity, there is in fact a growing despair about human life reflected in high suicide rates and the search for oblivion in drug-induced fantasies

At the same time, it is obvious that people are having greater and greater difficulties in relating to one another in families and neighbourhoods and in any community which requires long term commitment. There is no better nursery of confident individuals than a loving and stable family. Obviously, however, if the accent is on the rights of the individual to choose his pleasures without constraint then relationships of all kinds are undermined. Dis-related pleasure-seeking ultimately erodes the social institutions in which individuals are given a sense of personal worth and identity.

Modernity, however, was the outcome of a particular set of historical circumstances and spiritual options. It is not our inevitable destiny.

Its limits are being disclosed while at the same time we are learning again, sometimes painfully, that human beings without God are denied their full human potential. Does not sexuality become stale and meaningless when the reverberations between our intercourse and the great drama of love and the creation of life can no longer be heard? Can every rite of passage be abolished and every sanctuary demolished without humankind being degraded into a utensil? How long is it before we run out of arguments why clever machines should not inherit the earth from us? We have great power to explore outer space but the inner spaces are in great confusion. We have huge wealth and technical ability but we can only use it to construct a dome as a canopy to cover confusion.

I believe that in a world dominated by Prometheus, the Christ figure offers spiritual DNA of incalculable significance. I am by no means gloomy as I look to a new century. Prometheus stands for the individual isolate, the Forethinker all of whose powers of knowing have contracted to the rational calculating faculty. Christ is the bridge-builder who shows us the social nature of God and of the creation. Here is an integrative vision which values the uniqueness of every person but which sees that persons grow to their full stature to the extent to which they are in loving communion.

We have to admit, however, to a real problem in re-connecting in the West with the spiritual DNA conveyed by the Christ figure. We have turned our Promethean way of seeing, our manipulative gaze upon our own religious narratives and traditions. In becoming merely an object of our thought, God becomes implausible.

I have the privilege of being present when people are confirmed in the Christian way. I always spend time with them beforehand to elicit their understanding of what they are doing. Although the liturgy clearly asks them to confess that they 'believe and trust in God', an astonishing number of candidates seem to think that they are principally giving their assent to various mental notions about God. No wonder so many of them are disillusioned in this God of their own confection when they experience one of life's crises.

For so many people in the West, though not in the many parts of the world where the Church is expanding with astonishing vitality, the Christian way has become stale and excessively cerebral.

We are fortunate, however, in modern Europe in the presence of believers from many different faith traditions, Muslims from all over the world, and not least Christians with an African or Asian inheritance. They have offered a salutary challenge and wisdom which in my own experience is capable of recalling us to aspects of the Christian way which are present in the teaching and person of Christ but which have lain bedridden in the dormitory of the soul— to use Coleridge's expressive phrase.

We Europeans, however, cannot simply unlearn the critical approach to religious traditions. It is a tradition which has undermined bogus authorities and has liberated the Christ who was a captive of a power-hungry church.

There can be, however, more sinister results of the attempt to unlearn the critical approach. It can lead to the modern disease of fundamentalism which pays an unwilling tribute to the dominance of the scientific mode of establishing truth. Fundamentalism is the pretence that religious truth can be established in the same way as scientific truth by being measured, photographed and enumerated by any detached observer.

Alongside the new fundamentalism there is a new credulity. Since all the most important questions in life about its meaning and value have been emptied into the realm of unverifiable private opinion, then no one has the right to comment on the sincerely held beliefs of others, no matter how absurd. In Britain we have discovered that when you cease to believe in Christianity, it is not that you come to believe in nothing but that you believe in anything.

Take the phenomenon of astrology. There are ways of presenting astrology which offer us some sophisticated meditations on the dynamics of human affairs rather in the manner of the *I Ching*, but even knowledgeable astrologers will tell you that the value of generalised musings on our sun signs, the stuff of tabloid astrology, are of little value.

Yet the astrology sections of our popular publications certainly allow more space to fantasy than is ever given to expressions of the wisdom traditions of Islam and Christianity.

The Express newspaper is celebrating its victory over *The Mail* in luring away one of the highest paid seers in the country, Jonathan Cainer the astrologer. You have to take it seriously because there is so much money at stake and indeed frivolity is punished. A few years ago, according to an article in *The Economist*, embarrassed by the non-appearance of its regular astrologer, one newspaper handed the job over to a cynical hack. He relieved his boredom by writing under one sign, 'all the sorrows of yesteryear are as nothing compared with what will befall you today.' He was sacked when the switchboard was jammed with panicking readers.

Paul Ricoeur one of the most significant Christian theologians writing today suggests that the first naiveté of primordial openness to religious symbolism is not open to Westerners. A second openness of belief, flowing from the creative imagination working with the Biblical narratives, is, however, possible. More than that I believe that it illuminates the way in which Jesus himself taught and led his disciples not to the apprehension of a deposit of objective truths, but through a way which led into truth and life.

Christians understand the Bible as revelation, but I would argue that this is not so much as a deposit of specific timeless truths but as the arena for fission or sometimes fusion which occurs when the Biblical world and the world of the reader come into contact. Revelation is to be understood more in performative rather than in propositional terms.

I should like to reiterate that I find great hope in the unprecedented degree to which the great world religions co-exist. A period has already begun in which the major faith traditions influence one another, just as the religion of Zoroaster profoundly influenced the Jews of the period of the exile from Jerusalem. This is not a matter for fear. My own experience of genuine dialogue between adherents of distinctive faith traditions, who have become friends, is that such dialogue can very often bring into focus elements in the Christian faith which have become obscure in the West European milieu. Beloved Rumi says 'Faith consists in knowing who is one's true friend. When however a man has spent his life in the company of people who lack discrimination, his own discriminative faculty becomes feeble and he is unable to recognise that true friend of the Faith.'

It is sometimes suggested that proclaiming our faith must offend the adherents of other faiths. Speaking as a former Bishop of Stepney, I can say that Muslim friends are scandalised, not by our faith but by the torpor and tepidity of our convictions.

On one occasion, John Foster Dulles, Secretary of State and Eisenhower's right hand, invited an Israeli and a Syrian, a Jew and a Muslim, to meet him in a private heart to heart about the tensions in the Middle East. He began by warmly shaking them by the hand and then asked, 'Why can't we all sit down together and work this thing out like Christian gentlemen?' The anecdote may illustrate a certain cultural myopia but commentators on the negotiations between President Sadat and Mr Begin, which led to the Camp David Agreements, admit the role played by the genuine religious convictions of both men. The religious frame of reference let a little more space into the debate about competing national interests and was conducive to movement and risk-taking.

Experience gained over a number of decades, not least through the work of Prince Hassan and other participants has been fed into contemporary efforts to realise the potential of the faith communities for peace-making in the former Yugoslavia. There is now a carefully worked-out methodology for achieving this. The Centre for Strategic and International Studies has sponsored a project for representatives of faith communities to assist them to become active partners in preventing and transforming conflict. CSIS has held numerous seminars involving about three hundred people in Bosnia and the results of the exercise have been written up by David Steele in an important essay in *Peaceworks* published recently.

Nobody as far as I am aware is calling for the call-up of platoons of clerics and mullahs to shuttle between capitals like *Ersatz* diplomats but we must try to be practical. We must not just use the rhetoric of peace without willing the means and building institutions.

One of the besetting sins of much Christian talk about peace and reconciliation is what Professor David Martin calls 'hyper-moralism'. This stance 'first of all establishes a moral viewpoint sufficiently elevated above all the concrete choices to be made in proximate situations in which it never has to pay the costs of given policies ... At the point where the rapid and limited deployment of violence can avert future conflict say in the Rhineland in 1936, it refuses to act because it is paralysed by generalised guilt.' Hyper-moralism lacks practical wisdom. As we enter the 21st century together as people of faith we have to be clear that our wisdom traditions are imbued with that practical wisdom that is so clear and obvious on every page of the Holy Qur'an and the Holy Scriptures. It is always vital to hold in tension a clear vision of the 'Holy City' founded on blood willingly sacrificed for others with a practical wisdom about the needs of the 'Earthly City' which is built both on blood given and on blood taken. Both hyper-moralism and the complacency that confuses 'being realistic' with 'being imprisoned by the passing moment', are both alike to be avoided like the plague.

With all this in mind I was contemplating the rubble of one of the churches in the City of London, St Ethelburga's in Bishopsgate. The church survived the Civil War, the Great Fire of 1666 and the blitz but not the effects of an IRA bomb in 1993. In the explosion a journalist called Edward Henty was killed and 51 people were injured.

St Ethelburga's is a place which bears the scars of a conflict which does have a religious dimension. This is why, greatly encouraged by the late Cardinal Hume and other Christian friends, I determined to rebuild St Ethelburga's as a Centre for Reconciliation and Peace.

In particular the intention is to focus on the potential of the faith communities, worldwide, in preventing and transforming conflict. We hope to take our place as part of an emerging network devoted to matching means to rhetoric about preventing and transforming violent conflict. We are following here a path already opened up by His Royal Highness.

The partnership which has been established to rebuild the church is itself a sign of reconciliation within the Christian community. The work that is being planned, however, will involve from the outset partnership with members of other faith communities and individuals who simply acknowledge the spiritual dimension of peace-making without any particular institutional allegiances. Although it is a Christian partnership to put together this place, as it was blown to pieces by a Christian quarrel, the intention always is to involve from the outset partnership with members of other faith communities and individuals who acknowledge the spiritual dimension. I am particularly grateful for the support of Zaki Badawi and Professor Haleem of the School of Oriental and African Studies, co-author of a recent book about theories of the just war in Islam and Christianity.[2]

At the macro level the Centre will also be active in raising awareness of the resources offered by faith communities and religious institutions in situations of conflict, and also their potential for exacerbating problems. We all need to be more aware of our responsibilities as people of faith in these areas. As guardians, frequently, of important community symbols we need to be alert to the occasions when silence can make us into accomplices of a slide into violence or when, by what we say, we can contribute to an escalation of hostility by demonising the other side.

St Seraphim of Sarov said that one person with divine peace in the heart can convert the countryside for miles around. Some

---

[2] *The Crescent and the Cross: Muslim and Christian Approaches to War and Peace*, Macmillan, London, 1998.

people engaged in peace studies seem to be very angry and like you I am convinced that there must be a spiritual dimension to peace making. My prayer is that the peace of the all-merciful and compassionate God, the peace that passes all understanding, will irrigate and illuminate the century that lies ahead of us. The consequences if people of faith do not share their wisdom are too dreadful to contemplate.

FAITH IN THE 21st CENTURY
HRH Prince El-Hassan bin Talal

A few years ago, I was invited, as the grandson of a member of the Ottoman Emissaries Council, to visit the Turkish Parliament. After my statement, a Turkish parliamentarian asked, 'Why is it that the British always talk about our empire and their *Commonwealth*?' I thought for a moment. It occurred to me that the concept of the Ottoman empire was essentially a concept of *millet*/community.

I would like to suggest that being invited as an auxiliary speaker at a Commonwealth conference is significant in this context. My country fought alongside the allies in two World Wars, and although we do not actually lay a wreath on behalf of the Arab Legion on Remembrance Day, we identify with it. Further, in terms of both centrism, and moderation, many of us share the values of *millet*—of commonwealth, which is essentially, a read-across.

I would like to quote a former president of a Commonwealth country, President Mandela, who, speaking recently at the Oxford Centre for Islamic Studies, of the increasing recognition and acknowledgement given to African traditional religion for its contribution to humanity's spiritual heritage, said the following:

> The spirit of Ubuntu—that profound African sense that we are human only through the humanity of other human beings—is not a parochial phenomenon, but has added globally to our common search for a better world.[1]

---

[1] *Renewal and Renaissance: Towards a New World Order*—a lecture given in the Sheldonian Theatre, Oxford, 11 July 1997, by Nelson Mandela, President of the Republic of South Africa, published by the Oxford Centre for Islamic Studies.

It is that spirit of sharing in our common humanity that has encouraged me to develop a conversation within a specific framework. First, may I suggest that the emphasis of our conversations be on shared concerns between the adherents of the faiths; secondly, I would highlight the importance of recognising the relevance of culture in any conversation.

In the context of international initiatives, going as far back as the League of Nations, references are made to security and economy, with culture only as an afterthought. The UN is a cultural organisation, yet reference to culture is conspicuous by its absence in UNESCO's mandate. When I put this to Mary Robinson, the High Commissioner for Human Rights, she replied that in human terms culture is implicit in human rights. That is to say that there is no need for a new of independent forum for either interfaith or cultural conversation. I am not so sure.

I recall a thought-provoking discussion with the late Yehudi Menuhin at the time of the recent Balkan disaster in which we noted the references to working against antisemitism. Subsequently, in Runnymede, a stone's throw from here, we talked about working against Islamophobia. However, in Soweto, when I called on Walter Suzulu during a recent visit to that Chapter of the World Conference on Religion and Peace, it was clear that South Africans were tired then of working against *apartheid* and that today, they are tired of working against xenophobia. The time has come to work *for* something.

It is no longer enough to talk glibly of the need for tolerance, patting ourselves on the back all the while for being better than the fanatics. And it is misleading to talk of 'Islam and the West', or the 'West and the Rest', as if the two formed an irreconcilable geopolitical dichotomy.

We recently addressed this problem directly in the context of a meeting of the International Parliamentary Union, held in Amman, by calling for a Parliament of Cultures based on a collective consciousness of the following:

- Respect for life
- A responsibility towards future generations
- Protection of the human habitat/environment

• Altruism, nurtured by a sense of mutual interest and a recognition of human dignity and worth

Building upon this we developed, with the participation of twelve hundred participants in the IPU meeting, a concept based on an earlier intervention at the World Conference of Religion and Peace, under the rubric 'Action for Common Living', and which we hope can be carried to the Council of Europe, for a *Parliament of Cultures*.

In this context the Balkan example is worthy of consideration. We know all too much of the abuses of religion, and many of us recognise the importance of developing a moderate platform. I was heartened to find that Muslim, Orthodox, Catholic and Jewish leaders in the Balkans: were able to state publicly that 'we recognise the importance of the prophets in whom we share, and now the time has come to recognise the significance of the Covenant of Noah.' We talk much of the 'children of Abraham' and I too think that the time has now come to talk about his distinguished forebear as the *Ra'is al-'Ulama'* (the head of the scholars) in Sarajevo proposed at our meeting in the spring. He reminded us that Noah created an ark for the salvation of humanity. Can we now give of our shared humanity to build a new ark for the salvation of our common humanity?

This leads me to reflect on a telephone conversation I had with Richard Holbrook in November 1998, prior to the strike, in which he said that Kosovo reminded him of Somalia, rather than Sarajevo. I asked myself then what sort of hope there is, not for reconstruction, because reconstruction, in terms of bricks and mortar, will happen sooner or later, but for reconciliation.

In this context, I was happy to see that the same Bosnian leaders, who met in Amman, have worked with their sister communities in Kosovo to establish an Inter-Religious Council of Kosovo, dedicated to common living. Muslim-Christian cooperation is now commonplace among many Christian religious leaders who locked arms in solidarity to demand a halt to the almost decade long civil war. I see, therefore, an interplay, a read-across, between the inter-religious and inter-cultural.

In Jakarta I had the opportunity of meeting with a group of people I like to describe as 'positivists' (not activists, which can mean anything at all), but those who actively, or positively, stood up and called for conversation and reconciliation, and many of whom paid the price in one form or another. Their message was this: 'We have just emerged from a situation of martial law. We have freedom and we are trying to exercise it with responsibility, for as we know, freedom from responsibility is the worst form of freedom.' I was deeply moved and we carried on to discuss positive steps that could be taken in terms of crisis avoidance. This, I am glad to report, actually led, in due course, to their receiving the assistance they needed to begin reconciliation projects.

The activists by contrast seek a different end as was illustrated by a question I was asked whilst giving a lecture at the University of Indonesia. One of them stood up and asked stridently: 'How do we Islamise knowledge?', to which my response was that I do not know, but do we have to? This reassured others of my Muslim colleagues who fear, as at times I do, that true dialogue may give way to slogans: expressing extremism on all sides and that we shall continue to talk at, rather than to each other.

Recently, new multilateral and multicultural initiatives have evolved in the world. In our part of the world globalisation (*'awlamah*) is held in deep suspicion. It means material or economic order. Universalisation (*'alamiyyah*) however strikes a chord of recognition, being understood as a reference to universal values, the Universal Declaration of Human Rights.

In this respect it was interesting to observe the reaction of representatives, Indian, Chinese and African to the WIPO (World Intellectual Property Organisation), as regards globalisation. Their unanimous reaction was what is in it for nations? As a bridge-builder, I found that a hard question, post-Seattle.

The World Bank meeting in Seattle was convoked to discuss world trade, but ended up discussing this *ghoul* globalisation and the misunderstandings which resulted only emphasised how vital it is to take into account each nation's point of departure. It would, for example, be absurd when talking of 'intellectual property', to expect the Chinese, with their five thousand years of experience in jade production, to accept a Western concept of protectionism, rather, the conversation should focus on shared values, and a true recognition of the cultural contribution of the other.

In this context, I was fascinated by the attempts of two international institutions to bridge gaps.

First, the World Bank's Comprehensive Development Framework came as an interesting point of departure, which could have pre-empted Seattle. Development, the report suggests, includes all sections of society, most importantly, civil society.

In terms of religious values, it is significant that religious representation, as in the concept of building authority from the bottom up, is actually a part of civil society. But here I must stress again the importance of idiom. If you say *mujtama' madani* in Jakarta, it is understood as seditious, because *madani*/civil, is the opposite of *'askari*/military, thus one must elaborate the concept.

Moving on to the concept of security, I would like secondly, to applaud the work of the UN Human Development Report and its references to human security, not just hard, but soft security—globalisation with a human face. And I believe that this human security demands the convergence of various cultures within the scope of human civilisation, interacting without clashing, enriching and understanding one another.

In terms of culture, may I suggest that some thought too be given to the Erasmus and Socrates programmes, which were developed in Europe after World War II. Attention was given to extra-national cultural forms. Analogy *(qiyas)* was the point of departure.

In interfaith conversations (dialogue between Muslims, Christians and Jews), we have passed through three phases of fear: fear of the other; fear of the folks back home and finally, fear of peace. Sadly, we do not always have a vested interest in peace, for our cultures are so often cultures of exclusion, rather than inclusion, and here the inclusionist model of Erasmus and Socrates is worthy of consideration.

I would also put it to you that in this inter-religious, intercultural humanitarian read-across, the concept of a code of conduct which starts with the premise *la ikrah fi al-din,* no coercion in religion, and which recognises the importance of the relationship between theology and practicality, of a free flow of information, a re-visiting of the educational texts and the development of a framework for disagreement is worthy of consideration.

It was sad that during a recent meeting in Paris the concept of a European Muslim took on a frightening dimension—as a threat. On a more positive note, on a recent visit to Stockholm, I visited an exhibition called the 'Ninety-nine Names of God'. Bearing in mind that it was children, the future leaders of civil society, who acted as guides, I was amazed to find that each guide, whether Muslim, Christian, Jew or Hindu, was able to give a conducted tour of the mock-ups of temples, shrines, mosques etc. and to instruct the visitor in the different cultures and religions. I have not seen its like elsewhere. It represents that extraordinary, liberal other end of the spectrum.

But here I must add a note of caution. Allow me to refer to a warning, given by my dear friend President Vaclav Havel, at the opening of Forum 2000 in Prague. He warned of the increasing polarisation of rich and poor; the human impact of continuing population growth; the poison of ethnic hatred, and the insidious spread of weapons of mass destruction.

It was in the context of addressing these dangerous phenomena, that a report entitled *Winning the Human Race* was issued by the UN Independent Commission on International Humanitarian Issues (ICIHI). The report of the Commission, which I had the honour of co-chairing, proposed *The New International Humanitarian Order* which was adopted by the United Nations General Assembly.

It is important to bear in mind that we have to develop a comprehensive read-across: cultural, inter-religious and humanitarian. Equally important to remember is the fact that in our part of the world, the cluster of water, energy and the human environment is an essential ingredient in international thinking—i.e., thinking without a specific extra-national political agenda. It applies in the Danube Basin, in Kalinagrad, in the Great Lakes and elsewhere: we have to rise above the day-to-day strife, caused by the politics of exclusion.

I am not calling for a single world with a single agenda based on the value system of one culture. Such an agenda, excluding all others, would promote a world in which injustice and marginalisation lead inexorably to conflict and war. By contrast, 'One world with ten thousand cultures', as Professor Mircea Malitza of the University of the Black Sea in Bucharest put it, a world in which commonalities are the foundation, and particularities the cornerstones, will be characterised by cooperation. This is the only possible basis for common living and for the joint action necessary for the construction of a brighter future in which all individuals and communities have the means to achieve their potential.

That we have been able to gather here this week in Cumberland Lodge, in order to examine ways ahead for two of this world's widely distributed religious traditions, augurs well for the aspirations within that 'Variety of Unity' which we all seek.

THE ROLE OF RELIGION IN SOCIETY
Michael H Taylor

I

The scope of this paper must be severely limited from the outset. It cannot deal with religion in general, only with one religion in particular, namely Christianity. That is not of course to deny the significant roles that other religions and indeed non-religious or secular faiths have played in society. It is simply to acknowledge that, whilst I have experienced their almost overwhelming presence in countries like India, Bangladesh and Pakistan within the Commonwealth and Burma, Brazil and Haiti beyond it, and in my own city of Birmingham, I do not know enough about them to pass useful comments. I enjoy many friendships with people of other faiths but I am no expert in inter-faith dialogue. This Christian cobbler will have to stick to his last and hope that what he can say about his own faith tradition will not be entirely irrelevant to relations with the world of Islam or to the problems or opportunities of a multi-faith society, whether global or local, in which all of us increasingly live.

Let me begin from an historical perspective and say something about the role or rather roles that Christianity has played in the past.

Some years ago (in 1952) Niebuhr, an American Christian social theologian and brother of Reinhold Niebuhr (a subtle and forceful exponent of the ambiguous role that religion always plays in our human affairs), built on the work of Ernst Troeltsh[1] and produced a useful typology of the ways in which Christianity has

---

[1] *The Social Teaching of the Christian Churches*, George Allen and Unwin, London, 1931.

related to society. He called it *Christ and Culture*.[2] To my knowledge it has not been seriously challenged.

Niebuhr refers to 'Christ' and Culture rather than 'Christianity' and Culture to underline that Christianity is not a single entity but has taken many forms, all of them different but professing a common allegiance to Christ. Because it takes many forms Christianity has played many roles. The word 'Culture' is wider than the word 'Society' but includes it. It is what human beings have made out of the so-called 'natural' world which they did not make themselves. Clay soil is 'natural'. Bricks and houses are 'cultural'. The fact that we find ourselves in the company of other human beings in families and communities is 'natural'. The way we organise and regulate our life together including manners and customs, governance and law is 'cultural'. So a typology of Christ and Culture is not quite the same as a typology of the roles that the Christian religion has played in Society but it is near enough to count!

Niebuhr comes up with five types some of which are easier to explain than others. I shall list them only briefly since the details of his carefully measured and balanced account of them need not concern us here. It would be particularly interesting to know whether similar types are recognisable in the ways in which Muslims have related to society.

The first type Niebuhr calls Christ Against Culture. The role of Christianity is one of opposition and even hostility to worldly or secular society. It is represented by the monastic movements of the Middle Ages which called on believers to separate themselves from the world, and by outstanding thinkers such as Tertullian and Leo Tolstoy. The flavour of it can be found in the Sermon on the Mount[3] and the so-called 'hard sayings' of Jesus challenging would-be disciples to leave everything and follow him. In more modern times some missionaries have often demanded a break with indigenous, so-called 'heathen' cultures; and cults and sects (one in a village near to where I grew up) have corralled their followers away from everyday social life. Negatively this type of Christianity rejects everything to do with human society as evil. It is highly

---

[2] London, Faber, 1952.
[3] Matthew: 5-7.

sceptical, critical and separatist. More positively, which is where perhaps revolutionary and liberation theologies come in, with echoes of biblical, Magnificat songs about social reversal, it offers a radical alternative.

Niebuhr's second type is called the Christ of Culture. In direct contrast to the first, this form of Christianity lives fairly harmoniously with the society of its day. It accommodates to culture. There is no particular tension between them. The Christian Gnostics, Abelard, and Albert Ritschl are cited as examples. The type is also reflected in Western Christianity's close association with the Enlightenment and the Age of Reason and possibly the rise of capitalism (though that is not a point made by Niebuhr) and with democracy. Far from rejecting culture, Christ is the culmination of its development in the past and its guide for the future. This type of Christianity tends to identify itself with the surrounding society in a supportive, not to say legitimising way.

The third type, like all three remaining types, lies between these two extremes. It is called Christ Above Culture. It acknowledges that there is much good in culture and society. In them men and women can achieve both virtue and happiness. But they are not enough. Beyond them is the supernatural good obtainable not through the structures of the family and the state for example, but only through Christ. Nevertheless social structures are affirmed and upheld, even preserved (in the rather conservative way of those who emphasise what is 'natural' and therefore 'good'), contributing as they do to man's overall development. Clement of Alexandria (who wrote an interesting treatise on *How Can the Rich Man be Saved*—reassuring him that he could be, of course, without surrendering his riches!) and Thomas Aquinas are quoted as representatives of this type. It recognises the importance of upholding social institutions but also that more than what they can offer is required for salvation.[4]

The fourth type Niebuhr calls Christ and Culture in Paradox. Both Christianity and society are necessary. Both have a claim on

---

[4] See the paper presented to the Conference, and published in this volume, in which the Bishop of London echoed this 'type' when he castigated secular society's reductionist views of human nature and insisted there is more to human beings than what culture and society often make of them.

us: the laws of society for example and the 'law of Christ. Both exercise authority over us but there is an inescapable tension between them. We have to live in two worlds at once. Martin Luther is probably the most obvious example of this type with his doctrine of the two realms or Kingdoms: one of sin, and the law which deals with sin, saving us from the worst; the other of the Gospel and grace. Another way of putting it is to say that the role of Christianity is not to tell people how to be doctors, or builders, or legislators or bankers or whatever but to put a right spirit within them, above all a trustful orientation towards God, so affecting the quality of everything they do. This limited role of religion is reflected in the modem respect for the autonomy of secular disciplines. Christianity for example cannot dictate to the economist or scientist, they have a realm of discourse of their own. They are a law unto themselves which Christianity has to respect rather than change. Theology is not the Queen (or, to quote HRH Prince El Hassan: 'not all knowledge can be Islamicised'). This autonomous secular realm, however, can never entirely rule the roost. Science for example has its own procedures but cannot simply be left to go its own way regardless of the moral purposes for which its discoveries and inventions will be used. There is an inbuilt tension therefore and, at its most positive, an endless and healthy dialectic between Christianity and society.

Finally and perhaps more easily pinned down is Christ the Transformer of Culture. Without denying the good in it, there is a good deal wrong with society, but it can be redeemed and transformed. The earthly city can become the City of God. The Graeco-Roman empire centred on Caesar can become mediaeval Christendom centred on Christ. The kingdoms of this world can become the Kingdoms of our God. Augustine, Calvin, Wesley (with his doctrine of perfection) and F D Maurice and, I suppose, the Christian liberal optimists of the 19th and early 20th centuries, are all representatives of this type inspired as it is, by what T S Eliot called the *Idea of a Christian Society*.

So according to Richard Niebuhr Christianity, as one of the world's great religions, has typically played five roles in society: Hostile, Accommodating, Complementary, Dialectical and Transforming. I repeat: it would be interesting to know whether any similar typology holds good for other religions, especially for Islam.

If this helpful typology is understood to be 'descriptive', that is an account of the roles that the Christian religion has actually played in society rather than an account of the roles it has deliberately and self-consciously been encouraged to play, then it is obviously incomplete—as Niebuhr would be the first to acknowledge—and it is incomplete in at least three respects. First because rarely do we come across any of the five 'types' in its purest form. Instead we are confronted with endless combinations: a balancing emphasis here and a qualification there. More often than not the types represent different facets of a more complex role which is difficult to categorise and misleading to pigeon-hole.

Second, if each type has been advocated by its leading exponents in all good faith and for the best of reasons, each type is capable of being misused, and in any case the motives for adhering to it will often be mixed. Christianity has often upheld Western culture and civilisation for example, whether we are talking of its political institutions, its artistic and intellectual achievements, science and technology or free-market capitalism. It has zealously exported much of it to the rest of the world through colonisation, missionary endeavours and more recently development assistance. In part this is a case of 'The Christ of Culture' where there is little tension between the two and, indeed, culture can be seen as the flowering of Christian ideals. Such movements, however, are highly ambiguous. Without dismissing them as all bad, many in the so-called Third World experienced colonialism, missions and development assistance as exploitative and highly disrespectful of their cultures. The role being played was not so much a proper affirmation of the Christian way of life as an attempt to shape and operate the world and subdue it so that it favoured the rich and the powerful. Equally, many a liberation movement is easily associated with those role-types which contain a strong element of opposition to culture: against it, or in a dialectical and critical relationship with it, or out to transform it because, far from representing the flowering of Christianity, society's injustices and oppression fall far short of Christian teaching. Self-interest, however, is as much a factor here as before. It may be justified but the role that Christianity is playing is not simply to oppose a social arrangement that is contrary to Christ but to promote an alternative in the interests of those who are the losers. The outcome may or may not be an advance towards the Kingdom of God. Violent revolution may at times seem unavoidable but the outcome is rarely all that good.

Neither colonial nor revolutionary movements then are easily identified with Niebuhr's types except, shall we say, with their darker side. And all of Niebuhr's types are capable of perversion. Christ against culture can turn into arrogant self-righteousness. Christ of Culture can absolutise the *status quo* and descend into ultra-conservatism, as can Christ Above Culture. Christ and Culture in Paradox can pay its respects to the autonomy of secular disciplines and the various sectors of life, but it can also mount an argument for keeping 'religion' out of politics and reducing ethics to 'business ethics' and leaving the free-market well alone. And Christ the Transformer of Culture, far from enhancing human life, can turn itself into a process of subjugation by which one culture is advanced with missionary zeal and those in its path are treated with contempt.

The third way in which Niebuhr's typology is incomplete is suggested by the difficulty of actually establishing cause and effect in history. Christianity may set out for example to transform society. That is its stated intention, and society may indeed be changed. But whether Christianity was the prime mover or some other factor really made the difference is often hard to decide. The opposite may also be true. Christianity sets out to play one role but inadvertently plays another or finds itself confronted with a result it never intended. A recent example from Britain comes to mind. Oxford University was accused recently of elitism and prejudice when it refused to give a clever girl from a state school in the North of England a place in its School of Medicine. (As it happened the tutor involved turned out to be a prime mover in opening up the university.) What the subsequent debate suggested was that the real culprit was and remains the growth of private education which offers considerable advantages to its clients who are then better placed than state school pupils to win university places. The irony is that it may have been the campaign for comprehensive schools in the 1960s, which some of us Christians saw as an attempt to transform the education system and so make society in general more fair and just, which actually stimulated the very thing it wanted to avoid, namely a flight from the state system by those who could afford it and an increase rather than decrease of both privilege and disadvantage. Christianity on this comparatively small and on a much larger scale (maybe even as grand a scale as the historical divide between Eastern and Western Christianity) has accidentally or inadvertently and out of ignorance played roles that it never intended.

Finally Niebuhr's typology may be incomplete in the most straightforward sense. It may be possible to think of roles played by Christianity which he has not included. Two or three examples occur to me. First religion is often thought of as a cohesive force within communities. It is the glue that holds society together. Equally it has been seen in a more negative role as the cause of division and the perpetrator of conflict. In many cases neither may be true. Religion may simply be a label: the signifier of differences,[5] the real causes of cohesion and division lying deeper or elsewhere. Second there is Marx's description of religion as the opiate of the people. Thought of positively it can be the means by which people survive and cope in difficult circumstances whether of personal loss or deep poverty. The High Church movements in the city slums of 19th-century Britain can be seen in this light, as can the Pentecostal movements of Latin America. Thought of negatively an opiate can be the means by which a keen sense of injustice is blunted, the threat of revolution eased, or the downtrodden manipulated into accepting the unacceptable.

Third there is the long and interesting debate led by R H Tawney and others about the rise of capitalism and the role that religion played in developing an economic order which many in the non-Western world have long regarded as inextricably bound up with Western society and Western Christianity. Was Christianity responsible? It is impossible to tell though it has certainly gone along with much of it. One suggestion is that there were ideas in Western Christianity, like the Protestant work ethic, the Puritan streak which is reluctant to spend surplus money, and elements in Calvinism which at least encouraged entrepreneurs to seize with a good conscience

---

[5] See Martin Woolacott writing in *The Guardian*, 16 June 2000.

the opportunities which the industrial revolution and technological progress were offering. The Methodist, John Wesley, once famously said: 'Earn all you can, save all you can, give all you can.' He did not say: 'Spend all you can.' So there was every encouragement to work hard, make profits and reinvest capital. The role of religion was to provide an hospitable moral environment, an ethical seedbed, in which capitalism could flourish.

These three roles, as a cohesive social force, as the comforter or opiate of the people, and as fertile moral soil for social and economic developments, and doubtless other roles as well, may not readily fit into Niebuhr's typology but must be kept in line.

II

I turn now from a largely descriptive discussion about the roles that the Christian religion has played in society—upholding it, criticising and changing it for both good and more questionable reasons—to a more prescriptive discussion about the role or roles we think it ought to play. Here Niebuhr is quite clear and probably we would all agree with him. No single type will do on its own and for at least two inter-related reasons. First it is easy enough to see some merit in all of them. Why then cannot these five or more types or roles be held together by wise Christians in a single if complex whole? The answer is that it is relatively easy to see their merits when we are able to take a dispassionate, almost theoretical or academic view of these things, as we can now. It is far less easy to do so when we are under the pressures of history. If for example you have undergone a dramatic conversion experience you are unlikely to see much good in the world you have left behind. You are likely to be fairly 'against' culture where any hint of admiration will only look like compromise. If you are suffering poverty, oppression or violence you are even more likely to feel the same. Righteous anger will find little room for balance. If, again, your lines have fallen in pleasant places and life is good and, as far as you are concerned, you are blessed by God, you are unlikely to look on the society which structures that life as anything but providential. You will be firmly in the Christ of Culture camp. Or again if society appears to be in decline and fall, short of giving it up which is not in your long-term interest to do, you will tend to see your role not as a conservationist but as a transformer of culture. In other words the second reason why no single type will do is because all of them are relative to the people and circumstances in which they come to prominence and find favour. Persecution and misfortune will breed criticism. Peace and prosperity will breed affirmation.

In any prescriptive debate about what role the Christian religion should play in society it will be important therefore, if the debate is to be adequate, to stand back with a degree of detachment and test any proposed role for the Christian (or any other) religion against the most adequate typology or frame of reference we can put together out of our experience and our knowledge of the foundation documents and teachings of the Christian churches.

The framework we have already constructed (without suggesting it is complete) comprises: i) Niebuhr's five types, ii) their possible misuses, or uses for other than their stated purposes, iii) unintended roles for religion in society, iv) additional roles which could possibly supplement Niebuhr's typology. When we evaluate any role Christianity plays in society we shall need to ask how far it takes into account all these other possible roles and try to be acutely aware that motives are always mixed and the actual role being played is sometimes more covert than our protestations make out. The conclusion we reach is unlikely to be a comprehensive or balanced one if it is to be responsive to the swings and roundabouts of history and appropriate to the circumstances of the day. It will therefore be relative. It will not, however, be relativistic. It will not take the view that anything goes and that one role is as defensible (or indefensible) as another. The framework of reference will help Christianity to give reasons, rooted in scripture, tradition and experience, for the role it adopts.

I shall devote the remainder of this paper to the suggestion, hinted at in the papers for this conference, especially the statement about its objectives,[6] that the role of religion in society has to do with values: stating them, promoting them and doing what it can to

---

6 'How do Christians and Muslims help society to affirm the value of every human life, the need for tolerance, sympathy, community solidarity, individual self-

see that they are upheld. The values mentioned include 'the value of every human life, the need for tolerance, sympathy, community solidarity, (and) individual self-worth.'

Much the same suggestion about the role not just of Christianity but of religion in general shines through a project being jointly sponsored by the World Bank and leaders of the world religions chaired by James Wolfenson, the Bank's President, and George Carey the (Anglican) Archbishop of Canterbury. It is called *World Faiths Development Dialogue* [7] and it is interested in the contribution which religion can make to the struggle against poverty. For obvious reasons it should be of great interest to members of this Conference. The values, none of them peculiarly Christian, it seeks to uphold and promote in development include equality, fairness, cultural diversity; honesty (as against corruption), sustainability (and respect for creation) and the dignity of work. These values are of course deeply rooted in the belief systems which it is a primary task of religion to articulate and maintain. These beliefs express our convictions about the nature and purpose of our lives. For example, it is because we believe that all women and men are created and loved as the children of God that we value equality. It is because we believe the world has a sacred character as God's creation that we value sustainability and taking care of the earth. It is because we believe we are social animals made for each other and for love that we value solidarity and community. It is because we believe we are not just animals but beings capable of transcendence that we value intellectual and spiritual development and not just economic progress. This rooting of values in beliefs, what 'ought to be' in what we believe 'is the case', has its advantages in that it gives real substance to our goals

---

worth and the opportunity for redemption? Should religious groups work through the formal political structures of a society, or should they be independent of the state?

'Why do inter-religious tensions arise, when compassion is the essence of what both Christianity and Islam espouse? Why is religion often callously exploited for secular and political purposes? ' (from *Aims and Objectives ..., Muslim-Christian Relations in the Commonwealth: a dynamic role for the future*)

[7] Available from *World Faith Development Dialogue*, 33-37 Stockinore Street, Oxford OX4, UK.

in life. They are not merely 'utilitarian' or 'relative' values. They arise from a whole hinterland of what we believe life is all about. This deep rooting of values in religious beliefs can also of course make for difficulties when it comes to inter-religious co-operation since it may be more difficult for religious believers to negotiate their creeds than their values. Gender issues in development, especially attitudes to women, are one example of that. Religious beliefs breed seriousness but also conservatism in much the same breath.

How might the role of Christianity or religion as the upholder and promoter of values relate to Niebuhr's typology? The vocabulary suggests at first an additional type that we have not yet considered. On further reflection, however, it appears to be just that: a 'vocabulary' or a manageable and easily understood way of talking about all the different types and the search for a suitably measured position for our day and age. We can promote Christian or religions values in such a way as to appear highly critical of society where its values are not ours: Christ Against Culture; or we can be supportive and approving: Christ of Culture; and in so far as we might set out to change society's values, for example away from an obsession with consumerism and economic growth towards an overriding concern for the welfare and fulfilment of people, we might be seen to adopt the role of transformer of culture. All three of these notes, critical, supportive and transformative, are struck in the World Faiths Development Dialogue documents. So the language of values is a way of talking about all the roles that religion can play. It will be wise, however, to remember that it can, equally, be perverted along with any of these roles to become a subterfuge for achieving less desirable objectives. No one can be against honesty or in favour of corruption for example (the poor certainly aren't), but there is a certain ambiguity about Western capitalism's zeal for the present anti-corruption crusade; just as the drive to uphold democracy is not always born solely of enthusiasm for a more equitable society.

Promoting and upholding values can then be accepted as a handy way of talking about a role for religion which is clear and understandable whilst at the same time being necessarily complex. I want now to comment on three important issues it will have to face.

III

First, it sounds comparatively straightforward to say that religion should be the promoter and upholder of values but it begs the question as to which values it should promote and uphold, and why. I do not wish to sound over-sceptical about the possibility of reaching agreement. The World Faiths Development Dialogue documents for example comment on more than one occasion on the remarkable degree of consensus which the different faith traditions have achieved on the values which should be promoted in development. Nevertheless we live in a pluralistic age noted for its variety of opinions where, to quote the Bible, 'Everyone does what is right in their own eyes.'

Pluralism is the close-bosom friend of relativism and of the recognition that all our thinking is inevitably affected by our circumstances, our limited knowledge and by the kind of people we are, so that what is 'right' for one person is not necessarily 'right' for another. The other feature of pluralism is the lack of any authority which can cut through this variety of opinion. Social institutions for example, parents, teachers, politicians, religious and social superiors, no longer win our compliance simply because of who or what they are. They must make a case for themselves and their values along with the rest. Religious authorities like the Bible or the priest (pope) or the synods of the church can of course be handed authority. We can decide for our own good reasons to let them have the last word: to regard Scripture as fundamentally inerrant and the priest as infallible. But that is a choice we make. It is not a description of their own intrinsic characters. The Christian Bible for example is as deeply coloured by the people who wrote it, as sharply etched by historical circumstances, as inevitably flawed by the limited knowledge of the day as any other piece of writing. Whilst it remains an impressive witness to remarkable events and, although 'only human', a great nourisher and inspirer of faith, it is hardly a means of putting an authoritative end to debate.

One other 'authority', at least in the Western world, has fallen by the wayside, and that is the authority of 'reason'. In the days of the Enlightenment and the Age of Reason it exposed and undercut the oppressive social and religious authorities of the past.

As time went on its powers of observation, deduction and theorising triumphed in the rise of science. All sensible, rational people could agree about the best of all possible worlds if only they put their minds to it. But now we live in a 'post-modern' world where a common appeal to reason is no longer an obvious basis for agreement.

What values then are we to uphold? Even if we limit the discussion to Christianity and a shared appeal by Christians to teaching inspired by Christ, the answer is far from clear. If we take a wide historical perspective the values of the Western church and the values of the growing church of the South, rooted as they often are in their liberation theologies, are poles apart. If we take a narrow historical perspective what do we make of two leading British politicians of the day, the Prime Minister and the Leader of the Opposition, both agreeing that society should be value-led and both apparently agreeing that religion (for them both Christianity) has an important role to play; but one taking counsel from Hans Küng, the rebellious and rather liberal Catholic theologian, and the other from an American Conservative Evangelical. It is highly unlikely that they will return from such quests with the same values.

Agreement is not easy to come by and we cannot assume we know what these values are which religion is to promote and uphold.

Keeping our framework of reference in mind, and in particular Niebuhr's five types, the second, Christ of Culture, is at least worth contemplating at this point including its misuse, deliberate or otherwise. Margaret Thatcher, a former British Prime Minister, to illustrate the point, is famous for two incursions into the realm of religion and society when she appeared to approve of religion as the upholder of certain values. On, one occasion, outside 10 Downing Street, she quoted the prayer of St Francis of Assisi: 'Make me an instrument of your peace; where there is hatred let me sow love.' Like him, and Christ, she approved of peace, unity and love in society. On a second occasion when addressing the General Assembly of the Church of Scotland she referred to the parable of the Good Samaritan[8] and appeared to approve of the

---

[8] Luke: 10.

kindness and compassion that is ready to help our neighbours. But the values that she was in fact upholding turned out to be on the one hand the unity and peace that comes when troublesome elements in society like powerful trade unions have been firmly put in their place and, on the other, the wealth that comes from competitive business enterprises which enables the better-off to be charitable to the less fortunate: to pay as it were for the room at the inn or for private medical treatment for the unfortunate traveller. Margaret Thatcher's values were approved of by many but were not universally shared even by her fellow Christians and what we have here is a Christ of Culture type but in an ambiguous form. No great tension is felt between Christ and the culture or society of the day, but that has less to do with Christ bringing culture to its finest expression and more to do with Christ being used to sanctify and justify the culture and its social values that have been arrived at by a somewhat different route. Christ is not discovered in culture. Our cultural values are read into Christ. As we have already suggested, we cannot say that Christianity has nothing to do with the rise of capitalism, but we should recognise how easily it can be turned around so that Christianity simply approves of and supports the values our ideologies favour in any case.

If then religion is to play the role of upholding and promoting values it is not all that easy to know what those values are or should be, particularly when, in a pluralist world, there are no final authorities to arbitrate.

My own view for what it is worth is that we should not take an entirely negative view of disagreement over values either within or between religious traditions. We should be interested in those disagreements and explore the reasons for them. They represent something of a problem but also a wealth of varied insights from which we can learn a great deal. Agreement, however, still remains important. There is no way of reaching it without a prior and fundamental agreement that we want a value-driven society and that our overriding common concern is the well-being of all humanity. Only from that will other values flow, and they can only be established by a process of dialogue and consensus building. We must explain our values to one another and why we hold them, including the fact that they are rooted in our religious faith and what that faith has to say. We must recognise and respect that others may have different values, or the same values for different reasons, or both, and learn from those differences. We must exploit the evidence whether empirical, scientific, sociological or otherwise that may be open to all of us of whatever religious faith or none and which we can all respect, for example what we have learnt about the economic, social and spiritual needs of human beings on which we can construct notions of Human Rights. We must remember that people change their views less as a result of argument than of fresh experience; we need interaction, encounter and the building of relationships. Through these and other patient disciplines, where all of us are serious but no one assumes a position of overriding authority, we have to work by mutual persuasion towards consensus, in this instance about the values we wish to uphold. The present interest in global ethics, which I share, is a good example of this process. The end result is likely to be that we occupy common ground but often for somewhat different reasons.

IV

If religion is to uphold and promote values we not only have to come to some agreement about which values are to be upheld but about what it means to uphold and promote them, so that they actually influence and shape our common life.

One set of answers to the question seems comparatively easy and obvious. They should be promoted by 'moral' education in schools, religious centres and by voluntary organisations, by the example of parents and teachers and leaders, through the media, and by standards and codes of practice in public life. So far so good. The difficulty, however, is that these values are then confined to the personal realm and to individual responsibility. Society will be shaped by these values in so far as its individual members are taught to live by them. That is perfectly true but it is not enough (and too often in the Western world a 'privatised' version of Christianity has given the impression that it is enough). If we are serious about a value-led society, and for me that has meant a society that is just and includes the poor, our values have to be incorporated into social and economic policies, and that is far more difficult.

The difficulty can be illustrated by noting the 'distance' as it were between a 'value' and a 'policy', or rather the distances, since a shared value will often give rise to different, not to say diametrically opposed policies; one current and parochial example in the UK is the debate about fox hunting or 'hunting with dogs'. Everyone is agreed on the starting point. Nature is red in tooth and claw but when it comes to human beings they should be kind to animals and not inflict unnecessary pain and suffering. There is the value that all uphold. The resulting social policy, however, may be an outright ban on hunting, continuing acceptance or more careful controls. Another example of much more interest to me comes from the development world. Presumably we all share the view that abject poverty is a bad thing and should be reduced and as far as possible eliminated. That agreed starting point may, however, lead to economic policies in which the liberalisation of trade managed by the World Trade Organisation is seen as the best way to create wealth and opportunity for all or to policies which recognise that such a free-for-all in fact spells opportunity for the powerful to grow rich and disaster for poorer countries. And should Mr Blair and Mr Hague agree on their values, they will almost certainly come to different conclusions as to the implications for their political manifestos. Values are one thing. Implementing them in social policies is another.

This is partly due to the fact that our values—even more so the values that win consensus—are usually general and vague. They are 'universal' in a bland sense. The devil will lie in the detail. There is a considerable shift for example from upholding 'equality' to upholding 'equality of opportunity', and another one when it comes to answering the question: 'opportunity for what?' There is an even bigger shift between upholding 'love' as a value and spelling out what it means. But probably the main reason for the distance between our values and our social policies is that in arriving at those policies so many other considerations have to be taken into account. If you want to be rid of poverty you will not do so unless you discover and adopt workable economic policies and create appropriate social and governmental institutions to regulate them.

The same is true of adequate health care and a good education for everyone. We may all agree on the value we wish to uphold or the 'end' we wish to achieve. The 'means' to that end is more controversial and very often the other relevant factors which must be taken into account become more determinative than the values themselves. They will certainly occupy more of our time and intellectual energies.

For all its length and difficulty however the distance between 'value' and 'policy' has to be travelled. One reason why is firmly on the agenda of this conference and its call for a rediscovery of compassion.[9] I do not happen to believe compassion is in all that short supply though it can be brutalised out of us. Neither do I despise for one moment what is usually thought of as compassion, namely the immediate charitable response to human need. But compassion too easily descends to little more than sentiment and feeling sorry for unfortunate people. If we really care about them and want to put an end to their misfortunes then charitable responses are not sufficient and can in fact divert us from what is required. Food aid for the starving, for example, made possible by charitable donations, meets immediate need as it should but does nothing to reorganise the world so that everyone can enjoy a secure and sustainable livelihood. For that, workable social and economic policies are required, and compassion is not compassion unless it tries hard to construct them and put them in place.[10]

My own view is that the journey we have to make from values to policies includes a thoroughgoing interdisciplinary approach which considers with equal care what the different faiths have to say about human reality, about our goals and about the means of achieving them, and what the economist, scientist, political analyst and practitioner have to say about precisely the same subjects. The journey must involve an action-reflection model where intellectual effort leads to policy making and the lessons we learn from implementing those policies lead in turn to further reflection. We have to learn together as we go. The third feature of the journey

---

[9] It is mentioned in the *Aims and Objectives* and was the subject of two Conference papers.

[10] I probably share the Bishop of London's distaste for what he called 'hyper-moralism' as against 'practical-realism'.

will be what I might call 'prophecy' where we attempt to keep on seeing the wood for the trees by challenging ourselves not only to the deductive task of extrapolating policies from values but to the prophetic task of testing any policy for any connection between it and the values it professes to incorporate. Does, for example, an economic policy of wealth creation actually reduce poverty and enhance equality? The burden of proof must be thrown onto the policy.

If we put this debate, about how we move from the values we promote to upholding them in social policies, against our framework of reference which includes Niebuhr's typology, it throws up a number of useful points of which I will mention only two. One of Niebuhr's types is Christ and Culture in Paradox or tension, a leading representative of which was Martin Luther and his doctrine of the two Kingdoms or Realms. An interdisciplinary approach to policy-making upholds that doctrine in that it respects the autonomy of other disciplines like economic and social theory and development. A religious faith cannot dictate what they have to say but must come to terms with their independent voices ('not all knowledge can be Islamicised'). On the other hand we shall be wary of any absolute autonomy which leaves the economic and political realms of life to go their own way. They are never value free. They also have ends in view. They must always be open to the prophetic challenge as to whether those ends are acceptable or not.

The other point again relates to the statement about the objectives of this conference where it asks., 'Should religious groups work through the formal political structures of a society, or should they be independent of the state?' The answer, as they say, lies in both extremes. Our typology suggests that a measure of rigorous independence is absolutely necessary or we head towards too much respect for the state and its policies and even towards sanctifying a social structure which is inevitably imperfect and perverse. There is always a critical role to play (whether it can be played for better or worse by an 'established' church like our own Church of England or a state religion is another matter). On the other hand if religious groups, intent on upholding certain values, do not work through political structures, or get involved in all the messy and detailed business of creating and maintaining social policies and institutions, then in the long run they are not really serious about upholding those values at all.[11] Structures mediate values, otherwise they remain up in the air and of little real consequence.

V

Finally let me draw attention to a third issue that religion has to face in its role as upholder and promoter of values. In many religious traditions there is a strong awareness of what traditional Christian teaching calls 'sin'. The world is not full of 'nice' people, but not very nice people under pressure. Human beings at best are a disappointment, far less enlightened and compassionate than we had hoped. They are seduced by lesser concerns, trapped in their attachment to the material world or bound by narrow self-concern. At worst they are perverse and plagued not just by weakness but a hardened resistance to what many religions would call 'the will of God'. All of this casts considerable doubt on any attempt to promote and uphold values. If human nature is so flawed who can be relied upon to promote them, and once appealed to, who is likely to rise to this moral challenge or is capable of doing so?

History is the graveyard of values that have been highly recommended but disregarded or subverted or actively resisted. Given this reality, is society most in need of moral appeals or some kind of redemptive process? Some religions are more optimistic about our moral abilities than others. Islam I suspect is among them. Christianity does not deny them all together but is equally aware of a darker side to human nature which is in thrall to evil and from which it cannot extricate itself. We cannot be saved by efforts of our own, only by 'grace' which freely rescues us from our moral and spiritual predicament.

Christianity therefore, though morally serious, is to be understood primarily as a religion of redemption, saving us as it were from ourselves and enabling us to live the kind of value-driven lives which otherwise would remain desirable but beyond our reach. It is overtly transformative. It boasts the power to change

---

[11] See Niebuhr's fifth type: *Christ the Transformer of Culture.*

us. But in offering us this cure for our reluctance or inability either to promote values or to live up to them, Christianity only exposes itself to a further difficulty. History suggests that it has been better at diagnosis than at cure. During the two thousand years it has been at work in history it has manifestly failed to redeem the world. It may have assured numerous individuals of their forgiveness, delivering them from the fear of God's judgement, but, if it has seen itself, following Niebuhr's type five, as a transformer of culture, it has a very disappointing record indeed. Of course it has been influential and made an enormous difference but it is hard to see how it has improved the moral quality of life overall, especially as we look back over what the Dalai Lama described as the twentieth 'Century of Blood' including the Holocaust, wars on a vast scale, and repeated acts of genocide. Some things get better while others get worse. Some moral ground is gained whilst some ground is lost. The general level, however, remains much the same. Christianity has failed to make a new earth. Some will argue that the reason for its failure is the strength of the opposition coupled with the unwillingness of God to override our human freedom. Such arguments, however, only underline the problem. If the God who is like Christ cannot woo and attract recalcitrant humanity into joyful and willing co-operation that does not let Christianity off the hook. Rather it highlights its impotence. I suspect that this redemptive tale, that Christianity has to tell, has more to do with helping us to live with our perversity and poverty of spirit and come to terms with it, and not allow its persistence to paralyse us into thinking we can do no good, rather than with making us rid of it.

What then is to be done given the rather cynical judgement that, if presented with values such as equality for all and sustainability for all things, we are unlikely to live up to them or support them in practice? Four suggestions come to mind.

First it will be important wherever possible and appropriate to embody the values we say we wish to uphold in law. Where we are not willing to be just we shall have to make ourselves do justly (echoes of Luther's two realms). That will make us vigilant in ensuring that access to health care and education for example and a minimum wage are enshrined in law. It will also point us in the direction of understanding human rights, especially social and economic rights not as commendable goals which eventually the well-intentioned may achieve, but as legal claims which can be pressed under international law as of now.[12] Second, if we cannot achieve the best—and we should try—we must avoid the worst, which brings us back to what for me is a fundamental social strategy rooted amongst other things in what my Christian faith teaches me about human nature. We must always work to achieve a balance of power. Far from promoting the values of equality, freedom and fairness, the powerful will always prey upon the weak and take decisions which are to their own advantage. What is required is not a reversal of power but a balance. A generation ago that was understood very much in military terms. If societies were to become more equal, in South Africa for example, then the power of white regimes had to be matched by the power of the liberation movements. More recently the strategy has focused more on economic power, where poorer countries are so readily overwhelmed by the rich trading nations and the multi-nationals. The World Trade Organisation and all its works are a good example of that. A third example of the same strategy is to strengthen civil society as a third force to balance the power of the state and the power of the private sector, and to counter corruption. The more checks and balances the better. The third suggestion is not to let go of idealism but to match it with appeals to self-interest, making those appeals as enlightened as possible by helping everyone to recognise that if values, such as equal opportunities for the poorest and sustainability, are upheld the benefits will be enjoyed by us all.

In conclusion, I suspect that Christian teaching has paid too much attention to human perversity. I have seen that too often in the poor world—in Rwanda and the like. It has been too single-minded and narrow-minded in believing that history has gone wrong because sinful human beings have, for some incomprehensible reason, gratuitously decided to behave badly and to disobey God. It is difficult to see what they have to gain by doing so especially in the mythical context of an original Paradise. The roots of our perverse and destructive behaviour are far more likely to be found not in

---

[12] See B K Goldewijk and Bas de Gaay Fortman, *Where Needs Meet Rights*, World Council of Churches, Geneva, 1999.

wilful disobedience but in our insecurities: existential and spiritual insecurity, material and physical insecurity. We behave in highly egocentric ways and make every attempt to protect ourselves, even more so when we are together in social groups, because we do not feel safe. In which case it is at least worth considering whether some of the values under discussion as goals should be regarded not as ideals to which we aspire but as the essential preconditions of our surviving and prospering as secure human beings. They are not the moral icing on the cake but basic survival rations. They are not disinterested visions but highly and deeply self-interested pursuits. In our 'end', as the poet might have said but did not, is our 'beginning'.

In which case the role of religion in society, or at least the Christian religion, might be to work out a far more credible and maybe honest analysis of our human situation, drawing amongst other things on its deeply held convictions; out of which might come more truth and realism round which to organise our life together.

CHRISTIANITY AND ISLAM:
HISTORICAL ENGAGEMENT
THEOLOGICAL ENCOUNTER

THE PRESENCE OF 'SECULAR' IN CHRISTIAN-MUSLIM RELATIONS: REFLECTIONS ON THE *DA'WAH*, 'MISSION' AND 'DIALOGUE'

Ataullah Siddiqui

'For several centuries Western Christianity has allied itself with modern Western civilization with its essentially secularist outlook ...'

Seyyed Hossein Nasr

'Missionaries in India and Africa have been agents of secularization even if they did not realize it.'

Leslie Newbigin

In this paper, we will explore recent developments in Christian-Muslim relations against the backdrop of 'Secularism'. 'Secularism' is used in the much wider sense by Muslims to include materialism, modernity and the secularization of society.[1] One of the motivating factors behind Muslim initiatives to reform their own society was prompted by the fact that they faced the challenge of secularization. This they perceive as a 'corrupting' influence on their society. In this process they saw Christian missionary efforts in their midst as an extended arm of secularization. So whilst on the one hand they opposed the increasing prevalence of modern influences on society they also opposed whatever missionary activities were taking place amongst them. Ironically, they also held the hope that perhaps Christians, being believers in God, may be the best partners with which to forge an alliance against the growing process of modernization. They also hoped that Western Christians would in some way be able to help

---

[1] Though there is a difference between 'Secularism'—an extreme form of movement which opposes religion (here I have used Secularism with 'S' capital in this sense)—and 'secularization', the process that neither opposes religion nor envisages its disappearance but rather minimizes its role and significance in society. Largely, Muslims apprehend both as the two sides of the same coin.

them project their plight against political and social injustices. They hoped that with such an alliance they might be able to raise a common voice for justice. This, then, was the motivation behind their participation in Christian-Muslim dialogue during the mid-20th century.

I

The changing context in which Muslims have addressed the issue of *da'wah* (invitation) has largely been understood as a reform of the Muslim community itself. Muslim preachers (*da'i*) took a particular interest in instilling self-confidence with Islam amongst the Muslim masses but at the same time they were actively involved in raising Muslim awareness so as to face colonial challenges as well as the challenges posed by Christian missionaries. Muslims have interchangeably adopted the approaches of *da'wah* and *islah* (reform). They also, however, necessarily added *munazarah* (debate) especially in relation to Christians and this was understood as a vehicle of *da'wah*. The Muslim leadership also identified Western scholarship biased against Islam as a challenge that they must attend to and against which they needed to prepare the younger generation of Muslims so that they could rise up to the challenges. These then were a few dominant aspects of *da'wah* during the colonial period. Soon after Muslim political independence, a stark shift was noticed in the institutionalization of *da'wah*, and to this theme we will return briefly a little later.

A few explanations are now in order. The general meaning of *da'wah* is 'to call', 'to invite'. Invitees are all humanity and the invitation is towards God (*Fussilat* 41: 33-5). The invitation towards God is not seen as something new but rather as something which is eternal and known especially amongst the People of the Book (*al-Ankabut* 29: 46). Nor is this common understanding of God something new. The Muslims' invitation is to discover the path that has been lost (*al-Baqarah* 2: 136). In this invitation, respect for others and their beliefs need to be taken into consideration, even if the belief and practices of others contradict Muslim beliefs and practices (*al-Anam* 6: 108). The beliefs and practices of others are here seen as being unaware of what is in themselves (*al-Tawbah* 9: 6). Hence, *da'wah* is a call to return to his self or her self.

The term *islah* is understood as 'reform' or 'reconciliation'. It identifies people who are prepared to make amends in their life (*Al-i-Imran* 3: 89) or who repent and mend their ways (*An-Nissa* 4:146). This reform suggests a reform of the human being and should not convey the meaning that Islam needs *islah*. The term and its use become significant in so far as it implies a change in the ethical moral perception of Muslims and this is what many reformers envisaged. They encouraged the Muslim masses to return to the basics of Islam, to prayer and fasting and to face the new challenges. *Da'is* encouraged Muslims to purify the spiritual aspects of their life and emphasized that changes in society are possible once individuals change.

Perhaps it will help here to identify the meaning of *balagh* or *tabligh*. *Balagh* is understood as meaning 'to achieve an objective' or 'to come to hear'. According to this concept, the mere announcement of the message is sufficient for the fulfilment of this task. Words like *wa ma 'alayna ila'l- balagh*—our task is only to pass on the message—have, for instance, been widely used by Muslim preachers. As we pointed out earlier, the responsibility of preachers or communicators is guided by the principle that 'there is no compulsion in religion' and *balagh* fulfils this objective by 'informing', 'communicating' or 'warning'. The concept of *balagh* is guided by another verse in the Qur'an. Addressing the Prophet, the verse states that, 'We have not sent you as a keeper over them, nor are you responsible for them' (*al-Anam* 6: 106). Usually the content of *tabligh* is belief in the prophecy of the Prophet Muhammad along with the Oneness of God. Furthermore, the issue of salvation in the Hereafter is dependent upon this belief.[2]

The colonial expansion of European powers brought about a new era for Muslim countries. They faced a superior power equipped not only with new technologies and as a consequence a new economic power, but also a 'new' world view. Western man's world, for the Muslims, was full of dichotomy. One aspect of this was the seemingly dominant Christianity and Christian message, whilst the other aspect

---

[2] See Islahi, Amin Ahsan, *Call to Islam and How the Holy Prophets Preached*, Islamic Book Publishers, Safat (Kuwait), 1982 (Second Edition).

centred on 'reason' and a philosophy where God hardly appears. Despite these differences in the missionaries' language as also the language of the European colonizers, the Muslims saw some kind of understanding with Westerners and assurance that some sort of acting together was possible. For them they were hardly distinguishable.[3] Phrases such as 'conquering the world for Christ' '... and arouse the spirit of Christian chivalry in the hearts of young people ...' gave a military connotation to mission. The Muslim religious leadership at this juncture then had two priorities. One was reform or *islah* of the community in order to protect it from growing 'un-Islamic influences' and the other to challenge European scholarship which saw in their religion an amalgam of Christian heresy and animism. These two broad issues preoccupied Muslim *da'i* up to the first quarter of the 20th century. In the absence of clear political leadership, the *'ulama'* took their own stance and became the vanguard of community reform, especially in the areas of education and the preparing of Muslims to challenge European influences and the Christian mission in particular. In this respect *munazarah* became an important tool in reasserting Islamic identity and reforming the community. The need to do so was generated by Christian missionaries and their legacies, especially like those of Karl Pfander (1803-65). It was not so much *what* the Europeans and missionaries said but rather *how* they approached the Muslim community which became the focal point of the debate. As Powell remarks, the *'ulama'*, such as Rahmatullah Kairanwi (1818-90), 'had no complaint about the first phase of British rule and even tended moderate praise to the good organization and sense of security which [the] British presence had at first guaranteed. But the touchstone of this security had been the fact that there was no religious proselytism. He identified the beginning of the second phase of British rule with the abandonment of this religious neutrality in favour of support to missionary activity.'[4] This suspicion created a need for Muslims to establish their own schools and they began to prepare a

---

[3] See Tudesco, James Patrice, 'Missionaries and French Imperialism: The Role of Catholic Missionaries in French Colonial Expansion 1880-1905', PhD. thesis submitted at the University of Connecticut, 1980.

[4] Powell, A A, *Muslims and Missionaries in Pre-Mutiny India*, Curzon, London, Press1993. See also Gaudeul, Jean-Marie (ed.), *Encounters and Clashes: Islam and Christianity in History*, Vol. I (survey), pp. 256-261 and Vol. II (text), pp. 260-265, Pontificio Istituto di Studi Arabi e D'Islamistica, Rome, 1990.

host of *'ulama'*, to engage in *islah* and *da'wah*. Nonetheless, they also sustained the polemical and *munazarah* version of their engagements with other faiths especially with Christians but also with Hindus. The legacies of *munazarah* have continued ever since and continue to play a role in Muslim society. The origin of such *munazarahs*, as an approach to rallying Muslims around religious leadership, was meant to build confidence among the Muslims. This became all the more necessary when Christian missionaries began reaching the Muslim masses through religious tracts in Urdu and when they began addressing them in public places. The contents of such debates were overwhelmingly to 'establish' the 'authenticity' of the Bible and Jesus and, therefore, the 'falsity' of Islam. The *'ulama'* adopted a similar approach in relation to Christians and Hindus in India.

Da'wah at the academic level, however, took a different shape. In India, for example, Shibli Numani (1857-1914) began to address the issue of Western scholarship and Islam. The European's lead in the educational field in India and their superiority in administration and political control created a kind of inferiority complex amongst Muslims. They began to look to Western heroes and Western intellectuals as their guides. Numani emphasized the need to search deep into Muslim resources, and highlighting that there were, within Muslim history, those who could match and even surpass the Western thinkers and leaders. He wanted to reform and rebuild the crumbling Muslim society, especially the youth, and wrote *Al-Farooq, Al-Mamoon* and *Al-Ghazali*. A second approach he sought to confront centred around the increasing attacks made on the personality of the Prophet Muhammad, *viz.*, the legacies left by William Muir (1819-1905). Muir who wrote *The Life of Mahomet*,[5] which argued that the Qur'an was a document produced as a result of Muhammad's thought, prompted Numani to plan an extended biography of the Prophet Muhammad. In his introduction to the first volume, Numani narrates the reasons for writing such a biography. Here he summarizes Western scholars' arguments and demonstrates how they deliberately darken the image of the Prophet Muhammad. Though he was not able to complete his

---

[5] See Buaben, Jabal Muhammad, *Image of the Prophet Muhammad in the West: A Study of Muir, Margoliouth and Watt*, the Islamic Foundation, Leicester, 1996.

biography, his student Syyed Suleiman Nadvi continued the work according to the framework provided by Numani.

The Napoleonic invasion of Egypt created the same upheaval, which was witnessed in the Indian context. The Westernization of Egypt started by Muhammad Ali (1770-1849) continued despite the *'ulama*'s opposition, and both his son and grandson vigorously pursued this Westernization policy. This inevitably provoked a reaction from the *'ulama'*. Rifa'a al-Tahtawi (1801-73) suggested co-existence and convergence as a means to reform (*islah*) and *da'wah* which Jamal al-Din al-Afghani (1839-97) rejected. However, Muhammad Abduh's (1849-1905) approach was to rediscover the Muslims' own strength within their Islamic sources. He adopted a method that could establish the superiority of Islam *vis-à-vis* Christianity and Western political power on the other hand and prepared Muslims to assert themselves with vigour and self respect both within and outside the community. He saw in humanity a dialectic progression and Islam as a synthesis of all. He emphasized that in 'Childhood, man needed stern discipline which equated with the Law of Moses. During adolescence, man relied on feelings, the compassion being the Age of Christianity. But in maturity, when man relied on Reason and Science then his recourse was the Age of Islam.' Summarizing Abduh's approach to history, Gaudeul remarks that the 'Reform of Islam is not envisaged for its own sake only, but seeks to ensure that Christians will never again find reasons for criticizing Islam.'[6] In this respect it is important to note that Abduh deliberately avoided politics in his *da'wah* and *islah*. However, his student, Rashid Rida (1865-1935) was much more involved. In some way his writings encouraged a combative approach. In order to establish the 'authenticity' of Islam he sought to 'expose' Christianity's weakness and serialized the translation of the *Gospel of Barnabas* in his journal *Al-Manar*.

Developments in India and Egypt also had a significant impact in Indonesia, the *da'wah* and *islah* aspects especially highlighted in the *Muhammadiyah* movement (founded November 1912). The founder of the movement, Hadji Ahmad Dahlan (1869-1929), was greatly influenced by Abduh and Rashid Rida's approach to reform

---

[6] Gaudeul, *op. cit.*, Vol. I, p. 266.

in the Muslim community. His immediate target of reform was at grass roots levels. Basic items such as hygiene, the proper *Qiblah* of mosques and prayer, and education for younger children were given immediate priority. Civil servants were targeted especially and encouraged to learn about Islam. He also adopted some Western methods for engaging the youth elements, such as the Scouts, and created the *Hizb al-Wathan* (Party of the Fatherland). Essentially, he and his movement became very popular. However, while *Muhammadiyah* was engaged in social reform, Hadji Oemar Tjokroaminato (1882-1934) was engaged in a political crisis. He opposed the Christian mission in his country, but adopted their methodologies in order to train religious teachers. His organization, *Sarekat*, came into direct conflict with the Dutch Ethical Policy (1921). *Serakat* stated that Europe that had transformed 'almost all the people of Indonesia into labourers' including intellectuals who were 'only of value as tools of their capitalist'.[7]

So far we have assessed that *da'wah* and *islah* were the main preoccupation of Muslims and *munazarah* became an essential tool of *balagh* for many. There was, however, a sense of loss and humiliation. A need for self-reliance was widely felt and intellectual argument needed to be overcome. These multi-dimensional efforts, *da'wah, islah* and *balagh*, gradually created a new generation of Muslims who were concerned about Islam and wanted to change society but whose efforts were hampered by many variants and lack of a cohesive direction in Muslim thought. The hope of building and bringing the *Ummah* under one umbrella was dashed with the fall of the *Khilafah* in 1924 on the demise of the Ottoman empire and the establishment of the Turkish Republic. Therefore, the approach of *da'wah, islah* and *balagh* then inevitably followed a different route.

This second phase of *da'wah* and *islah* took a revivalist turn. Though many organizations and individuals emerged three organizations in particular had far-reaching impact. They, two in particular, became the inspiration for several other organizations all over the world. After the fall of the *Khilafah, Ikhwan al-Muslimin* was founded by Hassan al-Banna in 1927. This was an organized effort to

---

[7] See Noer, Deliar, *The Modernist Muslim Movement in Indonesia 1900-1942*, Oxford University Press, Kuala Lumpur, 1973, p.130, also pp. 166-170.

approach Muslims and to face contemporary challenges. The revival of Islam became its core, the cause, 'the reviving and revitalising [of] the religion' as Saeed Hawa put it, '[had] the understanding [of] the time and [the] feeling [of the] pulse.' This included constitutional change, and under the growing influence of Socialism, the *Ikhwan* took the initiative in reviving trade union laws. The family unit and the duty of *da'wah* were emphasized 'in order that Allah's Word may be raised in the world and His laws may reign supreme.' The *Ikhwan* accepted the fall of the *Khilafah* and the emergence of growing nation states in the Muslim world as a reality and they did not emphasize the 'formation of the World Islamic Bloc'. They nonetheless suggested that, in keeping with local customs and traditions, *fiqh* variations and local needs each Muslim community should adopt their own priorities but at the same time should strive for some sort of authority of the *Amir al-Muminin* (leader of the faithful). Changes were suggested at two levels, the 'revival and renaissance of Religion and change and revolution'. *Da'wah* in this context was understood as meaning 'to present Islam anew according to the demands of the time, and to transform Muslims from one condition to the other …' Hassan al-Banna placed much emphasis on *harkah* (movement), with the *da'wah* dimension as the essential tool. He emphasized three immutable resources in this respect: 1) deep faith, 2) effective organization, and 3) constant striving. The need for such organization in the *Ikhwan,* was 'to bring [about] a change in the Muslim individual and in all the Muslims'. Hassan al-Banna prescribed three stages of *da'wah*: an 'Introduction', where people formed a circle and acquaint themselves with the basic *da'wah* of the *Ikhwan* and where, from such a circle beginners would later be invited to become a part of the organization provided they could withstand all sorts of tribulations. In this process, for him, the mystical dimension of Islam was essential. Regarding its enforcement, al-Banna emphasized two aspects: one 'a daily routine [of spiritual development] and *da'wah*' and the other 'connected with the great organizational objectives'. 'The summary of your *da'wah*', Hassan al-Banna stated is: 'Allah is our objective; and the Prophet is our leader, the Qur'an is our constitution; Jihad is our method; and martyrdom is our earnest desire'.[8] The *Ikhwan* soon took root in

---

[8] See for a detail study Hawwa, Saeed, (translated by A K Shaikh) *The Muslim Brotherhood*, Hindustan Publications, Delhi, 1983.

Egypt and spread throughout the Middle East, and influenced the thinking of later Muslims the world over. The creation of the State of Israel in 1948 brought them directly into confrontation with the West. This was also became one of the reasons instrumentally behind the need to engage in dialogue with Christianity particularly when the call for dialogue came from the Western Churches.[9]

In the Indian subcontinent, Syyed Abul A'la Mawdudi formed the *Jamaat-e-Islami* in 1941 and quickly the organization found itself sucked into the socio-political and religious issues of India at large. *Jamaat*, like the *Ikhwan*, saw itself as the champion of Islamic revivalism. Mawdudi's *da'wah* concentrated on four broad areas: 1) the purification and construction of thought; 2) Reformation (*islah*) of the self; 3) reformation (*islah*) of society and 4) reformation (*islah*) of the system of government. Mawdudi expressed his views about these basic objectives in *Tarjuman al-Quran*. After nine years of personal effort, he invited people who were interested in his ideas to form an organization. Seventy-five people accepted his invitation and *Jamaat* was formed in 1941. But the four basic principles of *da'wah* remained central to Mawdudi and the *Jamaat-e-Islami*. His approach started within the context of an undivided India where Muslims were in the minority, addressed both Muslims and non-Muslims alike and identified 'root of corruption at all levels, and [the] lack of pious leadership'. Muslims, he argued, were unaware of the importance of ultimate change that is the change of leadership where 'the wicked and transgressed leadership will be replaced by leadership of the righteous.' The non-Muslims, he concluded, were unaware of the importance of such change, their views are based on prejudice and a lack of awareness of such a reality.

After the partition of India, the sphere of *da'wah* changed. The *Jamaat-e-Islami* Pakistan pursued a change in government and people, and planned their activities accordingly. The *Jamaat-e-Islami* *Hind* overwhelmingly diverted its *da'wah* efforts towards non-Muslims, *Iqamat-i-Din*, the total establishment of religion, being its overriding goal. *Da'wah* among non-Muslims and *Islah-e-Muasharat* (Reform of the Society) remain *Jamaat-e-Islami Hind*'s policy. In respect of non-

---

[9] See for details, *Continuing Committee on Muslim-Christian Co-operation: The Proceedings of the First Muslim-Christian Convocation*, Bhamdoun, Lebanon, April, 1954.

Muslims, the *Jamaat* constantly emphasized in its policy and programmes, brotherly relations and the removal of misgivings and misunderstandings about Islam. Its members argued the need and significance of the Oneness of God and its values in human life. They highlighted the need to uplift the backward classes and to help those who were burdened under the Hindu caste structure. At one of the meetings of *Jamaat-e-Islami Hind*, the *Jamaat* highlighted that it should concentrate all its efforts 'on *da'wah* of Islam in India … [and] should concentrate in translating Islamic literature in all major languages' of India. Apart from this, its policies and programmes concentrated on relief work, primary education and cottage industries, mainly among Muslims but also among non-Muslims.[10]

The atmosphere in India was such that though the Muslims wanted to educate their children, they were nonetheless suspicious about sending their children to secular schools and also reluctant to send them to *madaris* (seminaries). As a result a large number of young people were left out of both systems. Instead their parents preferred to send them to local mosques where the local imam would instruct them in basic religious education. There was though yet another problem. Though a large number of adults did not fit into any system, they nonetheless needed a basic Islamic education. Already considerable influences from local customs and traditions had crept into Muslim society and people adhered to these rigorously. For example in Mewat area in Gujarat, in India, the Muslims used to observe the local Hindu customs and festivals and adopted Hindu names for their children. In this respect Mawlana Ilyas (1885-1944) tried to introduce a different approach to reach mainly the adult Muslim population of the area. He toured Mewat regularly and inspired the people to change toward Islam. At least a hundred people accompanied him on those tours. Therefore, he formed a small number of *Tabligh* groups and assigned them to do the same as they had learned during their tours accompanying him. Once a viable group was formed that small group would do likewise. Mawlana Ilyas requested learned people to become involved in this movement and

---

[10] See Troll, C W, 'Islam as a Missionary Religion: some Observations with Special Reference to South and Southeast Asia', *Encounter*, No. 130 (November-December, 1986).

as a result Mawlana Muhammad Zakariyya of Saharnpur (d. 1982) gave his full support and eventually provided the basic syllabus. The system which Mawlana Ilyas devised and the syllabus provided by Mawlana Zakariyya formed the basis on which the *Tabligi Jamaat* have continued to work ever since. It became truly international under the leadership of Mawlana Yusuf, son of Mawlana Ilyas. The *Jamaat* has been successful in reforming Muslims' morals and uplifting their spirituality and imbibed amongst them a missionary zeal. In their approach, politics and power were of least concern. The Six Fundamentals were and remain the guiding principles of *Tabligh* groups. They are:

1. *Kalimah* (There is no God but God. This includes acceptance of the Oneness of God and the Prophethood of Muhammad).
2. *Salat* (Performing prescribed prayers).
3. *Ilmo-o-Dhikr* (Knowledge and remembrance of God).
4. *Ikram-i-Muslim* (To respect every Muslim).
5. *Ikhlas-i-Niyyat* (Sincerity in one's intention).
6. *Tafrigh-i-Waqt* (To spare time for *Tabligh*).

Apart from these, the *Tabligh* adopted, as a precautionary measure, avoidance of futile things *(tark-i-la yani)*. These basic methods of the *Tabligh* were disseminated far and wide and encouraged Muslims to participate in the movement.[11]

Although Mawlana Ilyas's reform movement avoided politics, his followers were keenly involved in polemics. Their overall perception of the West and Christianity was the same as that of the *Ikhwan* and *Jamaat-e-Islami*. The only difference one can point to between these groups and the *Tablighi Jamaat* was that others wanted to have some relations and engagement with Christianity. The *Tabligh*-ies, though, did not feel such necessity to speak to the Christians. Largely, the

---

[11] See *Six Fundamentals*, Ishaat-e-Dinyaat, New Delhi, n.d. For a biographical study of the founder of the *Tablighi Jamaat*, see Nadwi, Abul Hassan Ali, *Hazrat Mawlana Ilyas aur Unki Dini Dawat*, (Urdu), Ishaat-e-Dinayat, New Delhi, n.d.

Deoband School, and with them, the *Tablighi Jamaat* remain indifferent to Christians or have preferred to have a relation of *munazarah*. Even today, Rahmatullah Kairanwi's book *Izhar al-Haq* that he wrote in response to Karl Pfander's *Mizan al-Haq* is the standard book from which to understand Christianity.

By the 1960s, Muslim individuals and organizations began to feel a need to co-operate and support world-wide *da'wah* efforts, to prepare a team of *da'i* and send them to remote areas where they could impart Islamic knowledge to those who needed it most. With this in view, we would like to take note of two particular international organizations, namely *Rabitat al-Alam al-Islami* and *Jamiyat al-Dawah al-Islamiyah al-Alamiyah*.

The rise of nationalism and socialism in the Arab world during the 1950s and 1960s, especially in Egypt, where national identity quite often clashed with religious identity, produced a series of changes in the educational system of schools and universities including Al-Azhar. This alarmed the *'ulama'* who viewed these changes with scepticism. Saudi Arabia took the initiative to establish several universities and gave study grants to local as well as foreign students. The Saudis established the *Rabitat al-'Alam al-Isalami,* the Muslim World League, in 1962. One of the reasons behind its formation was the need to counter the Western influences and modern challenges. Nasser's nationalism was making inroads in the Arab world and influenced many Arab youths. It gave them a sense of pride and confidence. One such man was Mu'ammar al-Qadhdhafi of Libya. There was a desire in the minds of the Libyan leader to clarify misunderstandings about Islam, especially in the West, and to educate Muslims in general, and with this in mind *Jamiyat al-Da'wah*, The World Islamic Call Society, came into existing.

Both organizations were critical of the methods adopted by missionaries in the Muslim world. Ironically, however, they both modified the missionary approach and found it a convenient tool for use in the Third World countries. Their view of *da'wah* is much broader and encompasses a much wider scope than the *Tablighi Jamaat's* view. Their view is not simply the preaching and propagation of Islam but in some measure to prepare the Muslim community to counter the 'conspiracies of the enemies'. This institutionalisation of *da'wah* though is something that one needs to be concerned about.

The legacy of *munazarah* left by Pfander and Kairanwi has continued ever since. One such initiative which is alive and thriving can be found in the personality and activities of Ahmad Deedat and his organization, Islamic Propagation International. Deedat was born in Gujarat and migrated to Durban, South Africa, in 1927. He discovered his skills of debate and argument when American evangelical missionaries based across the road where he lived hounded him. The questions raised by the missionaries led him to search for answers and to question them in return. In time, this experience led Deedat to establish the Islamic Propagation Centre. In the *munazarah* spirit this organization provided 'combat kits' to challenge Christian evangelists and missionaries.

It was against this backdrop that the call for dialogue was made by the Christians in the mid 1950s.

II

Mission amongst Muslims is one of the most difficult issues of the contemporary relationship between the two communities, i.e. Muslims and Christian. As we have pointed out earlier one of the motivating factors behind the rediscover of Islam over the last hundred years or so has been secularization and mission.

The God of the Bible is a sending God and this sending act becomes a noble vocation for many.[12] Christians who took this responsibility on board and disbursed themselves throughout various parts of the world after Jesus. St Paul and St Thomas are early examples

---

[12] 'But when the right time finally came, God sent his own Son.' Galatians 4: 4.
Daw'ah is about invitation, mission is about 'sending'. The word 'mission' is derived from the Latin verb *mittere*, i.e. to send. The word 'apostle' also derived its meaning from the Greek root, *apostolein* meaning to send—an apostle is one who is sent. People or a group of people representing Jesus Christ and his Church sent with specific task are called 'missionaries'. The duty of Mission is based on the Biblical command: 'Go, then to all peoples everywhere and make them my disciples: baptize them in the name of the Father, the son, and the Holy Spirit, and teach them to obey everything I have commanded you. And I will be with you always, to the end of the age' (Matthew 28:19-20).

which motivated many subsequent generations of Christians to follow their path.[13]

Within the Protestant Churches, the issue of mission in the contemporary world was revisited against the backdrop of society's modern Secular outlook. The Western thinking like that of Kant, Darwin and Marx challenged the fundamental beliefs of Christianity. But Christians became uncomfortable when voices from within the Churches began to subscribe their values and ideas for them and hence, they began to question basic Christian beliefs. For example, Ernst Troeltsch (1865-1923), whose apparent denial of the absoluteness of Christian revelation and his doubts about the reliability of the biblical accounts, were seen as a new challenge to Christian mission. It signalled that the challenge was not only of how the message needed to be carried throughout the vast European empire, but also, in order to be effective in mission, there was yet another challenge and that was how to address the intra-Christian approach to mission and missionary challenge itself. The World Missionary Conference in Edinburgh in 1910 took the initiative in reviewing the mission field worldwide. The Conference's major concern was 'evangelization and unity' but it also looked very closely at the issue of the missionary message in relation to non-Christian religions. The preparatory committee did extensive home-work and prepared a survey of the world situation. John R Mott (1865-1955) collected the necessary material for the commission that was responsible for 'Carrying the Gospel to All the Non-Christian World'. He perceptively reported to the Conference about the situation of the Muslim world. 'Nationalism in Egypt' he found 'is in most respects [a] pro-Moslem movement, and therefore intensifies the dislike of the Egyptian towards the foreigner and the Christian.' He was aware of Western imperialism and its economic power that deliberately 'defraud', 'oppress' and 'degrade native races, because of greed.' His analysis of the Muslim society of the time is equally relevant for mission. He wrote: 'Of all the non-Christian religions, Mohammedanism exhibits

---

[13] For the history of missions, see K S Latourette, *A History of the Expansion of Christianity* (7 Vols.), Zondervan Publishing House, Michigan, 1939-45, and Neill, Stephen, *A History of Christian Missions*, Penguin Books, London, 1977.

the greatest solidarity and the most activity and aggressiveness, and is conducting a more widespread propaganda at the present time than any other religion save Christianity.'[14] A few years later, reflecting on the Jerusalem Conference 1924, Mott's remark seems to confirm the view of missionaries that they are happy to see the Muslim world becoming more secularized and Westernized rather then remaining within the 'sacred universe' of faith and belief. He wrote: 'the conferences revealed unmistakable evidences of the weakening or disintegration of Islam. This is true politically. Generally speaking nationalism is taking the place of Pan-Islamism. The Turkish Moslem, for example, is becoming more Turk than Moslem. The abolition of the Caliphate has had a profoundly disturbing effect not only in Turkey but also throughout the Mohammedan world. There are sign on every hand of the weakening of the social hold of Islam … The spread of Western industrialisation and the startling development of the material aspects of modern civilization have had a marked disintegrating influence. I asked one of the most eminent professors of Al-Azhar in Cairo what gave him greatest hope for Islam. He replied, "I see no hope; materialism is overwhelming us." He further remarks that a "new mentality is being developed as a result of contact with Western science and civilization during the war. Above all, one is impressed with the religious unsettling among Moslems."'[15]

One of the most poignant remarks that I have come across is that of Baron Carra de Vaux (1867-1953). He was one of the founders of the *Revue de l'Orient chrétien* and worked for the organisation of Congrès Scientifiques Internationaux des Catholiques. He was one of the experts on Ibn Sina who openly associated the colonial powers with Christian powers and with reference to Christianity he stated 'I believe that we should endeavour to split the Muslim world, to break its moral unity, using to this effect the ethnic and political divisions … Let us therefore accentuate these differences, in order to increase on the one hand national sentiments (*sentiment de nationalité*) and to decrease on the other that of religious community (*communauté religieuse*)

---

[14] See Cracknell, Kenneth, *Justice Courtesy and Love: Theologians and Missionaries Encountering World Religions, 1846-1914*, Epworth Press, London, 1995, p. 182, 184.

[15] Mott, John, R (ed.), *The Moslem World of To-Day*, Hodder and Stoughton, London, 1924, pp. 363-364.

among the various Muslim races. Let us take advantage of the political condition. Egypt, for example, governed today by British power, must form a moral entity clearly distinct from French Sudan or from Egypt a barrier between African Islam and Asian Islam. In one word, let us segment Islam and make use, moreover, of Muslim heresies and the Sufi orders.'[16]

Missionaries perhaps unconsciously believed that the increasing Westernization of the Muslim world might speed up its Christianization as well. The 'emancipation of women' and the increasing numbers of Western/Secular educated elite amongst Muslims were seen as steps in the right direction. But these very measures made the Muslims suspicious of Christianity. They saw them as an expansionist arm of Westernization. These fears had some basis. When the young Charles Lavigerie (1825-1892) was sent to Algeria in 1869 to be the new archbishop. He immediately confronted the 'reality' that the conversion of Algerians to Christianity was not something for the future, but the immediate requirement for him, like the French colonialist, was to 'civilize' the native Algerians. He even criticized the French authorities for not doing enough to 'civilize' the Algerians. He remarked that the 'sad sight of blindness and impotence that we have seen for thirty years in Africa [i.e. from the beginning of French colonization of Algeria] is only explained by the calculated absence of all Christian thought in the administrations of Algeria, which instead of assimulating [sic] these Berber populations by leading then to our civilization keep them their barbary and their Koran.'[17]

After World War I the Christian mission arguably became much more introspective without losing its strategic edge over the Muslim world. The Edinburgh Conference subsequently gave birth to three organizations: The International Missionary Council (1921), The Life and Work Movement (1925) and The Faith and order Movement (1927). The last two organizations merged in 1948 to form the World Council of Churches. Later, in 1961, the IMC merged

---

[16] Quoted in Buheiry, M R, 'Colonial Scholarship and Muslim Revivalism in 1900', *Arab Studies Quarterly*, Vol. 4, No. 1-2, (Spring 1982), p. 5.

[17] Quoted in Schissel, GregoryA, SJ, 'The Quest For Common Ground: The Roman Catholic Church and Islam After the Second Vatican Council', Ph.D. thesis submitted at Harvard University, Cambridge, Massachusetts, 1998, p. 39.

with the WCC. The WCC was instrumental in organizing intra-Christian debate about dialogue with people of other faiths.

The three examples selected here demonstrate that the Muslim fear of missionaries as Secularization agents is somewhat justified. Today, the mission is perceived in Muslim society largely through the commercialism and through the 'charity' organizations represented by the various non-government organizations (NGOs). They too have been referred to as the arms of Westernization in the Muslim world.

The Roman Catholic Church's approach to the duty of mission is largely be found in Church's documents like *Lumen Gentium*, *Nostra Aetate* and *Evengelii Nutiandi* as well as in the Pope's various Encyclicals particularly *Redemptoris Missio*. These documents were produced against the background of increasing secularization and the Church's urgency to readjust itself to the new post-world war world. Essentially, the Church was self-consciously aware of its perception amongst the people of other faiths, particularly amongst the Jews. It wanted to dissociate itself with its perceived past and was keen to start a new chapter of mission-renewal as well as forge better relations with people of other faiths.

These documents suggested that the Church wanted to address in its relationship with other faiths in an open and frank manner. He signalled that a closer relationship was desirable and that in the process the Church was willing to forget the past and urge others to do the same. Furthermore, in this new relationship the Church did not want to lose sight of the centrality of Jesus and the Church and its own missionary obligation. The Church would see others from its own standpoint and as far as other faiths were concerned Pope John Paul VI stated that each 'contains sparks of light within itself which must neither be despised nor quenched, even though they are insufficient for giving clear vision.'[18] The pope makes it clear that the Christians should not forget to 'declare openly ... that there is but one true religion, the religion of Christianity ...'[19] The problem the Church encountered though was how to reconcile dialogue and mission. The increasing expectations that dialogue

---

[18] Easter Homily, 29.3.1964.
[19] *Ibid.*

generated in the 1970s gave the impression that the Church and its mission would largely be one of 'involvement in the world'. Some members began to state clearly that the '[n]on Christians do not need membership in the visible Church in order to be saved; they do not need the Church to arrive at a deeper awareness of the saving mystery by which they are continually embraced.'[20] On the other hand, the Church was under constant pressure both from within and from outside to clarify its position regarding mission and dialogue. Finally in 1991, the pope's Encyclical, *Redemptoris Missio*, stated clearly that dialogue is 'a part of the Church's evangelizing mission. Understood as a method and means of mutual knowledge and enrichment, dialogue is not in opposition to the mission *Ad Gentis*; indeed it has special links with that mission and is one of its expressions '… the Church sees no conflict between proclaiming Christ and enjoying inter-religious dialogue. Instead she feels the need to link the two in the context of her mission *Ad Gentes*.'[21]

III

What we have said so far is that the dialogue between the two communities has been strongly influenced by the presence of the Secular. Indeed the Revd Dr Charles Amjad Ali, former Director of the Christian Study Centre Rawalpindi (Pakistan), argued that the word 'dialogue' as it has been used and understood is deeply flawed and heavily influenced by Western Secular discourse particularly in Christian-Muslim relations. He finds that both 'the concept and practice' of dialogue is rooted in Western philosophical traditions and 'in the Enlightenment and related traditions which provide epistemological foundations.' This poses, in his view, 'three conceptual problems'. First, 'the self-sufficiency of the thinking subject to determine the world in the Cartesian *cogito ergo sum*. The second is the Kantian emphasis on transcendent reason unimpeded by

---

[20] Quoted in Glasser, A F, 'Vatican II and Mission 1965-1985', *Missiology*, Vol. XIII, No. 4. (October 1985), p. 491.

[21] *Redemptoris Missio*, pp. 70-71. Muslims have generally associated dialogue with *da'wah*, see for one such approach Denffer, A V, *Some Reflections on Dialogue Between Christians and Muslim*, the Islamic Foundation, Leicester, 1989 (reprint).

determination of location and identity. And the third is the liberal political theory which emphasizes the discrete, vying and entitative existence of people, reducing (if not negating) community and religious identities.'[22] He forcefully argues that because of this dislocation of the meaning 'it is no wonder then that we have seen dialogue at the periphery of the theological task rather than as its very foundation.' Due to this bent of mind, he remarks, dialogue has always been 'something we do after our theology.' Hence it minimizes 'the identity of people'. He then goes on to explain how the word 'dialogue' is 'misconstrued'. 'The preposition *dia* (going through) has, in fact, been replaced by a numerical prefix *di* (two) by a purely mental process (*res cogitans*). And the word *logos* has changed from its original meaning of "principles and significant cohering realities" simply to mean "word exchanged." This is clearly evident from how we pose the opposite of *dia*logue by using *mono*logue.'[23] He emphasizes that by adopting the meaning and practising the 'dialogue' with the prefix *di*, dialogue has become a dialogue of two individuals and not a dialogue of two communities. As a result dialogue has become a contractual relationship 'as in politics', where the only possibility of 'the common existence of two discrete, vying and isolated entities [can] be achieved through "social contact." ' Hence through dialogue with its acquired meaning a 'religious contract' is sought. He defines dialogue as a 'foundational process of discourse in which the communities involved go through their own respective *logos* in order to come to some common understanding of certain social and political problems and issues. In achieving this common understanding, the very *logos* through which one has proceeded into dialogue in the first place itself undergoes changes.' Once this definition is accepted 'then the opposite of dialogue is not *monologue* but *metalogue*, which means going beyond one's *logos*, or achieving a transcendent reason through escaping or overcoming the prejudices of one's own *logos* and locatedness.'[24] The

---

[22] Amjad-Ali, Charles, 'Theological and Historical Rationality Behind Christian-Muslim Relations' in Rajashekar, Paul, and Wilson, S H (eds.), *Islam in Asia: Perspectives for Christian-Muslim Encounter*, Lutheran World Federation, Geneva, 1992, pp. 5-8.

[23] *Ibid.*, p. 6.

[24] *Ibid.*, p. 6-7, See also Podgorski, F R, 'Towards a Catholic Theology of Missionary Dialogue and Dialogical Mission with other Religions', A Doctoral dissertation submitted at Pontificiae Universitatis Gregorianae, Rome, 1987, pp. 61-63.

problem is highlighted forcefully. For the Muslim, Christians have proposed the dialogue, perhaps unconsciously, in *di*logue sense where the art of bargaining between the people was more prevalent than the art of collective participation. In the light of the definition that Amjad-Ali proposes—'going through'—living and participating in the world was the meaning that the Muslims took and understood.

Although the basis of *hewar* (dialogue) is rooted in the Qur'an, particularly with the Christians, however, Muslim participation in dialogue, in general, has been less 'theologically' oriented. For a Muslim, strictly speaking, dialogue in the 'theological' domain is a return to God and that is perhaps the only reason to enter into dialogue. The basic element in dialogue, as Seyyed Hossein Nasr argues is 'faith in God'. He emphasizes that the last few decades of Christian-Muslim dialogue shows that the 'complete accord between religions is not possible in the human atmosphere but only in the divine stratosphere.' The approach to the theological problems in his view 'have not received a proper solution in the present-day context by those seeking common accord between Islam and Christianity.'[25]

For their part Muslims have seen dialogue, in some respect, as a plea to explain their faith, but more than that they have viewed dialogue as an opportunity to face the growing challenge presented by atheism and materialism. Therefore, the theological dialogue for Muslims has received little attention. Lately, it was the urgent challenge they faced in the shape of materialism and Secularism in general, that they wanted to confront. They saw the critical use of reason against the Divine and material powers as seeking to fold their faith. In all this, it was not only the outside world that saw religion as a lingering force from the past, but both Christians and Muslims themselves also observed that such 'philosophies ... have [had] crept into the lives of those who profess to be the followers of Islam and Christianity.' The growth of 'materialism', 'irreligion' and 'atheism' are being seen as 'the breeding grounds for social, spiritual and moral anarchy.'[26]

---

[25] Nasr, Seyyed Hossein, *Islamic-Christian Dialogue—Problems and Obstacles to be Pondered and Overcome*, Center for Muslim-Christian Understanding History and International Affairs, George Town University, Washington DC, 1997, p. 4.

[26] Declaration of the Executive Board of the Continuing Committee on Muslim-Christian cooperation at Alexandria, Egypt on 14 February 1955. See Haddad, J N ed., *op. cit.*, p. 23.

Though both Christians and Muslims somehow acknowledged that priority in their relations should be given to socio-cultural issues, nonetheless the emphasis they sought to assert was different. Firstly, we find the Churches—both Catholic and Protestant—wanting to justify their involvement theologically even in a *di*logue sense. In other words, they wanted to be sure that their involvement with other faiths and particularly with Muslims had theological underpinnings. This was also necessary because the Churches were under constant pressure from their own members not to abandon the duty of mission in their new relationship. Relatively speaking the Muslims were not under such pressure because the issue of relations with the Christians was not an urgent one nor indeed was the issue of survival. Hence, they hardly even discussed this issue among themselves. Thus, there was no urgency to open-up *Shari'ah, fiqh* or even the nature of *hewar* to be considered with immediate priority.

Today, in dialogue, we need to look at the perception of religion itself. Muslims have no choice in a new world that they are living in. The West and its perception of religion have been moulded by the Christian interpretation of faith. Historically and culturally, Christianity has played a significant role here. The Muslim assertion of faith, in public life, is measured on the criteria provided by Christianity. Therefore, there is an urgent need to enter into a dialogue with that perception of religion. By entering into dialogue with Christianity, Muslims would be entering into debate with Western society's perception of faith and belief. Muslims are asked to take Christianity seriously, both in its history and thought and not just at dialogue gatherings and conferences. Once this aspect becomes important for Muslims then the debate between Christians and Muslims will perhaps be a dialogue of 'equals'.

Today, dialogue between the two communities has to move away from the mission and *da'wah* circuit. Muslims in some respect need to re-examine how they are going to address the issue of living together and the *'ulama'* and imams, in the mosque in particular, are placed with significant responsibility. They have great influence on Muslim society. This influential group is almost unaware of dialogue, instead they are aware of *munazarah* and the history of polemical debates. The development between Christians and Muslims is seen only through the polemist's eye. Invariably, they do not see the need and necessity for such dialogue as they see this as a mechanism that will only help reduce *iman* (faith) and compromise their own religion. This situation could be addressed if Muslims looked into their own tradition where studying Western, including Christian traditions, customs and practices could become part of syllabus. Special care has to be taken where customs and traditions and understanding of faith are to be taught, as they are understood in that culture and belief and not simply from a Muslim's view of the faith. After all an *'alim* or a *mufti* is required to have some basic knowledge and needs to have some awareness of the 'custom' *('urf)* and 'practice' *('adat)* of the people where he lives and works. Any religious opinion must carry the weight of these facts behind it.

Although the creation of a Christian-Muslim Council at international level may be desirable, the establishment of a Council at Commonwealth level is somewhat urgent. Such a Council could provide a platform to discuss contemporary issues that Muslims and Christians are facing in a number of Commonwealth countries such as Pakistan, Nigeria, or countries such as Australia that is hit in some respect by the conflict in neighbouring countries like Indonesia. Or issues such as the role of NGOs in countries like Bangladesh could be discussed. Such a Council could help at local level in organizing Christian-Muslim groups or helping existing groups and these could address both historical and contemporary issues that hamper relations.

The Christian-Muslim dialogue today seems to have moved away from a simple religious discourse between the two communities. The *new world order* debate combined with Huntington's 'Clash of Civilization' proposal generated a passion amongst Muslims who were until then passive participants in dialogue. They all became alert to the prospect of a clash. Various groups—religious and non-religious—all became interested and involved. It created a dialogue market in the 1990s which has continued ever since. Now that the United Nations also had declared year 2001 as the Year of Dialogue among Civilizations, the bi-lateral dialogue and its boundaries are now increasingly blurred. There is a lot more overlapping and sometimes it is difficult to differentiate the boundaries between Christian-Muslim dialogue and the Islam and the West dialogue. Now, countries like Saudi Arabia, Kuwait, Jordan, Turkey, Indonesia, Morocco, Iran and others are all involved in this dialogue of culture and civilization. The European Council is equally involved. For Muslims and Christians this is perhaps an opportunity to divert our attentions away from issues such as *da'wah* and mission and focus instead on a new dialogue where the two communities can speak plainly and openly without theological constraints.

Finally I would like to conclude from a recent presentation by Professor Walid Saif in a Muslim-Christian Consultation where he stated: 'Muslim-Christian dialogue should not be promoted by common and shared fears from non-religious or anti-religious discourses. Our common grounds and concerns should be defined in positive terms, stemming from our own initiative as faithful Muslims and Christians— from our awareness and moral obligations dictated by our religions. We do not meet to defend our religions, but rather to defend the rights and welfare of all people out of our religious ideals, and exactly through that we extend our religious message and promote our religious advocacy. Great ideals and convictions can only be communicated through tangible models. And we can, somehow, observe with some rejoice and confidence, the growing revival of religiosity throughout the world as a testimony to the ever-lasting endurance of religion in the face of materialism and extreme secularism. But, exactly at this point, we may want to stop fearing for religion from secular extremism, and start fearing for our religions from religious extremism. I strongly believe that the growing religious sentiments in different parts of the world lays more responsibility on our Muslim-Christian dialogue as on each of our religious communities; and both intra-religious and inter-religious efforts are certainly interlinked. The harm which can be done to religion by religious extremism may well surpass any such harm by secular extremism. In fact, historical experiences show that anti-religious trends often breed on and gain, or regain, legitimacy from the atrocities and injustices made in the name of religion. If not rationalised by enlightened and inclusive religious perspectives, the growing religiosity may well be translated into both inter-religious and intra-religious conflicts, exclusion and coercion. The most dangerous division may not be religion vs. religion. Religious freedoms across religious communities or within the same community can be more suppressed by zealous, narrow-minded and exclusivist interpretations of religion.'[27]

---

[27] This paper was submitted at the Christian-Muslim Meeting, Amersfoort (The Netherlands), organized by the World Council of Churches (7-12 November 2000). Published in *Encounters: Journal of Inter-Cultural Perspectives*, Vol. 7 No. 1 (March 2001), p. 97.

CHRISTIANS AND MUSLIM-CHRISTIAN RELATIONS: THEOLOGICAL REFLECTIONS

Anthony O'Mahony

> I have been on my guard
> not to condemn the unfamiliar.
> For it is easy to miss.
> At the turn of a civilisation
> > *The Sleeping Lord*, David Jones (1895-1974),
> > Anglo-Welsh Christian Poet and Artist.

Crossing frontiers

Never before has history known so many frontiers as in our contemporary world, and at no period has there been such a frequent violation of frontiers as happens today. It would seem that the establishment and removal of frontiers is the order of the day. This contradictory process is a window into the plight of humanity in these times: a dialectical tension between demarcation of particular identities and crossing over to the other shore. If the consolidation of frontiers is characterised as ethnicity, tribalism, nationalism and religious exclusiveness; the crossing of them is known as globalism, the mixing of cultures, trans-nationalism and expression of world religiosity.[1]

We are struck by the ambiguity of the phenomenon of frontier crossing. Crossing over could mean a march of aggression

---

[1] Felix Wilfred, ' The Art of Negotiating the Frontiers', *Concilium: Frontier violations: the Beginings of new identities*, no. 2 (1999), pp. vii-xiii. Several Muslim-Christian frontiers have been outlined in Asia and Africa and the Mediterranean by M Marion, 'Les sept frontières chrétiennes devant l'Islam', *Esprit*, vol.116, no.10 (1986), pp. 39-59 and Anthony O'Mahony, 'Islam in Europe', *The Way: Contemporary Christian Spirituality*, vol. 41, no.2 (2001), pp. 122-135.

that infringes upon the freedom and autonomy of the realm invaded. It could be overt and violent, as when a power intrudes into the territory—physical, cultural, spiritual—of the other; or it could be covert and subtle, nevertheless destructive, as in the transnationalization of capital and homogenisation of cultures. A sense of ambiguity marks the affirmation and negation of frontiers.[2]

The violation of frontiers is often a matter of creativity. This aspect can offer great hope for the emergence of refreshing new identities and encounters and the envisioning of alternatives. To be able to cross over, one has to locate oneself at the margins or at the edges of present identity. To position oneself at the frontier can be to adopt a very advantageous standpoint inasmuch as one can assess one's identity in a very creative and critical way. This in no way requires the rejection of tradition, but an affirmation of its continuing relevance and ongoing unfolding. There is a great epistemological potential in being positioned on the outer edge, where the view of things is bound to be quite different from the centre where one may not understand what it means to come face-to-face with another identity another spiritual or religious territory.

It is important to note that the crossing of frontiers and the birth of the new are a sheer necessity for a new historical period or a particular context. The reality or the search for authentic renewal from within tradition outgrows the existing bounds and frames and forces the crossing of frontiers and the breaking of the frame. A re-mapping of the territory and a re-drawing of the frontiers follow it.

However crossing, of course, is not simply an external event. It is also a spiritual experience. This journey as an enriching spiritual endeavour has been taken up by the American Catholic theologian, David Burrell who writes:

> We are, invited, in our time, on a voyage of discovery stripped of colonizing pretensions: an invitation to explore the other on the way to discovering ourselves. The world into which we have been thrust asks nothing

---

2   Claude Geffré, 'Christianity and Culture', *International Review of Mission*, vol. 84 (1995), pp. 17-32 and Cl Geffré, 'Mission Issues in the Contemporary Context of Multifaith Situations', *International Review of Mission*, vol. 86 (1997), pp. 407-409.

less of us; those of us intent on discovering our individual vocations cannot proceed except as partners in such a variegated community. And as that journey enters the domain of faith, our community must needs assume interfaith dimension. What once were boundaries have become frontiers, which beckon to be broached, as we seek to understand where we stand by expanding or minds and hearts to embrace the other. Put in this fashion, our inner journey can neither be syncretic nor procrustean: assimilating or appropriating. What is rather called for is mutuality of understanding and of appreciation, a critical perception which is already incipiently self-critical. Rather than reach for commonality, we are invited to expand our horizons in the face of diversity. The goal is not an expanded scheme, but an enriched inquirer: discovery of one's own faith in encountering the faith of another.[3]

In the Christian tradition, the centre also determines the circumference. The body of Christ can be the body of Christ if it has limits. To keep the unity of faith, the primitive Church was to promote different types of mediations: summaries of the Easter faith; a practice of exchange and mutual verification without fear of polemic; the recognition of authentic charisms; the authority of the scriptures, the practice of baptism and the eucharist; the setting up of the apostolic ministry. Later there would be more developed creeds, the holding of councils, the development of tradition of faith, the recognition of primatial centres. In this way the Church was to show itself as a communion: a vertical communion of God and a horizontal communion among believers; the universal communion of the local churches.

Felix Wilfred has observed several distinct moments in the early history of Christianity when identity recorded a shift in its self-understanding. Thus Christianity has re-drawn its own frontiers several times. This has always been a critical act at crucial times. One could

---

[3] David Burrell in the preface to Roger Arnaldez, *Three Messengers for One God*, University of Notre Dame Press, 1994, pp. VII.

highlight several moments. The first crisis is connected with the times when disciples of Jesus stood on the crossroads of forging their identity either as a group within Judaism, with strict Jewish membership and following its customs and traditions, or opening up the way of Jesus beyond ethnic frontiers. What was achieved after many struggles was in fact a frontier-moving act. The widening of the circumference of the group led to the re-positioning of its identity. If the first re-drawing of frontiers was thus a matter of *ethnos*— overcoming the tendency of a reduction of Christianity within ethnical bounds.

The second frontier moving act had to do with the *chronos*: against the apocalyptic background of the imminent expectation of the Risen Christ, Christian discipleship was viewed as a matter for a brief period. A realisation of the delayed *parousia* pushed the temporal frontiers of Christianity with very significant consequences. It paved the way not only for the consolidation of ecclesial structures providing for an indeterminate period, but also for shaping the Christian identity anew.

Today we are witnessing a further shift or movement in Christian history which witnesses to profound deepening of self-understanding in relation to other religious traditions. This not only engages the Christian tradition in a reassessment of its own fractured oneness—that is how it understands itself from within, and how others bear witness to that tradition from without. This is of particular importance in the relationship between Christianity and Islam, as the Muslim tradition grasps within itself a particular understanding of Judaism and Christianity. It is thus linked into the Jewish-Christian *other*, and is thereby held hostage. Christian theologians are now becoming aware of *a* Christian identity within Islam, and what that says to the Christian tradition.

A global theological encounter

A theologian and scholar of Islam once told a story to convey a warning. Once upon a time an itinerant grammarian came to a body of water and enlisted the services of a boatman to ferry him across. As they made their way, the grammarian asked the boatman, 'Do you know the science of grammar?' The humble boatman thought for a moment and admitted somewhat dejectedly that he did not. Not much later, a growing storm began to imperil the small vessel. Said the boatman to the grammarian, 'Do you know the science of swimming?'[4]

Thus we are reminded that at beginning of the new millennium too much of our theological activity remains shockingly introverted. Instead of allowing an inherent energy to launch us into the larger reality of global religiosity, we insist on protecting our theology from the threat of contamination. If we continue to resist serious engagement with other theological traditions, our theology may prove as useful as grammar in a typhoon. One of the most important tasks of theology today is to develop strategies for determining how to enter into the meaning system of another tradition, not merely as a temporary member of that tradition, but in such a way as to see how the two traditions bear upon one another.[5]

As has been observed by Fr Patrick Ryan, there is an important sense in which the Christian tradition has to become more *catholic*, in the root sense of the word: embracing the whole of human experience.[6] Any form of Christianity in the future will face two major challenges, each of which has theological and philosophical implications. The first of these challenges is polycentrism of intellect and the second one could be summed up under the heading of the unity of humankind.

---

[4] John Renard, 'Islam and Christian Theologians', *The Catholic Theological Society of America: Proceedings*, vol. 48 (1993), pp. 41-54 and p. 41.

[5] Emilio Platti, of the Dominican Institute for Oriental Studies in Cairo, has written two interesting accounts of how this might be observed in relation to Muslim-Christian relations: *Risques respectifs du souci de fidélité dans l'Islam et dans le christianisme, Christianisme, Judaisme et Islam: Fidélité et ouverture* (sous la direction de Joseph Dore), Editions du Cerf, Paris, 1999, pp. 223-242, and 'Islam et Occident: "Choc de theologies?"', *Mélanges Institut Dominicain d'études orientales*, vol. 24 (2000), pp. 347-379.

[6] Patrick J Ryan, 'Sailing Beyond the Horizon: Challenges for the Third Millennium', *America*, May 23, 1998, pp. 14-28. See also his 'Is Dialogue Possible with Muslims?', *America*, 31 December, 1994, pp. 13-17; 'The Monotheism of the Excluded: Towards an Understanding of Islam', *The Month*, n. s, vol. 16, no. 8 (1983), pp. 264-267, and 'Creative Misunderstanding and the Possibility of Jewish-Christian-Muslim Trialogue', *The Month*, n. s, vol. 31, no. 7 (1998), pp. 267-274.

Augustine in the first millennium of the Christian era and Aquinas in the second lead the honourable procession of Christian intellectuals of those two millennia who retrieved the thought of Plato and Aristotle, the fountainheads of philosophical speculation in the millennium before Christ. These two doctors of the church reinterpreted pre-Christian Greek thought in terms of their own respective grasps not only of that philosophy but also on the cumulative Judeo-Christian traditions of faith and hope and love.

As we start the third millennium, it might be suggested that those who would follow Augustine and Aquinas in the next thousand years would have a task somewhat similar to that of their intellectual ancestors. But they will have to retrieve from many more non-Christian intellectual and faith traditions of past centuries new ways of thinking about the experience of Christian revelation. They will also have to do philosophy and theology and work out ethics that borrow categories from broader perspectives. One most notably dimension is the inter-faith encounter. One could be tempted to say that the future of theology depends upon a more intensive 'inter-penetration' of systematic theology and the history of religions.

Some do not hesitate to speak of a new planetary ecumenism. We must agree with them inasmuch as the dialogue between religions coincides with the keener awareness of the unity of the human family and a more acute sense of the common responsibility of religions for the future of humankind and its environment.

But it would be absurd to think that the 'new ecumenism' makes Christian ecumenism in the primary sense obsolete or secondary. The ecumenical dialogue within the Christian community, which began to take shape in the early decades of the 20th century and started to mature after the Second World War, has shattered a certain type of absolutism and has generally promoted the dialogue of the Church, first with the other two monotheistic religions, and then with the great Eastern religions.

The theology of religions has become an important chapter in Christian theology, but once again we find ourselves stammering because it takes time to shed our old habits and to understand that frank and open dialogue does not necessarily lead to false ecumenism, that is, to religious indifferentism.

A widespread consensus exists today among theologians that

any exclusive model for understanding Christianity must be qualified, whether it be that of ecclesio-centric absolutism or that in which Christianity is the only source of grace. On the other hand, it is not enough to adopt an inclusive religious model—Christ fulfils everything that is good, true, and holy in other religions—to believe that we have thereby demystified the absolute character of Christianity as an historical religion. Indeed, a fundamental tension remains between the demands of equality and reciprocity inherent in true dialogue and the apostolic claim of Christianity to be the religion of the absolute and definitive manifestation of God in Jesus Christ. If Jesus himself is only one mediator among others and not God's decisive manifestation for all men and women, then we can seriously question whether we have not already discarded the faith inherited from the apostles.[7]

For religions as well as cultures, globalisation presents a double reef or dialectic: it can only lead to destructive syncretism but also to fundamentalist reactions.[8] However, it should be able, nevertheless, to favour an inter-religious engagement on a planetary scale, without falling into the myth of world religion. Each religion, faithful to its proper identity, can witness to the universal search of the Ultimate or Last Reality, which no religious system can exhaust.

In other words, it is not at all certain that we yet possess an adequate theological response, which takes seriously the implications of interreligious dialogue without sacrificing Christian identity. In any event, it is not sufficient to go from Christocentrism to theocentrism as the adepts of a pluralistic theology of religions suggest. Every responsible Christian theology must maintain the normative character of Christology. Rather than adopting some general theocentrism, we must start at the very centre of the Christian message, that is, God's manifestation in the historical particularity of Jesus of Nazareth, and find there the justification for the dialectical nature of Christianity.

Without having the pretension of installing a New World

---

[7] My own reflections here owe much to the thought of the French Catholic theologian Claude Geffré, 'Pour un christianisme mondial', *Recherches de Sciences religieuses*, vol. 86, no. 1 (1998), pp. 53-75; 'Le pluralisme religieux de l'indifferentisme ou le vrai défi de la théologie chrétienne', *Revue théologique de Louvain*, vol. 31 (2000), pp. 3-32.

[8] Cl. Geffré, 'La rencontre du christianisme et des cultures', *Revue d'Ethique et de théologie morale. Le Supplément*, no. 192 (1995), pp. 69-91.

Order, Christianity holds a prophetic and counter-cultural power against the risks of, not only dehumanisation, but also fragmentation between persons and ethnic and religious communities. As a religion of incarnation, Christianity not only announces to every human being the gratuitous salvation of God, but it works in healing cultures and all creation. The Church announces Jesus Christ as an event of universal salvation for all humanity, including those who belong to other religious traditions. But the witness of the Gospel must learn not to confuse the universality of the mystery of Christ with that of a Christianity understood as a historical religion inseparable from its Western form, and must learn to maintain a distance between the Church as means of salvation and the Kingdom of God, which never ceases to go beyond its frontiers.

In theology, paradox is not contrary to the demands of logical reason. Paradox does not result from logical contradiction, but from the fact that an event transcends all human expectations and possibilities.

Any dialogue requires respect for the dialogue partners and interest in their beliefs—especially if these beliefs are culturally and religiously different from our own. At the same time we must retain our own cultural and religious identity. Lack of commitment under the pretext of openness leads to no real dialogue, or to sham agreements. We cannot put our faith in parentheses in order to connect with another's faith.[9] This is especially true with regard to Muslim-Christian encounters, when what is at issue is not only the identity of each tradition, but the future character of an engagement which encompasses nearly half of humanity.[10]

Christian-Muslim relations in all their multi-faceted complexity (religious in the strict sense, cultural, societal, economical, political) are fundamentally an encounter of believers called to give, through life and word, a witness. Contained in these two living traditions is the giving of a witness in and of faith. Members of these traditions know themselves to be called in faith to witness faith. The meeting of these two distinct overall witnesses, Christian and Muslim, is lived in countless

---

[9] Cl. Geffré, 'La portée théologique du dialogue islamo-chrétien', *Islamochristiana*, vol. 18 (1992), pp. 1-23, and 'La théologie des religions non-chrétiennes vingt ans après Vatican II', *Islamochristiana*, vol. 11 (1985), pp. 115-133.

[10] Thomas Michel, 'Christian-Muslim dialogue in a changing world', *Theology Digest*, vol. 39, no. (1992), pp. 303-320.

concrete practical ways and adaptations and, hence, produces an endless number of encounters, both by individuals and by groups.[11]

Fr Christian Troll has reminded us that Franco-Algerian Jesuit, Henri Sanson,[12] suggested that we should reflect on our Christian vocation towards Muslims 'in the mirror of Islam', that is, taking into account at every step the missionary vocation which our Muslim partners, in faith, know themselves to be charged with. We shall then reflect on our mission to Islam in the light of that of Islam, i.e. the Muslims' consciousness to be called by God, individually and collectively, to witness the Truth, to proclaim it, to establish the true religion and to invite all and everyone to membership in the *umma muslima*. This encounter with Islam as a missionary religion will lead us to greater precision in the grasp of the distinctive features of our Christian missionary vocation and message, and of appropriate ways to respond to them today. For Islam is more than a social and political, a religious and humanitarian phenomenon, it is more a challenge to the growth of the Church. It is ultimately a theological issue as the heart of the *missio Dei*.[13]

Muslim-Christian relations

The historical study of the relationship between Muslims and Christian communities, between Islam and Christianity is by necessity still in its beginnings. It cannot be otherwise, since Islamic history itself as well as the history of those Christian communities that have been in contact with Islam in different times and places, is still being written. Islamic-Christian relations are as old as Islam. In the course of thirteen

[11] Jacques Waardenburg, 'Critical Issues in Muslim-Christian Relations: theoretical, practical, dialogical, scholarly', *Islam and Christian Muslim Relations*, vol. 8, no. 1 (1997), pp. 9-26, and Thomas Michel, 'Social and religious factors affecting Muslim-Christian relations', *Islam and Christian Muslim Relations*, vol. 8, no. 1 (1997), pp. 53-66.

[12] Henri Sanson, *Dialogue intérieur avec l'Islam*, Centurion, Paris, 1990). no. 12: Henri Sanson, *Christianisme au miroir de l'Islam: essa sur la rébcontre des cultures en Algérie*, Editions du Cerf, Paris, 1984; *Dialogue intérieur avec l'Islam*, Centurion, Paris, 1990; 'Universalite du christianisme et universalite de l'Islam', *Islamochristiana* (Rome), vol. 13 (1987), pp. 47-59.

[13] Christian W Troll, 'Witness Meets Witness: The Church's Mission in the Context of the Worldwide Encounter of Christian and Muslim Believers Today', *Encounter*, vol. 4, no.1 (1998), pp. 15-34.

centuries of history they have been manifested in the most varied and even contradictory ways. There have been hard and painful periods. But there have also been periods of frank and fruitful collaboration and even moments of sincere friendship, which have not been overcome by conflict.[14] The relationship between Christians and Muslims over the centuries is a long and tortuous one. Geographically the origins of the two communities are not so far apart—Bethlehem and Jerusalem are only some 800 miles from Mecca—but as the two communities have grown and become universal rather than local influences, the relationship between them has sometimes been one of enmity, sometimes one of rivalry and competition, sometimes one of mutual influence, sometimes one of co-operation and collaboration.[15] Different regions of the world in different centuries have therefore witnessed a whole range of encounters between Christians and Muslims.

The Muslim and Christian worlds have known violent confrontations. Muslim conquests which brought parts of the Christian world under Muslim domination; the Crusades still vividly remembered today; the expansion of the Turkish Ottoman empire with its threat to Christian centres; the Armenian massacres and

---

[14] In an effort to respond to an increasingly religiously pluralistic situation, perhaps Christians need to explore friendship with non-Christians as a theological virtue. Virtues are enduring aspects of character that incorporate values and skills, have histories, and often act as correctives to vices. Inter-religious friendship in particular can be seen as an example of human excellence, a new virtue that incorporates values and skills and helps Christians in resisting the vice of despising, ignoring, or caricaturing their non-Christian religious neighbours. See James L Fredericks, 'Interreligious Friendship: a new theological virtue', *Journal of Ecumenical Studies*, vol. 35, no.2 (1998), pp. 159-174. For a interpretation of the origin of the theology of friendship, see L Gregory Jones, 'The Theological Transformation of Aristotelian Friendship in the Thought of St Thomas Aquinas', *New Scholasticism*, vol. 61 (1987), pp. 373-399; for the application of Aquinas' thought to Islam, see David Burrel, 'Friendship with God in al-Ghazali and Aquinas', (ed.) L Rouner, *The Changing Face of Friendship*, University of Notre Dame Press, 1994. However, there are limitations to friendship in interreligious engagements, see Anthony O'Mahony, 'Mysticism and Politics: Louis Massignon, Shi'a Islam, Iran and Ali Shari'ati: a Muslim-Christian Encounter', *University Lectures in Islamic Studies*, (ed.) Alan Jones, WIFT, London, vol. 2 (1998), pp. 113-134.

[15] Hugh Goddard, 'Christian-Muslim relations: a look backwards and a look forwards', *Islam and Christian Muslim Relations*, vol. 11, no.2 (2000), pp. 195-212; H Goddard, *A History of Christian-Muslim Relations*, Edinburgh University Press, Edinburgh, 2000, and Alan M Guenther, 'The Christian Experience and Interpretation of the Early Muslim Conquest and Rule', *Islam and Christian Muslim Relations*, vol. 10, no.3 (1999), pp. 363-378.

genocide; European colonialism of the 19th-early 20th centuries; the rise of Christian missions; the continuing difficult situations in which Christians find themselves in dominant Muslim societies. It would be petty to try to figure out who is more guilty in these conflicts. History should make us all a little more humble.

The weight of this history may be why few approach Islam without strong feelings one way or the other. Sound spiritual teaching, as witnessed by the teaching of Pope John Paul II, reminds us that something must be clarified and freed within us in regard to Islam. The Spirit of Jesus is the Spirit of peace and charity. To quote a sage: 'We cannot change the past, but we do have a responsibility of how it is remembered.'

Originating on the Arabian peninsula in opposition to the polytheism of Mecca, Islam at its birth could have seen itself as a close or distant relative of Judaism, which held sway at Medina and other cities. It could also have regarded itself as a neighbour alongside the Monophysite Christian communities of Yemen and Ethiopia, or the Nestorian Churches of the Sasanian empire, or the Jacobite and Melchite Churches of the Byzantine empire. It was not long, however, before anathemas and excommunications were being exchanged. It was in 631 with the Mubahala of Medina (3.61) when the Christians of Najran came into contact with to the young Muslim state and its 'covenant of protection' *(dhimma)* that Muslim-Christian dialogue could be said to have began in dramatic fashion. Thereafter it took the form of a long series of political, cultural or religious confrontations and encounters.[16]

---

[16] Muslims are in general very sensitive to Christian and Jewish criticism of the Islamic imposed status of *dhimmis* and nearly all-Muslim apologetic literature contains discussions of this subject.

For a general account of the Christians and Jews under Islamic rule see: Bat Ye'or, *Le Dhimmi: Profil de l'opprime en Orient et en Afrique du Nord depuis la conquête arabe*, Edition Anthropos, Paris, 1980, and translated into English as: *The Dhimmi: Jews and Christians under Islam*, Fairleigh Dickinson University Press, 1985, and *idem, Les Chrétientés d'Orient entre Jihad et dhimmitude*, Cerf, Paris, 1991, translated into English as *The Decline of Eastern Christianity under Islam: From Jihad to Dhimmitude Seventh-twentieth Century*, Fairleigh Dickinson University Press, 1996. See also Bat Ye'or, *Juifs et Chrétiens sous l'Islam—les Dhimmis face au défi intégriste*, Berg, Paris, 1994; Alain Brissaud, *Islam et Chrétienté: treize siècles de cohabitation*, Robert Laffont, Paris, 1992; Berthold Spuler, 'L'Islam et les minorités, *Die Islamische Welt zwischen Mittelalter und Neuzeit'*, *Festschrift für Hans Robert Roemer zum 65 Geburtstag*, (eds.) Ulrich Haarmann and Peter Bachmann, Kommission bei Franz Steiner Verlag-Wiesbaden, Beirut, 1979, pp. 609-619; Bernard Lewis, 'L'Islam et les Non-Musulmanns', *Annales: Economies, Sociétés, Civilisations*, 1980, pp. 784-800.

The position of Christianity in Muslim doctrine in the Arabian peninsula is extremely complicated. It depends largely upon the treatment of Muhammad and his successors of Christians there, upon what Muhammad said about the presence of Christians, upon what he meant when he said it and upon the interpretations subsequently put upon his words.[17]

The Qur'an does not always lay down many clear guidelines for the treatment of Christians in a Muslim community. Initially, Muhammad and the early Muslims regarded the 'People of the Book' (i.e. Christians and Jews) as potential allies, and this is reflected in the *Surahs* (chapters) of the Qur'an which were revealed early in Muhammad's mission. Subsequently the Jews and then the Christians were viewed with less favour as they resisted conversion to Islam or actively opposed Muhammad and the growing Muslim state. Late *Surahs* instructed that Muslims should not take Jews or Christians as friends or allies, an injunction used in later times to exclude Jews or Christians from employment in official positions in the Islamic state.[18]

As the Muslim domain expanded it came into contact with well-established Christian communities within Arabia and around its northern borders. Some arrangements had to be made to accommodate Christians who would not convert to Islam, and yet who were recognised as sharing the same revealed religious tradition as Muslims. Initially, treaties were made with Christian (as with Jewish) communities, the

---

[17] See also the following works on the evolution of the status of non-Muslims within the Islamic world: Antoine Fattal, *Le statut légal des non-musulmans en pays d'Islam*, Beirut, 1958); *idem*, 'Comment les dhimmis étaient jugés en terre l'Islam', *Cahiers d'Histoire Égyptienne*, vol. 3 (1951), pp. 321-341; *idem*, 'La nature juridique du statut des dhimmis', *Annales de la Faculté de Droit, Université de Saint-Joseph*, Beirut (1956), pp. 139-154; A S Tritton, *The Caliphs and their non-Muslim Subjects: a critical study of the Covenant of Umar*, Oxford, 1930; and N Edelby, 'L'autonomie législative des Chrétiens en terre d' Islam', *Archives d' Histoire du Droit Oriental*, vol. 5 (1950-51), pp. 307-351.

[18] We know that the composition of the Qur'an as it now exists does not follow the chronology of the life of Muhammad and the recitation of the Qur'an. The shortest *surahs*, which correspond to the Mecca period, are put at the beginning. It is these latest *surahs* which are most violent about Jews and Christians. Emilio Platti notes: 'Whereas in the first Mecca period the recitation of the Qur'an came close to the biblical tradition, with Moses as the main figure, the late *surahs* of the Qur'an (3-4-5) attack Judaism violently and distanced themselves from the Christian presentation of Jesus Christ, to such a degree that at this moment the Qur'an no longer included Judaism and Christianity in the authentic monotheism of Islam, as was the case in the early period at Mecca', *Islam ... étrange*, Editions du Cerf, Paris, 2000, p. 152.

earliest being with the important Christian community of Najran. Such treaties specified the rights of Christians and the restrictions imposed upon them. The communities with whom these treaties were made received protection from the Muslims in return for the payment of a special tax, i.e. the *jizyah*, Qur'an 9.27/9.29.

The development of Islamic policy towards Christians in the Arabian peninsula after the death of Muhammad appears to have been initiated by the action of the second caliph, 'Umar b. al-Khattab, who expelled the Christian community of Najran to Iraq and Syria, deriving his authority from an instruction which was reported to have been given by Muhammad. The early Islamic sources record a number of variants of this instruction.

Whatever Muhammad may have said, and whatever he may have meant, his immediate successor, the first caliph, Abu Bakr, seems not to have seen any need to put it into effect, since he renewed Muhammad's treaty with the Christians of Najran. 'Umar's expulsion of the community soon after he became caliph (only two years after the death of Muhammad) seems to have been motivated less by a desire to execute his instructions than by immediate strategic or political concerns (a number of which are alluded to in the early Muslim histories) with Muhammad's instruction serving as authorisation for his act. Owing to the lack of any very clear guidelines on the treatment of Christians in the Qur'an and the *sunnah*, and the unclear precedents set by the earliest Islamic rulers, it took some time for the position of Christians within the Islamic state to become formalised. As Islamic law came to be codified, a broad consensus was reached among the four Sunni schools of law (Hanbali, Hanafi, Maliki and Shafi'i) about the rights of, and restrictions placed upon, *dhimmis*, i.e. those protected people, Jews and Christians, who were recognised as sharing in the same religious traditions as the Muslims. Even so, it is worth stating at the outset that the treatment of Christians, whether within or outside the Arabian peninsula, depended as much upon the whims of rulers as upon the prescriptions of any of the major schools of law. The codification of the laws relating to Christians was probably complete by the beginning of the 9th century AD, but according to Tritton 'it depended on the temper of the monarch or the political exigencies of the time whether they were enforced or not.'

A starting point for the legislation regarding the treatment of Christians and those of other religions was to be found in a document referred to as the 'covenant of 'Umar', supposedly made at the time of the Muslim conquest of Jerusalem in AH 15 (AD 637). This laid down some broad guidelines on the rights granted to and restrictions imposed upon non-Muslim subjects. Because the 'Covenant' exists in a number of different rescensions, however—probably because it was set down in writing very much later—its soundness as a source of authority is questionable. It is perhaps to be regarded as a description of the general terms applicable to the treatment of non-Muslim subjects.[19] The question of the status of Christians (and Jews and other non-Muslims) still haunts Christian-Muslim relations and requires much more discussion and engagement. Historical record will be part of the debate, but also now the evolution of religious thought within the Islamic tradition will enable a more robust engagement around this issue.[20]

In Christian-Muslim relations polemical argument and ideological challenges resulted in innumerable misunderstandings and prejudices: and these, despite the efforts of great personalities in every century to tone them down and to solve the problems continued to grow.

In Christian counties, knowledge about Islam has varied with the times: it has depended most of all on how well the Arabic language

---

[19] See also the several thoughtful and suggestive works by Andre Ferre, 'Muhammad a-t-il exclu de l'Arabie les juifs et les chrétiens?', *Islamochristiana*, vol. 16 (1990), pp. 43-65, idem, 'Protégés ou citoyens?', *Islamochristiana*, vol. 22 (1996), pp 79-117) and Jean-Marie Gaudeul, 'The correspondence between Leo and 'Umar: 'Umar's letter re-discovered?', *Islamochristiana*, vol. 10 (1984), pp. 109-157; *La correspondance de 'Umar et Leon (vers 900) (Presentation et notes par J-M Gaudeul)*,: Pontifcio di Studi Arabi e d'Islamica, Rome, 1995, and Seth Ward, 'A fragment from an unknown work by al-Tabari on the Tradition 'Expel the Jews and Christians from the Arabian peninsula [and the Lands of Islam]', *Bulletin of the School of Oriental and African Studies*, vol. 53 (1990), pp. 407-420.

[20] For a Christian perspective, see the work by Samir Khalil Samir, 'Le débat du délit d'apostaise dans l'Islam contemporain', *Faith, Power and Violence: Muslims and Christians in a Plural Society. Past and Present*, (eds.) John J Donohue and Christian W Troll, Pontifico Istituto Orientale, Rome, 1998, pp. 115-140; 'Une Théologie arabe pour l'Islam', *Tantur Yearbook, 1979-1980*, Jerusalem, 1980, pp. 53-84; 'Liberté religieuse et propagation de la foi, chez les théologiens arabes chrétiens du IXè siècle et en Islam', *Tantur Yearbook, 1980-1981*, Jerusalem, 1981, pp. 93-164; 'Pour un thélogie arabe contemporaine. Actualité du patrimoine arabo-chrétien', *Proche Orient Chrétien*, vol. 38 (1988), pp. 64-98, and 'Il dialogo tra Cristani e musulmani nell'oriente arabo', *La Civiltà Cattolica*, no. 3517 (1997), pp. 41-47.

was known. From the fall of Jerusalem in 636 to that of Constantinople in 1453. Muslim-Christian dialogue was mainly a theological matter. In this dialogue, the Christian Middle East had as its main representatives the Melchites John of Damascus (655-749);[21] Theodore Abu Qurra (740-820/825);[22] the Jacobites Abou Ra'ita (early 9th century), Yahya Ibn 'Adi (893-974) and 'Isa Ibn Zur'a (943-1008); and the Nestorians Patriarch Timothy I (728-823).[23] Nicetas of Byzantium (842-912) and Manuel II Paleologue (1350-1425).[24]

The Latin West, through its lack of knowledge of Arabic, was at a disadvantage and fully engrossed in translation work. Peter of Cluny produced the first Latin version of the Koran (1146). Anselm of Canterbury (1033-1109). Peter Abelard (1079-1142). St Bernard (1091-1153) and Roger Bacon (1214-1294) spoke out on Islam. Ramon Lull (1235-1315), a Franciscan tertiary from Mallorca, in his

---

[21] Daniel J Sahas, *John of Damascus on Islam: The 'Heresy of the Ishmaelites'*, Brill, Leiden, 1972; *idem*, 'John of Damascus on Islam: revisited', *Abr Nahrain*, vol. 23, (1984-85), pp. 104-118, and *idem*, 'The Seventh Century Byzantine-Muslim Relations', *Islam and Christian-Muslim Relations*, vol. 2, No 1 (1991), pp. 3-22.

[22] Sidney H Griffith, *Arabic Christianity in the Monasteries of Ninth Century Palestine*, Variorum, London, 1992; *idem*, 'The Monks of Palestine and the growth of Christian literature in Arabic', *The Muslim World*, vol. 78 (1988), pp. 1-28, *idem*, 'Stephen of Ramlah and the Christian Kerygma in Arabic in 9th century Palestine', *Journal of Ecclesiastical History*, vol. 36 (1985), pp. 23-45; *idem*, 'Anthony David of Baghdad, scribe and monk of Mar Sabas: Arabic in the monasteries of Palestine', *Church History*, vol. 58 (1989), pp. 7-19 and *idem*, 'The View of Islam from the Monasteries of Palestine in the Early 'Abbasid Period: Theodore Abu Qurrah and the Summa Theologiae Arabica', *Islam and Muslim-Christian Relations*, vol. 7, no 1 (1996), pp. 9-28.

[23] S H Griffith, 'Disputes with Muslims in Syriac Christian Texts, from Patriarch John (d. 648) to Bar Hebraeus (d. 1286)', *Religionsgespräche im Mittelalter*, (eds.) B Lewis and F N Niewöhner, Otto Harrassowitz, Wiesbaden, 1992, pp. 251-273; Habib ibn Hidmah Abû Râ'itaha, 'Christian *Mutakallim* of the First Abbasid Century', *Oriens Christianus*, vol. LXIV (1980), pp. 161-201; Michel Hayek: 'Ammâr al-Basrî. La première somme de théologie chrétienne en langue arabé ou deux apologies du Christianisme', *Islamochristiana*, vol. 12 (1976), pp. 69-113; Hans Putman: *L'Église et l'Islam sous Timothée I (780-823). Etude sur l'eglise nestorienne au temps des premiers 'Abbâsides avec nouvelle édition et traduction de dialogue entre Timothée et Al-Mahdi*, Dar el-Machreq, Beirut, 1975.

[24] Adel Theodore Khoury, *Polémique byzantine contre l'Islam (VIIIe-XIIIè siècle)*, Brill, Leiden, 1972); *idem, Manuel II Pelelogue: Entretiens avec un Musulman 7è controverse* (Introduction, critical text, translation and notes by A. Th. Khoury), Sources Chretiennes No. 115, Editions du Cerf, Paris, 1966); *idem, Les Théologiens byzantins et l'Islam, textes et auteurs (VIIIe -XIIIe siecle)*, (Thèse faculté des lettres et sciences humaines de l'Universite de Lyon) Edition Louvain, Nauwalaerts, 1969; *idem*, 'Apologétique byzantine contre l'Islam (VIIIe-XIIIe siecle)', *Proche-Orient Chrétien*, vol. XXIX (1979), pp. 242-300, vol. XXX (1980), pp. 132-74, vol. XXXII (1981), pp. 14-47.

time achieved the ideal of peaceful dialogue whose aim was to mediate between the two cultures and the two religions. St Thomas (1225-1274), William of Tripoli (13th century) and, above all, Nicolas of Cusa (mid-15th century), transcending controversy, paved the way for a serious and respectful encounter.[25] This early Muslim-Christian dialogue, which went on throughout the Middle Ages, is of interest because of its readiness to rely on philosophical reasoning, to have recourse to scriptural texts, and to investigate them methodically. The motives behind the dialogue were many—ranging from mere witness or polemical intent to eschatological perspectives or papal political initiatives against Islam.[26]

The modern experience is, inevitably, rather different. The 20th century opened with independence of many new nations and the general re-awakening of Islam called more urgently than ever for a global re-evaluation of this thirteen-centuries-old dialogue and a systematic renewal of theological views in order to reassess the place of that dialogue within the history of salvation.[27]

There was, first of all, the Belgian Jesuit Henri Lammens (1862-1937)[28] who dedicated his whole life to the study of Islamic sources at St Joseph's University, Beirut (Lebanon). Through his endeavour—a Christian Orientalist reading of Islam—he examined Islam in its environment to its limit, and perhaps to its extremes. His aim was to

---

[25] Aquinas: J Waltz, 'Muhammad and the Muslims in St. Thomas Aquinas', *The Muslim World*, vol. 66 (1976), pp. 81-95; Nicholas of Cusa: N Rescher, 'Nicholas of Cusa on the Qur'an: a 15th Century Encounter with Islam', *The Muslim World*, vol. 55 (1965), pp. 195-202; J Biechler, 'Christian Humanism Confronts Islam: Sifting the Qur'an with Nicholas of Cusa', *Journal of Ecumenical Studies*, vol. 13 (1976), pp. 1-14; Raymond Lull: Dominique de Courcelles, *La parole risque de Raymod Lull, entre le judaisme, le christianisme et l'Islam*, Vrin, Paris, 1993; Dominique Urvoy, *Penser l'Islam. Les présupposés islamiques de l'Art de Lull*, Vrin, Paris 1980; *idem,* 'Ramon Lull et l'Islam', *Islamochristiana*, vol. 7 (1981), pp. 127-146.

[26] David B Burrell has shown us how such interreligious dialogue was immensely productive in the Middle Ages and how a renewal of such conversations might be productive for current theological engagement among Jews. *Jews, Christians and Muslims: Knowing the Unknowable God. Ibn Sina, Maimonides, Aquinas*, University of Notre Dame Press, Notre Dame, Indiana, 1986, and *Freedom and Creation in Three Traditions*, University of Notre Dame Press, 1993.

[27] Maurice Borrmans, 'The Muslim-Christian Dialogue of the Last Ten Years', *Pro Mundi Vita Bulletin*, 74 (1978). Brussels; M Borrmans, 'Le dialogue islamo-chrétien des trente dernières années', *Studia Missionalia* (Rome), vol. 43 (1994), pp. 115-137.

[28] Youakim Moubarac: Henri Lammens, *Récherches sur la pensée chrétienne et l'Islam. Dans les temps modernés et á l'époque contemporaine*, Publications de l'Université Libanaise, Beirut, 1977.

make clear, from an historical point of view, firstly who Muhammad was—was he sincere?, secondly what was primitive Islam—a revision of the myth of Abraham that keeps most closely to Judaism and treats in a Judaic manner what Christian truths it adopt?, and thirdly what the Umayyads of Damascus were—the pride of the Syrian nation and the glory of the Arab empire. Credit should be given to Fr Lammens for raising the serious study of Arabic and Islamology to its highest point and for his courage in asking the most fundamental questions and proposing valid answers, even if his critical spirit did lead him into the very controversy and polemics he wanted to avoid.

In Spain, Fr Miguel Asin y Palacios (1871-1944),[29] a very good friend of Louis Massignon—the master figure in the Christian theological engagement of Islam—and fervent student of Pascal and St John of the Cross, developed Christian Orientalism along lines well suited to the Spanish genius and the renewed challenges of the Gospel. His academic research and teaching led him to pursue the comparative study of Islam and Christianity very far along the following lines: primitive Islam is deeply influenced by Christianity, particularly by oriental monasticism; Islam systematises and perfects Christian data pertaining to dogmatics, ethics, asceticism and mysticism; Western Christianity is influenced by oriental Christianity through Islam and the impact of Arab influence on medieval scholasticism. Studying the Muslim-Christian similarities in the fields of philosophy (St Thomas and Averroes), mystical theology (St John of the Cross and Ibn Abbad of Ronda), mystical confraternities (Shadhilis and Illuminati), spirituality (Pascal and Ghazali) and eschatological poetry (Dante and Ibn 'Arabi), this Madrid priest-professor came to a positive appreciation of the dogmatical and mystical values of Islam. Asin Palacios's tendency to connect too readily parallel texts comes from his general view which he himself expressed thus: 'It must not be forgotten that Muslim mysticism in general, and the Shadhili form of it in particular, is the heir of oriental

---

[29] Mikel de Epalza, 'Algunos juicios teologicos de Asin Palacios sobre el Islam', *Pensamiento*, vol. 25, nos. 97-98-99 (1969), pp. 145-182, and L Massignon et Asin Palacios, 'Une longue amité, et deux approches différentes', *Louis Massignon. Le cahier de l'Herne*, (ed.) J-F Six, no. 13 (1970), pp. 157-169, and for the general context, see Francisco de Borja de Medina, 'Islam and Christian Spirituality in Spain: contacts, influences, similarities', *Islamochristiana*, vol. 18 (1992), pp. 87-108.

Christianity and at the same time of Neoplatonism'. Applying this principle to St John of the Cross, he writes:

> If the hypothesis of literary transmission be confirmed, it would be a question of a normal case of cultural restitution; an evangelical and Pauline thought grafted on Islam in medieval times would have acquired, in these surroundings, so rich a development in new ideological nuances and such a wealth of unusual forms and expressions that, transferred to the soil of Spain, our sixteenth century mystics would have not have disdained to draw on it for their works.[30]

His work could be called a Muslim-Christian 'osmosis' or 'transubstantiation'. He was the first to show how Islam and Christianity are ineluctably linked together in the religious history of mankind. Therefore, what can they contribute to each other? Can they come together? And how, from the viewpoint of Christian theology, can all this be accomplished? Never before had a Christian, in full loyalty to his own religious tradition been so aware of this.[31]

The Second Vatican Council's view of Islam and Christian-Muslim relations

During the second session of that Second Vatican Council (October 1962—December 1965), the project of a text about Judaism was presented, the Catholic Oriental patriarchs and bishops living in Muslim countries asked for 'balance', in other words, that justice should be done not only to the reality of Judaism but also to Islam.[32] This demand issued in two relatively short but important and decisive texts.

---

[30] M Asin Palacios, 'Un précurseur hispano-musulman de saint Jean de la Croix', *Études carmélitaines*, vol XVII (1932), pp. 113-167; *Saint John of the Cross and Islam*, Vantage Press, New York. 1981.

[31] Maurice Borrmans, 'The Muslim-Christian Dialogue of the Last Ten Years', *Pro Mundi Vita Bulletin*, 74 Brussels, pp. 8-9.

[32] Robert Caspar, La réligion musulmane, 'Les relations de l'Eglise avec les réligions non-chrétiennes', *Collection Unam Sanctam Vatican II*, Editions du Cerf, Paris, 1966, pp. 201-236, and 'Le Concile et l'Islam', *Etudes*, janvier (1966), Paris, pp. 114-126.

Although they are primarily concerned with the Catholics' practical attitude towards Muslims, they imply elements of a fresh Catholic theological view of Islam. Number 16 of the 'Dogmatic constitution on the Church' *Lumen Gentium* declares:

> But the plan of salvation also embraces those who acknowledge the Creator, and among these the Muslims are first; they profess to hold the faith of Abraham and along with us they worship the one merciful God who will judge humanity on the last day.

The study of the proceedings of the Council makes clear that it did not want to state an objective link between Islam, Ishmael and the biblical revelation. The reference to Abraham is put on the subjective level: 'They profess ...' Islam is situated first among the non-Biblical, monotheistic religions and it is audaciously stated that the Muslims adore the same God as the Christians.

The second text of the Council is longer and more substantial. It constitutes paragraph three of the 'Declaration of the Church's relation to the non-Christmas religions' *Nostra Aetate* in which were put together the schemata for Judaism, Islam and the other religions. After stating in paragraph two the principles of the Christian vision of the religions in general: to accept all that they contain of the true and good as coming from God, without however falling into syncretism, the Council fathers state:

> The Church also looks upon Muslims with respect. They worship the one God living and subsistent, merciful and almighty, creator of heaven and earth, who has spoken to humanity and to whose decrees, even the hidden ones, they seek to submit themselves whole-heartedly, just as Abraham, to whom the Islamic faith readily relates itself, submitted to God. They venerate Jesus as a prophet, even though they do not acknowledge him as God, and they honour his virgin mother Mary and even sometimes devoutly call upon her. Furthermore they await the day of judgement when God will require all people brought back to life. Hence

they have regard for the moral life and worship God especially in prayer, almsgiving and fasting.

Although considerable dissension and enmities between Christians and Muslims may have arisen in the course of the centuries, this synod urges all parties that, forgetting past things, they train themselves towards sincere mutual understanding and together maintain and promote social justice and moral values as well as peace and freedom for all people.

Two characteristics of this text are immediately evident: first, it highlights the common or related points between Islam and Christianity, noting at the same time the essential difference: the Christian profession of the divinity of Jesus. Second, it opens up the possibility of collaboration between the two religions, at the service of the most pressing needs of contemporary humanity.

The opening sentence of the paragraph, apparently a trite formula, in fact constitutes a unique statement and an absolutely new beginning insofar as it is an official declaration about Islam issued by the highest teaching authority of the Catholic Church. The faith in God as One and His adoration are the centre and heart of Islam. It has been set out by the Jesuit thinker, Christian Troll. In discussing Christian attitudes to Islam, he mentions that the first article of the Christian faith, *Credo in unum Deum*, is the same, even if, for Christians, the divine Oneness opens itself to the trinity of the three persons. Muslims and Christians adore together the one God, but they do not always give him the same 'names', nor do they give the same meaning to apparently similar 'names'.[33]

It fell to the popes and in particular to Pope Paul VI[34] and Pope John Paul II,[35] to oversee the application of the Second Vatican

---

[33] I owe much to the extended reflection by Christian W Troll, 'Changing Catholic views of Islam, Islam and Christianity. Mutual Perceptions since the mid-20th century', (ed.) Jacques Waardenburg, Peeters, Louvain, 1998, pp. 19-77; Christian W Troll, 'Catholic Teachings on Interreligious Dialogue. Analysis of Some Recent Official Documents, with Special Reference to Christian-Muslim Relations', *Muslim-Christian Perceptions of Dialogue Today: Experiences and Expectations*, (ed) J Waardenburg, Peeters, Louvain, 2000, pp. 233-275.

[34] Maurice Borrmans, 'Le Pape Paul VI et les Musulmans', *Islamochristiana*, vol. 4 (1978), pp. 1-10.

[35] Thomas Michel, 'Pope John Paul II's Teaching about Islam in his Addresses to Muslims', *Pro Dialogo* , No. 62 (1986), pp. 182-191.

Council teaching on the relationship between Christianity and other faiths. This can be seen from the fact that during their apostolic journeys to different countries time has always been set aside for a meeting with the leaders of other religions, including Muslims. They have also received Muslim leaders in the Vatican and taken the opportunity of talking over matters of common concern. Worthy of special mention are the visits of Pope John Paul II to Morocco (1985) where he addressed a large gathering of Muslim youth, and to Tunis (1996) where he laid special emphasis on dialogue within the Mediterranean region. Nor should one forget the initiative of Pope John Paul II in inviting religious leaders to come to Assisi in 1986 to pray for peace in the world. A number of Muslims accepted the invitation. The common commitment to pray for peace was shown again in 1993, when John Paul II and the Catholic Bishops of Europe called for a special weekend of prayer in Assisi to pray for peace in Europe, and especially in the Balkans, Muslims from nearly every country of Western Europe, as well as a delegation from Bosnia, took pains to be present.

To carry through his plans after the Vatican Council Pope Paul VI set up *The Secretariat for Non Christians*, later to become *The Pontifical Council for Interreligious Dialogue*, as one of the organs of the Roman Curia. The purpose of this body was to promote among the Catholic community this new attitude of dialogue. This entailed first of all reflection and writing so that false ideas might be dispelled and prejudices overcome. As part of this effort a book of *Guidelines* for dialogue between Christians and Muslims was published in 1969. It was later revised and a new edition brought out in 1981. This has been translated into a number of different languages, including Arabic.[36] There was too a desire to be in direct contact with Muslims. As has been mentioned, many spiritual leaders came to Rome and were received by Pope Paul VI. They were also welcomed at the Secretariat. Special mention could be made of a delegation from the Supreme Council for Islamic Affairs, in Cairo, which paid an official visit in December 1970. This visit was reciprocated in 1974 by Cardinal Pignedoli, Msgr Rossano and Fr Abou Mokh (an Arabic-speaking,

---

[36] *Guidelines for Dialogue between Muslims and Christians*. Prepared by Maurice Borrmans, translated from the French original (published in 1981) by R Marston Speight, Paulist Press, New York, 1990.

Greek Catholic Melchite from the Middle East and now Patriarchal Vicar of His Beatitude Maximos V of the Greek Catholic Melkite Church). Opening the way for this exchange there had been the visit of Cardinal König to Cairo in 1965 and his historic lecture on monotheism at Al-Azhar. Since 1968, the Secretariat had begun the habit of addressing a message to Muslims for the end of Ramadan. In recent years care has been taken to have this message translated into the various languages used by Muslims, not only Arabic, English and French, but also Turkish, Urdu, Bengali, Bahasa Indonesia and others. The message is signed by the President of the Council. In 1991, because of the suffering caused by the Gulf War, the message was signed by Pope John Paul II.[37]

Louis Massignon: witness to Muslim-Christian relations

During the decades preceding the Council no scholar had so intensely and persistently tried to transform the Christian community's view of Islam as French Catholic Islamicist, mystic and priest Louis Massignon (1883-1962).[38] By the force of his personality and the originality of his

---

[37] Pontifical Council for Interreligious Dialogue, *Recognize the Spiritual Bonds that Unite Us. Sixteen years of Christian-Muslim relations*, Vatican City 1994; Michael Fitzgerald, 'The Secretariat for Non Christians is Ten Years Old', *Islamochristiana* 1 (1975), pp.87-95; M Fitzgerald, 'Twenty-five Years of Dialogue: the Pontifical Council for Interreligious Dialogue', *Islamochristiana* 15 (1989), pp.109-120); Thomas Michel, '25 Years of Letters to Muslims for Id Al-Fitr', *Pro Dialogo*, no. 84 (1993), pp. 300-302, and 'The Vatican and the Gulf War', *Encounter: Documents for Muslim-Christian Understanding* (Rome), no. 174 (1991), pp.1-14.

[38] A H Hourani, *Islam in European Thought*, Cambridge University Press, 1990, pp. 43-49. Louis Massignon's bibliography as a scholar is impressive. For the complete bibliography, see Youakim Moubarac, *L'Oeuvre de Louis Massignon; Pentalogie Islamo-Chrétienne I*, Éditions du Cénacle Libanais, Beirut, 1972-73. Amongst his studies, the first place must go to his two doctoral theses of 1922: *La Passion d'al-Hosayn-ibn Mansour al-Hallâj, martyre mystique de l'Islam*, Geuthner, Paris, 1922, First Edition, 2 vols. Massignon continued to work on a new edition of this work until his death in 1962. After his death, the new edition was assembled by a group of scholars working together with the Massignon family and friends, which was published as *La Passion de Husayn ibn Mansur Hallâj, martyre mystique de l'Islam*, Gallimard, Paris, 1975, Second Edition, 4 vols. The second edition was translated into English by Herbert Mason as *The Passion of al-Hallâj: Mystic and Martyr of Islam*, Bollingen Series XCVIII, Princeton University Press, 1982, 4 vols. An abridged version appeared as *Hallâj: Mystic and Martyr* edited and translated by Herbert Mason, Princeton University Press, 1994. And *Essai sur les origines du lexique technique de la mystique musulmane*, First Edition,

ideas Louis Massignon was perhaps the only Islamicist scholar who was a central figure in the intellectual life of his time.[39] The renewal of Massignon's Christian religious consciousness was directly linked in his own mind to Islam. Having discovered his Christian faith through the study of the great Muslim mystic al-Hallaj, Massignon found that he had moved forever beyond the realm of mere academic interest to become an actual guiding fraternal force. Their extraordinary friendship: 'filled the heart of Massignon and shaped his mind so thoroughly that he can be seen as the greatest Muslim among Christians and the greatest Christian among Muslims'.[40]

A clear record of how Massignon reconciled his scholarly work on Islam with his Orthodox Catholic beliefs is found in *Les trois prières d'Abhraham: Seconde prière*, which is a meditation on Abraham's prayer for Ishmael, as reported in Genesis. He stresses that Ishmael's exile took place after he had been circumcised and had received God's blessing in response to Abraham's prayer (Genesis 17: 18-20). Massignon sees in Muhammad's own forced emigration, or *Hijra*, from Mecca, a repetition of Ishmael's banishment at the instigation of Sarah. He suggests that, when Muhammad encountered the Jews in Medina, he therefore declared before God that he drew his inspiration from

---

Geuthner, Paris 1922; Second Edition, Vrin, Paris, 1954; Third Edition, Vrin, Paris, 1968. Now being translated into English by Benjamin Clark as *Essays on the origins of the technical language of Islamic mysticism*, University of Notre Dame Press, 1999. Secondly, there are the editions of religious texts, most of which are related to al-Hallâj: *Kitâb al-Tawâsîn d'al Hallâj*, Geuthner, Paris 1913; *Quatre textes inédits, relatifs à la biographie d'al-Hallâj*, Geuthner, Paris, 1913—including *Akhbar al-Hallâj*, which was re-edited with new materials in several editions: Paris, 1936, and Vrin, Paris, 1957; *Diwân d'al-Hallâj*. First Edition, *Journal Asiatique*, Paris, 1931; Second Edition, Geuthner, Paris, 1955; Third Edition, Documents spirituels des Cahiers du Sud, Paris, 1955. One important edition to this bibliography is *Testimonies and Reflections: Essays of Louis Massignon* (selected and translated by Herbert Mason), University of Notre Dame Press, 1989.

[39] On Louis Massignon, see the following: *Présence de Louis Massignon: Hommages et témoignages. Textes réunis par Daniel Massignon à l'occasion du Centenaire de Louis Massignon*, Éditions Maisonneuve et Larose, Paris, 1987; J Moncelon: 'Louis Massignon' *La Vie Spirituelle*, vol. 680, 1988, pp. 363-379; J Moncelon, *Massignon: l'Ami de Dieu*. Thèse de doctorat, Nanterre, 1990; C Destremau and J Moncelon, *Massignon*, Plon, Paris, 1994; Maurice Borrmans, 'Louis Massignon, Témoin du dialogue islamo-chrétien', *Euntes Docete*, vol. XXXVII, 1984, pp. 383-401; Mary Louise Gude, *Louis Massignon: The Crucible of Compassion*, Notre Dame University Press, 1996; and Anthony O'Mahony, 'Le pèlerin de jerusalem: Louis Massignon, Palestinian Christians, Islam and the State of Islam', *Palestinian Christians: Religion, Politics and Society in the Holy Land*, (ed.) A O'Mahony, Melisende, London, 1999, pp.166-189.

[40] I Madkour, 'Louis Massignon', *L'Herne: Massignon*, (ed.) J F Six, Ed. l'Herne, Paris, 1970, p. 68.

Abraham and claimed all of Abraham's spiritual and temporal heritage for the Arabs alone.[41] In later years, he became particularly interested in those phenomena which show a convergence or dialogue between Islam and Christianity: the meeting of Muhammad and the Christians of Najran, the cult of Fatima as a parallel to the veneration of the Virgin Mary, the veneration of the Seven Sleepers of Ephesus by Christians and Muslims alike, vocations within Islam of mystical compassion and substitution like that of al-Hallaj. Massignon, who was very interested in biography, liked to plot on the graph of what he called 'the curve of life' of the life stories which attracted his attention. He also thought that there are Christic figures within Islam who could ultimately play a role in bringing Muslims to confess the divine sonship of Jesus, the Christ, if only at the last judgement, such figures included Salman Pak,[42] al-Hallaj,[43] al-Ghazali and others. Massignon was above all an eschatological thinker.

Massignon became convinced that Christians had to accomplish what amounted to a Copernican re-centring in order to understand Islam.[44] In other words, Christians had to place themselves at the very axis of Muslim doctrine. Massignon was open to the Muslim notion that the three religions issued from the same source. He accepted the connection of Muslims to Abraham via Ishmael: they were the heirs of his blessing, and of his vocation of being specially chosen.[45] He viewed Muhammad as *prophète negatif* in the sense that

[41] Sidney H Griffith, 'Sharing the Faith of Abraham: the "Credo" of Louis Massignon', *Islam and Muslim-Christian Relations*, vol. 8, no. 2 (1997), pp. 193-210.

[42] Jean Moncelon, 'Salmân Pâk dans la spiritualité de Louis Massignon', *Luqmân*, Tehran, autonme-hiver, 1991-1992, pp. 53-64.

[43] R Arnaldez, *Hallaj ou la religion de la croix*, Plon, Paris, 1964; Herbert Mason, *Al-Hallaj*, Curzon Press, Richmond, 1995; and Herbert Mason, *The Death of al-Hallaj: a dramatic narrative*, University of Notre Dame Press, Notre Dame, 1979.

[44] P Rocalve, *Place et rôle de l'Islam et de l'Islamologie dans la vie et l'œuvre de Louis Massignon*, Thèse de doctorat, Sorbonne, 1990, which has now been published as P Rocalve, *Place et rôle de l'Islam et de l'Islamologie dans la vie et l'œuvre de Louis Massignon*, Institut Français de Damas, Collection Témoignages et Documents, No 2, 1993.

[45] Neal Robinson: 'Massignon, Vatican II and Islam as an Abrahamic Religion', *Islam and Christian-Muslim Relations*, vol. 2, 1991, p. 182-205, and Robert Caspar, 'La vision de l'Islam chez Louis Massignon et son influence sur l'Eglise', *L'Herne Massignon*, (ed.) J-F Six, Paris, 1970, pp. 126-147; Roger Arnaldez, 'Abrahamisme, Islam et christianisme chez Louis Massignon', *L'Herne Massignon*, (ed.) J-F Six, Paris, 1970, pp. 123-125, and R Arnaldez, 'Figures patriarcals et prophétiques', *Lumiere et Vie*, no.188, 1988, pp. 81-96.

he denies God being more than what he affirms him to be. Muhammad is the herald of intransigent monotheism.

For Massignon, Muhammad is no longer the 'Antichrist' as a certain section of the Church had presented him in the past. He rather is the one who expects Christians and Jews to put themselves in the place of the Muslims in order to join in the one salvation proposed by God. This substitution implies that Christians take on themselves the sins, the insufficiencies, the sufferings, and the limitations of its doctrines and its legal prescriptions. It implies that Christians live dependant upon Islam in order to save it in the same way in which Christ depends on those whom he saves. If Christians had been faithful to their calling, would Islam have been born? Massignon saw Islam as the claim of the heritage of Abraham against Christians unfaithful to Jesus and against Israel unfaithful to Jesus and the covenant.

Massignon's *témoinage*, his deep personal commitment to Muslims and Islam have profoundly influenced the course of Muslim-Christian dialogue and has at times directly influenced how some Islamic thinkers have understood in their own reflection the relationship between religion and politics.

The important Iranian Islamist activist and thinker Ali Shari'ati[46] recalled:

> The most remarkable lecture by professor Massignon I ever attended was not held at the Sorbonne or at the College de France ... but at the foot of the columns of the mosque of the Muslims of Paris. He was sitting there, with a few vegetable salesmen and some unhappy Algerian Arabs who had, in colonialist France, forgotten even their religion and their language; and he taught them the Qur'an.

As a Muslim, Shari'ati could not help asking himself the following question with regard to Massignon: was he, in the eyes of

[46] N Yavari-d'Hellencourt, 'Le radicalisme shi'ite de 'Ali Shari'ati', *Radicalismes Islamiques I: Iran, Liban Turquie*, (eds.) Oliver Carré and Paul Dumont, L'Harmattan, Paris 1985, pp. 83-118, and Ali Shari'ati, *Histoire et destineé, textes choisis et traduits du persan par F Hamed and N Yavari-d'Hellencourt*, Sindbad, Paris, 1982.

God, an infidel (a *kafir*) or a believer? In other words: was he saved or not? In 1967, in *Kavir*, he composed a long prayer where he talks very freely with God, 'just like a child with its Father' and gave up to him all his questions and hopes. In one passage, he asks God as follows:

> O God, who is an infidel *(kafir)*? Who is Muslim? Who is Shi'a? Who is Sunni? What is the exact border that separates each of them? ... Massignon, that ocean of science, who for 27 whole years has plunged into the life of Salman, the first historical founder of Shi'ism in Iran, who throughout his life researched the personality and posthumous influence of Saint Fatima in the history of the people, gathering all information which in the course of history had been dispersed in Arabic, Persian, Turkish, Latin and even Mongol sources, he whose whole being took fire each time he spoke about Fatima, Islamic mysticism or Salman ... is he an infidel? (...) Oh God, tell me, how you see things? How do you judge? Falling in love with 'names' is that Shi'ism? Is it not rather to know those who are called these names? Or, more even, to imitate their manners?

Four years later, in 1971, when performing a pilgrimage to Mecca, Shari'ati gave a lecture to Iranian pilgrims in Medina. He came to speak of 'Professor Massignon, my master, a Christian and European Orientalist' and of his work on Salman. In the published version of this talk, Shari'ati added the following note:

> 'How lucky it is that I should remember him in this circumstance [in Medina]; assuredly, God, who does not judge by appearances but by the heart, has undoubtedly forgiven him and given him a great recompense.'[47]

---

[47] Michel Cuypers, Une rencontre mystique: 'Ali Shari'ati—Louis Massignon', *Mélanges de l'Institut Dominicain d'Etudes Orientales*, vol. 21 (1993), p. 330, and *idem*, 'Une rencontre mystique: 'Ali Shari'ati—Louis Massignon', *Louis Massignon et ses contemporains*, (ed) Jacques Keryell, Karthala, Paris, 1997, pp. 309-328.

The personality and spirituality of Massignon was inseparable from his mysticism. His approach was of a Christian benevolently encountering Islam, of which he had made himself the host. That the love and charity does not only address itself to those who in some way or other are already one with me, but it finds its supreme accomplishment in the love of the other as such, in total respect of his/her 'otherness'.

Islam as a challenge to Christianity

As Anthony Johns has reminded us,[48] the challenge of Islam is total— it presents itself as the primordial authentic religion per excellence. The final, complete form in which this religion lives and is taught today is guaranteed by the Qur'an, the book revealed to Muhammad by an angel. It proclaims the God of Abraham, Isaac and Jacob, who first revealed himself to Adam, father of mankind, and made a covenant with him and his descendants.

Even if the Qur'an praises the humility of certain Christians, Mohammed seems to have encountered a Christianity which gave the impression of having betrayed Jesus, of worshipping three gods and especially of being greatly divided. The Qur'an puts this terrible pronouncement about Christians in God's mouth:

'We estranged them, with enmity and hatred
Between the one and the other
To the day of judgement' (Surah 5:14)

Apparently Christians showed no signs they would ever be able to get along with each other. Opposing this kind of Christianity, Islam proclaims the absolute oneness of God and unity among believers. Whatever the case, Islam has been a challenge to Christianity since its origin. Our histories were and continue to be intertwined.

The relationship has been ambiguous. For the Muslim, Islam proclaims the ultimate and total truth about humanity and its history,

---

[48] Anthony H Johns, 'Islam as a Challenge to Christianity', *Concilium: Christianity Among World Religions* (1986), pp. 13-21. See also Guy Monnot's description of Islam, 'Ce que l'Islam n'est pas', *Communio: revue catholique internationale*, vol. 16 (1991), pp. 28-41.

about Jesus Christ (as servant, not as God; as a prophet in the Islamic understanding of that term), and about Christianity (which tampered with Scripture and/or its interpretation and so represents a continued deviation from Christ's teaching). To Islam, Christianity has changed so completely, it is hard to recognise it as Christianity. Everything about it is interpreted from that standpoint.

The Christian Islamicist Fr Jacques Jomier has reflected upon these themes. In the context of interreligious dialogue and the encounter between Christians and Muslims, how does the Islamic *umma* define itself *vis-à-vis* the other, non-Muslim communities? Can Muslims today, with good Qur'anic conscience, as it were, attribute to non-Muslims, including those who freely reject the message of Islam, the same message of Islam, the same human dignity as to the Muslim believer? What practical consequences follow from this teaching in the contemporary context? This is a crucial and decisive question of contemporary interpretation and readings of the Qur'an. Or, are all non-Muslims to be viewed—Qur'anically—as somehow deformed by their erroneous beliefs and their refusal to adhere to Islam? Do they merit to be treated as human beings of equal dignity and rights?

Jomier discusses the possible reasons for this Islamic 'psychological assurance'. He observed that to many, the Muslim appears uniquely sure of his faith, convinced of the truth of Islam being evident to the point of suspecting those who do not accept it, of acting dishonestly. Is that certitude linked with the specifically Qur'anic view of man as believer? ... and if so what is the consequence for the Muslim and the Christian in Muslim-Christian relations today?[49]

Kenneth Cragg, has well summed up this dilemma for Islam:

> The Muslim sense of being completely equipped by final truth, and sustained by 'the religion of God' . . ., traditionally left little room for introspection or self-doubt. While these may still not be conspicuous in contemporary Islam, there is no denying that Islam is more vulnerable today in spiritual terms than in earlier

---

[49] Jacques Jomier, *Dieu et l'homme dans le Coran. L'aspect religieux de la nature humanie joint à l'obéissance au Prophète de l'Islam*, Cerf, Paris, 1996.

times. While it has not been rich in sceptics, there are aspects of the present that more readily evoke them.[50]

For the Christian, Islam is hard to make out. What is the meaning of this religion which on the one hand came after Christ and is related to Christ and Christianity, but on the other hand does not seem to be acquainted with true Christian teaching or the authentic Christian view of the living person of Jesus Christ? Some (e.g. John of Damascus) saw Islam as a Christian heresy; the medieval Christian saw it as a diabolical work—not very helpful for seeing its values.

The prism through which others view the nature of the unity and diversity of Islam as a global tradition continues to inform encounter and dialogue. In their views of Islam, both Muslims and non-Muslims seem on the whole to gravitate toward the notion that all Muslims are really the same, but they say so for very different reasons. For non-Muslims—especially some European and American secularists—images of a monolithic Islam often arise out of a fear of the unknown or of organised religion, or autonomous spiritual values, that encourages oversimplification in dealing with 'the other'. That fear is in turn exacerbated by long-standing stereotypes of Muslims as bellicose and generally given to religiously motivated and sanctioned violence.

For their part, Muslims tend for several reasons to dismiss the notion that there are varieties of Islam. One is that their tradition's characterisation of Christian disunity poses an unacceptable image of a religious community; another is that their own understanding of, and wish for, a truly global community of Muslims leaves no room whatsoever for any significant diversity within it. If non-Muslims' consistent attribution of a seamless unity to Islam rests on an unjustifiably negative reading of Muslims as humanly homogeneous, that of Muslims is built on an equally uncritical idealisation of Islam as religiously uniform. The first characterisation is unfair, and the second unrealistic.[51]

In August 1986, addressing young Moroccans gathered in Casablanca stadium, Pope John Paul II did not hesitate to tell them:

---

[50] K Cragg, 'Islam and Other Faiths', *Studia Missionalia* (Rome), vol. 42 (1993), pp. 257-270, p. 263.

[51] John Renard, 'Islam, the One and the Many: Unity and Diversity in a Global Tradition', *Concilium: Islam: A Challenge for Christianity*, no. 3 (1994), pp. 33-40.

'We believe in the same God, the one God, the living God, the God who creates the world and brings the world to their perfection.'[52] This is an indubitable affirmation of the existence of one and the same creator God. But one also has to add that Christians and Muslims who worship the same God have very different conceptions of God's unity. One could even say that the monotheism, which is a common heritage of all children of Abraham, has at the same time divided them for centuries.[53] Muslims cannot accept Christian monotheism as Trinitarian monotheism, and that is a direct consequence of their rejection of the divine sonship of Jesus.

So we should remember how by its radical nature, Islamic monotheism differs from Christian monotheism, and note that in Muslim eyes the sin par excellence, that of idolatry, is committed not only by pagan polytheists but also by Christians themselves.[54] But at the same time, over and above engaging in a secular polemic, Claude Geffré has asked whether in the age of interfaith dialogue this difference should not lead both sides to vie with each other in seeking a God who is always greater.[55]

David Burrell suggests, 'the experience of complementarily may prove a more reliable guide than a quest for commonality, when it comes to understanding other religions, and our own'.[56]

---

[52] John Paul II and Morocco, 'The Speech of the Holy Father, John Paul II, to Young Muslims (Casablanca, Morocco, August 19, 1985)', *Encounter: Documents for Muslim-Christian Understanding* (Rome), No. 128 (1986).

[53] However, one would do well to listen to the warning of Roger Arnaldez, 'Hence, the problem of the diverse messages stubbornly remains. There is no way of reducing it to a common core so long as we situate ourselves within one of the three religious families. [Judiasm, Christianity, Islam] One must be Jewish, Christian, or Muslim, adhering to a faith that excludes the other two. If we want to extract some monotheism-in-itself, a monotheistic theology or morality as such, we must simultaneously depart from the three monotheistic religions and place ourselves outside or above them. To put it most forcefully, we would have to neglect the particularities of their messages, ignore the characteristics of each, and repress the very notion of a Messenger.' *Three Messengers for One God*, University of Notre Dame Press, 1994, p. 3.

[54] Robert Caspar, 'The Permanent Significance of Islam's Monotheism', *Concilium*, no. 177 (1985), pp. 67-78, and, for an Arab Christian perspective, see Samir Khalil Samir, 'L'Unicité absolue de Dieu: regards sur la pensée chrétienne arabe', *Lumière et Vie*, no. 163 (1983), pp. 35-48.

[55] Claude Geffré, 'The One God of Islam and Trinitarian Monotheism', *Concilium*, 2001, no. 1, pp. 85-93.

[56] David Burrell, 'Naming the Names of God: Muslims, Jews, Christians', *Theology Today*, vol. 47, no. 1 (1990), pp. 22-29. p. 29.

The denial of the fundamental dogmas of Christianity, the incarnation and the Trinity makes Muslim-Christian dialogue particularly difficult. However, this dialogue always remains open for we have not yet reached the end of the historical reasons for such a misunderstanding between the two monotheisms. If we remember that in the Qur'an the specific function of Muhammad, as of the former prophets, is not to give a prediction about the future but to issue both a reminder and a warning—a reminder of the identical Word of God and a warning of the new signs of God's rights— we may think that Islam as a revelation and a practical attitude serves as a warning about the inadequate conceptions and practices of Christians where monotheism is concerned. Christian Trinitarian monotheism seeks to be no less intransigent than that of Islam.[57]

However, in the age of interfaith dialogue, has not the time come to go beyond a polemic which gets nowhere and to see how the difference between the monotheism of Islam and Christian monotheism can help both sides to get a better grasp of the meaning of the true transcendence of God? Do we not have a shared responsibility to confess a personal God in the face of modern unbelief and the increasing attraction of transcendences without God? Christians with a Trinitarian faith must allow themselves to be asked questions by Muslims, to the degree that Islam demands strict monotheism. Provocatively asked by Claude Geffré, conversely how could the doctors of Islam, who proclaim the uniqueness and greatness of God, so passionately ignore the revelation of the Fatherhood of God in Jesus Christ? Rather preserve in a banal and ultimately incorrect contrast between the distant God of Islam and the near God of Christianity, we should take account of the tension between two radically different conceptions of the divine oneness and investigate their historical and philosophical roots. Even if the Qur'anic revelation seeks only to be the confirmation of the biblical revelation of the exclusive unity of the creator God, we can seriously ask whether the transcendence of the God of Islam does not finally obey the philosophical logic of the Absolute: that the identity which excludes all difference and is the expression of its self-sufficiency. Geffré asks whether we must follow Louis Massignon in discerning in the Qur'anic

---

[57] Claude Geffré, 'The One God of Islam and Trinitarian Monotheism', *op. cit.*, p. 88-89.

revelation a natural theology which differs from the salvation-historical theology developed by the sacred writers of Israel?[58]

Roger Aranaldez' reflections, albeit with a different accent, closely relate to this theme:

> But the God of Islam is no more identical to the God of the philosophers than is the God of Judaism or of Christianity. Doubtless a superficial knowledge of the Qur'an can create this illusion; such superficiality characterizes the judgement of certain *philosophes* of the eighteenth century who saw in Islam the expression of 'natural religion'. But in fact, Muslim theology does not recognize natural law, natural morality, or natural religion. What is called *fitra*—sometimes translated 'nature'—is in reality only the mark of creation on the creature, the opening of human beings to their Creator. Reason is given in order to receive and understand the Word of God, not to engage in autonomous speculations. Finally, the Qur'an brings a positive law, set of commandments whose sole justification is the absolute will of God, who legislates as He will. Nothing is farther removed from a natural law. Consequently, from this point of view, it would falsify Islam to reduce it to a kind of common denominator among all monotheisms, for the Qur'an preaches more than the unicity of God. His omnipotence, His omniscience, and other attributes—truths that are in fact already present within the Old and New Testaments. Islam teaches a law that is not that of the Bible, and less still that of the Gospels—a law that repeals all those preceding it and will never be repealed, Islam calls for obedience to a prophet whom neither Jews nor Christians recognize; moreover the definition of prophet and of prophecy varies among the three religions.[59]

---

[58] *Ibid.*, 90-91.

[59] Roger Arnaldez, *Three Messengers for One God*, University of Notre Dame Press, 1994, pp. 2-3.

On the other hand, if we follow Christian monotheism through to the end as an affirmation of the uni-trinity of God, we discover that the uniqueness of God must be thought of as unity which assumes differences. The God of trinitarian monotheism is a life differentiated in communion. It is there that the originality of the God of Christians proves to be so different from the God of natural theology.[60]

The theme of *différance* is developed by Christian de Chergé, the prior, theologian and mystic of the Cistercian community of the Atlas-Tibhirine, whose Martyrdom has come to symbolise the dilemma and drama of contemporary Muslim-Christian dialogue.[61] Fr. de Chergé, has extremely provocatively captured the dilemma: 'Do our differences have the sense of a communion?'[62] The greatest difference should allow us to think of the least difference. For Christian de Chergé, diversity is a basic characteristic of creation. In his ministry, Jesus was attentive to all those who were not 'as the others'. He himself was seen by his fellow citizens as someone with an intolerable difference: he made himself 'equal to God' (John: 5.18). Yet he claimed to gather all God's children in this difference (John:17:21). This is a gathering-in which does not kill diversity: 'In my father's house there are many mansions' (John: 14:2). To be the Church is to see oneself invited constantly to enlarge the space of one's heart by discerning the traces of the Spirit. Islam, with the words of the Qur'an, offers itself as a difference which needs to be examined. The person who is 'like' is different, and such persons are not constituted just by any fingerprints. Genesis proclaims this infinite variety of the created world with a series of plurals: the waters, the lights, the birds, and the plants. These remarks by the Prior of Tibhirine fit perfectly with the shift of contemporary awareness, which has made the other and

---

[60] Claude Geffré, *op. cit.*, 91.

[61] Bernardo Olivera, 'Monk, Martyr and Mystic: Christian de Chergé (1937-1996)', *Cistercian Studies Quarterly (CSQ)*, vol. 34 (1999), pp. 321-338; Donald McGlynn, 'Atlas Martyrs', *CSQ*, vol. 32 (1997), pp. 149-194; and Marie-Christine Ray, *Christian de Chergé, Prieur de Tibhirine*, Paris, Centurion-Bayard, 1998.

[62] Text published in *La Lettre de Ligugé*, no. 227 (1984), pp. 21-37 and no. 228 (1984), pp. 25-42. Reprinted in Christian de Chergé, *L'invincible espérance*, Centurion-Bayard, Paris, 1997, pp. 109-166. For another collection his writings, see *Sept vies pour Dieu et l'Algérie*, Centurion-Bayard, Paris, 1996, both edited by Bruno Chenu, editor of *La Croix*.

différance major intellectual and existential categories. A particular category of globalisation allows for a revaluation of the particular, whether cultural or spiritual. The new feature of the present time is the recognition of the other as other and the emphasis on the other's particularity. The challenge is to convert a pernicious fear of difference into delight in a difference, which enriches. As Christian de Chergé has emphasised, a true theology of creation allows a positive appreciation of *différance*. To echo this sensitive reflection by Christian de Chergé, Bruno Chenu writes regarding *différance* within Christian history:

> We have again become aware of the cultural, liturgical, canonical and theological diversity which has run through the history of the Church. We have not stopped meditating on the significance of a remark of St Irenaeus about the question of Easter: 'The difference in the fast confirms the agreement of faith' [Eusebius of Caesarea, *Ecclesiastical History*, Book V, 23, 13]. And St Augustine can only conceive of the church with the finery of a glistening diversity, leaving it to love to weave the links between the differences. If uniformity is going to override Christian freedom, we must never forget that the liturgical diversity which remains has always been more attractive than a panoply of rites: a certain image of God and of the relationship with God, a face of Christ, a conception of the church. And the Catholic Church has always had an East, even when it was becoming polarized on its West. Down the centuries the church has been polyphonic. Certainly there are limits to the hospitality that the church offers to multiplicity. Respect for the other cannot silence a concern for the truth and the aim of unity. However, we could speak of a hierarchy of differences in ecclesial life. In the nineteenth century the only difference that Johann-Adam Möhler recognized was the difference that is incompatible with ecclesial polyphony. False notes excluded themselves as a matter of course. For the risk of the fragmentation of the church is not utopian, as history bears witness. That is why the

last word of the Christian is not 'difference' but 'coherence', 'harmony': in a word communion.[63]

However, whilst the supreme corruption might be considered idolatry, negation of the one. It has to be acknowledged that the Christian community has not been able to bear an incontestable witness to love as unity down the centuries, so much so that the division of Christians 'has served as an apologetic argument in favour of the authenticity of the Qur'an.'[64]

Anthony H Johns has reminded us there is much that Christians may find unacceptable in the formulations of emphases of Islam. The spiritual insights of certain passages in the Qur'an and the sense of near ecstasy that it sometimes expresses are inspiring. Other parts, however, particularly those stipulating punishments do not immediately command assent or respect. At the same time they will miss certain emphases central to the Christian tradition, such as the sacral and sacramental potential of created things and the work of human hands. This is exemplified in the communion with the Holy enshrined in the ritual of sharing of bread and wine which is at the heart of the central act of Christian worship. So far from having a ritual meaning, wine is forbidden in Islam, and the very act of eating or drinking breaks ritual purity. In such matters there are problems that cannot be resolved in the short term, any more than can the mystery of religious pluralism in the wider sense. There is the constant

---

[63] B Chenu, *Do Our Difficulties have the Sense of a Communion?*, pp. 128-129, and B Chenu, 'L'unité sous forme de communion. L'objectif du mouvement oecuménique', *Recherches de science religieuse*, vol. 89 (2001), pp. 247-270. In two particularly fruitful papers, William T Cavanagh has argued that the process of globalization is not, as the word implies, merely a process of universalization, the dominance of the one over the many, but a peculiar proliferation of the many, still ultimately absorbed into one. He turns to the Catholic theologian Hans Urs von Balthasar to argue that only Christ adequately solves the problem of the one and the many. Christ is the key, therefore, to the sustenance of a sane culture in a globalizing world. The Christian is called not to replace one universal system with another, but to attempt to 'realize' the universal body of Christ in every exchange. W T Cavanagh, 'Balthasar, Globalization, and the Problem of the One and the Many', *Communio: International Catholic Review*, Vol. 28 (2001), pp. 324-347, and 'The World in a Wafer: a Geography of the Eucharist as Resistance to Globalization, *Modern Theology*, Vol. 15 (1999), pp. 181-196.

[64] Bruno Chenu, 'Do Our Difficulties have the Sense of a Communion? In Memory of Christian de Chergé, Prior of Tibhirine, Algeria', *Concilium*, 1999, no. 2, pp. 125-136.

danger that argument on such points of disagreement in attempts to prove by natural reason whose morality is better, will lead to a bitterness, if not downright hatred and destructive personal relationships. When so much is shared, the primary human responsibility is to seek wisdom in the quality of commitment to the source of every moral sense, God. Non-Muslims, by definition, do not see the Qur'an and Muhammad in the same light as do Muslims. They cannot refuse to learn from the testimony of Muslim living.[65]

Conclusion

Christians and Muslims must strive with patience to remove the misunderstandings as well as the completely false ideas which too many Christians have of Islam, as well as certain presentations of Christianity which the Muslim finds in his own tradition and which the Christian cannot recognise or accept at all.

Thus the Christian has the task not only to show, but also to make the people he speaks to and his Muslim friends realise that his faith is truly monotheistic and that it too demands a very pure interpretation (which will not cover the Islamic conception as stated in Muslim tradition, but is no less exacting) of God's transcendence. And further, the relation between the spiritual and the temporal is regarded differently in different traditions. It follows that the joining of the spiritual and the temporal in Islam is not confusion and that their separation in Christianity is not in fact a separation. That *mystique et politique* engage with a similar intention but they may join at a different juncture.

In different places, the emphasis varies, ways of explanation and references to the Word of God diverge, and the mystery of salvation does not unfold according to the same divine Economy. It is right to be clear about this. But sincere exchanges are none the less possible and highly desirable. There must be on all sides a desire, a wish for sympathy and intellectual fairness, an anxiety to understand precisely the other's thought. And perhaps, in doing this, we shall see more than once the dialogue breaking off in favour of a common

---

[65] Anthony H Johns, 'Islam as a Challenge to Christianity', *op. cit.*, p. 21.

task of philosophical exploration.

It is indeed a task, which requires staying power, and there is no lack of obstacles. Real mutual knowledge of Christianity by Muslims and of Islam by Christians is already a difficult thing. But we believe that it is only the interior living-out of faith in God and the theological meaning of the destiny of man, which can assign to such enquiries their rightful place; and, without denying or in any way minimising the differences and divergences, we must learn sympathetically and with respect how to use them to further mutual understanding and, if God wills, a common love of the Truth.

In his first encyclical of his pontificate, *Redemptor hominis*, John Paul II referred to the religious map of the world and underlined the importance for the Church in taking account of religious plurality. John Paul II has devoted more attention to the relations between Christians and Muslims than any of his predecessors. His overriding attitude is one of respect for the valid religious experiences of Muslims. He wants Christians to approach Muslims, not merely eager to speak and give but also to be open to learn, being aware that they can be challenged and enriched by them.[66]

Michael Fitzgerald, the Pontifical Council for Interreligious Dialogue has made the following observations about the future of Muslim-Christian relations:

> When mention is made of dialogue it is usually formal discussion between experts that comes to mind. It must be stated clearly that this is not the only form of dialogue, but it does have its own importance. It should serve to facilitate the dialogue of life and the dialogue of deeds by clarifying ideas and dissipating prejudices. From what has been said ..., it will have been noted that much formal dialogue concentrates on social issues. It is useful to examine different religious perspectives on these issues in order, precisely, to build up mutual

---

[66] See the following essays: M L Fitzgerald, 'Pope John Paul II and Interreligious Dialogue: A Catholic assessment'; pp. 209-222; M Ayoub, 'Pope John Paul II and Islam', pp. 171-186; and Ibrahim M Abu-Rabi, 'John Paul II and Islam', pp. 187-208—in *John Paul II and Interreligious Dialogue*, (eds.) Bryon L Sherwin and Harold Kasimow, Orbis Books, Maryknoll, New York, 1999.

confidence. On theological matters it will be hard to come to agreement. From this point of view, interreligious dialogue differs from the ecumenical dialogue among Christians, which aims at bringing about a unity of faith. It is obvious that Christians and Muslims will continue to differ on essential matters of faith. For this reason the purpose of theological dialogue will not be to prove that one side is right and the other wrong, but rather to explore respective positions in order to understand them better. When this is done many prejudices, built upon half-truths, will fall by the wayside. Since delicate issues are involved here, it is particularly useful that they be studied by groups, which have certain stability. This allows for questions to be re-examined, looked at in new ways, with a readiness to go beyond ready-made formulas, which often falsify the other's position.

The dialogue of religious experience is sometimes merely a special instance of the dialogue of discourse. What distinguishes it is that the matter under examination is the spiritual tradition of Christianity and Islam respectively. Attention may be paid to the spiritual message of the Bible and of the Qur'an, but also to the writings of spiritual authors, of sufis and mystics. Such exchanges, especially when they take place in an atmosphere of faith and silence before God, can be of immense help in building up mutual respect. Some groups engaging in such spiritual exploration do exist already, but there would surely be room for more in the current efforts at Christian-Muslim dialogue. Within the realm of religious experience other possibilities may also be mentioned. There are occasions for being present during the worship of the other community. A Muslim may be invited to a baptism or a wedding in a Christian church. A Christian may at times be invited to be present during the performance of *salat*. Reverent observation, while uniting the heart in prayer to God, can surely help to deepen appreciation for the spiritual riches of the other tradition. There are times too when Muslims and Christians may want to join in common supplication to God. During the Gulf War, in a number of places Christians and Muslims, and Jews too, came together to pray for peace. When praying together in this way, care has obviously to be taken not to cause embarrassment by the choice of inappropriate formulas or gestures. Where such care is taken, and particularly when the planning is carried out jointly, the common standing before God does help to knit minds and hearts. To my mind all these forms of dialogue can be contributions towards peace in the world. The dialogue of life will provide an understanding and a harmony between individuals and communities strong enough to resist being broken by outside influences. Dialogue of deeds, with a common response to the effects of war, will reinforce the will to ban armed conflict as a way of resolving disputes. The specialist dialogue will help to clarify issues, and also to plan strategies. The dialogue of religious experience will help to provide motivation and will also be a source of strength to persevere. All this may seem very idealistic. It is true that we have to take reality into account that we have to take people as they are. Nevertheless we have to keep ideals before us, we have to maintain a vision, otherwise we shall just resign ourselves to constant conflict. As a new millennium approaches, should we not set our sights higher?[67]

---

[67] M Fitzgerald, *Encounter: Documents for Muslim-Christian Understanding* (Rome), no. 247 (1998), pp. 13. See also M Fitzgerald, 'The Spirituality of Interreligious Dialogue', *Origins. CNS Documentary Service*, 28, 36 (February 25, 1999), pp. 631-33.

THE NEED TO
REDISCOVER COMPASSION

THE NEED TO REDISCOVER COMPASSION—AUSTRALASIA

Anthony Johns

'... for those occasions on which
we have failed in compassion ...'
Ordinary of the Mass

Introduction

Compassion is in some ways a problematic word. *The New Shorter Oxford English Dictionary* (1993) gives as its meanings: (Obsolete) 1. Participation in another's suffering, fellow-feeling sympathy. 2. Pity, inclining one to show mercy or give aid, have compassion on. (Obsolete) 3. Sorrowful emotion, grief. The entry closes with the combination ' "Compassion Fatigue", indifference to charitable appeals resulting from the frequency of such appeals.'

The indication that the first meaning is obsolete, like reports of Tom Sawyer's death, appears to be exaggerated. 'Participation in another's suffering, fellow-feeling, sympathy' are still among its current meanings—that the Conference uses it in this sense is proof enough that this is the case. But even so, it is not quite adequate to our needs. The aspect of reciprocity is lacking. Ideally, there should be a word that expresses not simply fellow-feeling on the part of the speaker for one worse off than his/herself, as in 'I have compassion on you', but a mutual recognition of the plight all are in, a common response to the inadequacies we all share. The Qur'an puts it succinctly, prefaced by the formula, 'In the name of God, the Merciful, the Compassionate. By the declining day! Humankind is indeed destitute, apart from those who believe and do good deeds, counselling each other with Truth, counselling each other with Patience' (Sura 103).

131

This is my point of departure, together with a whimsical reflection on the tantalizing quest the title suggests. How can one rediscover what has never yet been fully realized. Such a compassion, in its fullness, is at best, something only dreamt of; or like the lost chord, is heard but once, and then vanishes into silence. Yet the memory of its haunting beauty has such power that it compels all who have ever heard it, to search to recover it without ceasing.

*   *   *

Islam is a new arrival in the world of Australasia. Yet in saying the words 'Islam' and 'arrival' without further qualification, we are on dangerous ground. It may be overlooked that 'Islam' is used in two senses: as a verbal noun, signifying a commitment to God alone, recognition of His prophet Muhammad, and dedication to divine and human values this commitment requires; and as an abstract noun, a convenient piece of shorthand no doubt, but often with a pejorative connotation that implies distrust and fear. Phrases such as 'The development of Islam as the language of insurgency' and the like from journalists and would be social scientists are not that uncommon.

To stress this distinction is not pedantry. The word Islam as loosely used in the media needs rehabilitation. To use it with care is one step towards recovering the compassion we seek, by a careful, sensitive, use of language.

*   *   *

It is helpful to establish some general perspectives. Geographically, Australia like Europe, faces a domain of Islam, the Islam of Southeast Asia—not that of West Asia and North Africa. It is sometimes known as the land of the second expansion. Islam came there relatively late, Muslim principalities and port-cities not making an appearance until the 13th century, though this appearance marks the climax of centuries of involvement in the trading system of the Indian ocean, the spice islands of the West Pacific and the South China sea.

Geographically, it lies between the Indian sub-continent and China, and is tenuously linked to the Great South Land. It was without a name of its own until the term Southeast Asia was invented in World War II. It took some time for it to become established in general discourse, and even then, its significance as part of the world of Islam long went unacknowledged. The map on the inside covers of the Festival of Islam volume, has the Islamic world ending with the eastern borders of Bangladesh!

Australia's immediate contacts with the Islamic world are through its neighbours, the nation states of Indonesia, Malaysia, Singapore and Brunei. This cluster of nation states is collectively home to the largest community of Muslims of closely related ethnicities and a common language in the world, more numerous than that of the Arabs and speakers of Arabic. In the pre-World War II world of high colonialism, Australia was able to ignore this world. In fact it was not a case even of ignoring it. There was the total, invincible ignorance that such a world existed.

In all these states except Singapore, Muslims are a majority, and for the most part ethnically related, being either Malay, or other sub-groups of the West Austronesian family. About 60 percent of the population of Malaysia is Muslim, with over 90 percent of Muslims being Malay. According to the constitution, only a Muslim can be a Malay. The remainder of the population are Chinese and Indian, religious adherence in varying proportions being to Buddhism, Hinduism and Christianity. Singapore is predominantly Chinese. It has a small Muslim minority, almost exclusively Malay. Brunei is the most ethnically homogenous state in the region, both in terms of ethnicity and religion, being Malay and Muslim. Only in Indonesia—89 percent Muslim—is there no necessary nexus between ethnicity and religion.

Australia, according to the 1996 census has 200,885 Muslims, or 1.1 percent of the total population (but 2.1 percent of the population of Sydney, and 1.6 percent of the population of Melbourne). There are reasons for regarding 400,000 as a closer estimate, but even on the lower figure of 200,000, Islam is the religion with most adherents in Australia after Christianity.

In contrast with its Southeast Asian neighbours, Australia has only a tiny minority of Muslims. But if Muslims in southeast Asia are largely of a common West Austronesian stock with a common language, Islam in Australia is represented by at least 45 ethnic groups each with its own language, for most of whom their ethnicity is as much part of their self definition as the profession of Islam. Alongside them are a number of converts from older-established Australian communities.

Muslims come to Australia

Muslims entered Australian history in 1866 with the arrival of 124 camels and 34 Afghan attendants to assist in transport across and exploration of the desert interior of the country. These Afghans were not brought to Australia because they were Muslims, but because they could handle camels. There was but little concern with Islam among those who brought them, and little realization then that they were the forerunners of a new faith community in Australia. They came, largely on a short-term basis, to serve the economic needs of the separate colonies that constituted Australia at that time. Even so, culturally they left memorials of their presence and their religion. These included mosques. One of the oldest, built in 1889, and still in use, is in Adelaide. Another built in 1891 was at Broken Hill in New South Wales, now a museum maintained by the Broken Hill Historical Society. The remains of other mosques can be seen on the old route to the northwest between Adelaide and Brisbane. A few devotional books belonging to them still survive, collections of Arabic prayers and invocations, bound in rough leather to protect their pages from the dust and grit of the desert. And street names: In Alice Springs, (Central Australia), there are street names that attest their one time presence, Mahomet Street and Khalick Street, and a school called the Charlie Sadadeen School. The trans-Australian railway is known as the Ghan—an abbreviation of Afghan, commemorating the transport system across arid central Australia managed by the Afghans in 1879.

A living link with these Afghans survived until 1962, when one of them, who arrived in 1885 died at the age of 106.[1] And a descendant of one of the north Indian families who followed in

---

[1] Laurence P Fitzgerald, 'Christians and Muslims in Australia', in *Islamochristiana*, 10 (1984), p. 163.

their wake, Hanifa Deen, has given a vivid account of them in her book *Caravanserai Journey Among Australian Muslims.*[2]

The White Australia Policy, applied by the notorious dictation, test was introduced on Federation in 1901. It was designed to exclude Asians from Australia, and almost by definition Muslims. Although there was a slight relaxation in its application during the 1920s which allowed a number of family reunions for Indians who had followed the Afghans into Australia prior to Federation, this acted as an effective brake on the development of Muslim communities in Australia. But during the same period, a number of Albanian Muslims, being European in physiognomy, were able to enter the country. In the 1940s there was the migration on a small scale of Turkish-Cypriot Muslims, facilitated by the fact that they had British passports.

It was not until the 1950s, with the emergence of new nations to Australia's north, and Australia's engagement with them at a diplomatic level, that their peoples, hitherto unknown, found their way into the Australian ken. This was through a growing presence, although largely transitory, of Asian individuals, consisting of a growing diplomatic community, and increasing numbers of students coming to Australia and New Zealand under the Colombo Plan. Many of them were Muslims from Malaysia and Indonesia.

To meet their religious needs and serve as a sign of the presence of a Muslim community, the diplomatic missions of Muslim countries collaborated to build a Mosque in the National capital. It was opened on 26 January 1960/27 Rajab 1379, the feast of the Mi'raj, by the then Indonesian Ambassador A Y Helmi (whose wife was Turkish). During this period a number of Asians with professional qualifications were granted 'Certificates of Exemption' from the dictation test to enter Australia to take up professional appointments. Among them were Muslims, two of them appointed to university posts, to teach the languages and cultures of Asia, an initiative of the Menzies government of that time designed to extend the scope of university education beyond the traditional parameter of the humanities, by including in it the languages and cultures of

---

[2] Hanifa Deen, *Caravanserai—Journey Among Australian Muslims*, Allen and Unwin, Australia, 1995.

135

Asia. Thus middle-class Muslim intellectuals began to find a place, and make their mark as significant members of the Australian professional and educational elites.

There was a radical new development in immigration policy in 1968. In that year, an immigration agreement was signed with Turkey, the first time one had been made with a non-European state, to bring Turkish working class migrants to Australia. They were to come, it should be emphasized, not as in Germany, as guest workers, but as migrants with prospective rights of citizenship. The first planeload of 186 Turks arrived at Sydney airport in November 1968. They were dispersed in automotive assembly lines, clothing and textile factories. Between 1968 and 1971, over 10,000 of them were to emigrate from Turkey. They came to meet the labour needs of Australia in an expanding economy. That they were Muslims was fortuitous. Again, there was little if any realization that their arrival was to extend the new faith community first brought to Australia by the Afghans.

They came as Turks, not as Muslims, though Muslims they were. And a bipartite symbolism was seen in their arrival. On the one hand the migration agreement struck resonances with Australian memories of the Turks at Gallipoli in 1915. Remarkably few grudges followed that defeat, indeed there was a mutual respect between the soldiers of both sides. In the light of it, the welcome of Turks as new Australians had an almost poetic irony.

On the other hand, members of the small, older community of Muslims welcomed them as brothers, seeing in their arrival a link with the arrival of the Afghan Muslims a century before, and they gave them a ceremonial welcome at Sydney airport.

There is a further historic irony in that it was an Australian need that brought the Afghans to Australia a hundred years before, and likewise a need for labour, after the traditional sources of migrants had dried up, that brought Turks to Australian factory floors.

With the formal abolition of the White Australian Policy in 1972, race was no longer a barrier to acceptance as a migrant. In the wake of it, Muslims were among the various peoples coming to Australia. The continuing migrant program was based on an annual quota, and filled according to a mix of criteria which varied from year to year on the basis of which points were awarded on the basis of professional skills, knowledge of English, sponsorship, family reunions and age, to which were added persons granted refugee status. These migrants included Muslims of various ethnic backgrounds. A large number came in the wake of war and civil unrest: in the wake of the Arab Israeli war in 1967 and the continuing Palestinian tragedy, the war in Cyprus in 1974, the break-up of Pakistan in 1975, and the outbreak of civil war in Lebanon followed by the Israeli invasion. By 1981 Australia had received about 16,500 Lebanese born Muslims. The initial numbers may seem small, but it should be remembered that in 1945, Australia had a population of only 9 million, and by the end of the seventies not much over 12 or 13 million.

Immigration is a dynamic and continuing process with an important role in Australia's development. The current target is 80,000 per year, and there is discussion of raising it to 100,000 in 2001. More recent migrants include refugees from Somalia, Afghanistan, Iraq and Bosnia. Over the past few years, numbers of illegal refugees have arrived in Australia, some of them 'boat people' including 1675 Iraqis and 1164 Afghanis. A number of these are professionals, including mechanical engineers and medical practitioners. Of those who had been processed up to 1999—up to 917 Iraqis and 713 Afghanis, none have been sent back.[3]

Together with the new immigration policy, there was a change in the attitude of the Australian government to new migrants. Hitherto it had regarded their assimilation into the Australian community as it then was, as a matter of course. There was a tacit assumption that 'they will become like us.' A policy of multiculturalism was now established This was in large part due to the representations of an emerging vocal migrant community. Government policy now recognized the value of diverse cultural traditions and so provided opportunities for giving a voice to the various ethnic, linguistic, cultural and religious minorities for whom Australia was now home, and assisting them by providing them the means to retain their distinct identities within an Australian context.

The late 1970s saw the appearance of a number of publicly

---

[3] *The Australian*, Monday 17 January, 2000, p. 4.

funded multicultural institutions designed to support this multicultural idea: A government Department of Multicultural Affairs, government funded research projects on settlement in Australia, the establishment of the Special Broadcasting Service (the SBS, jocularly referred to by older Australians for some of whom the various codes of Rugby had a semi-religious status, as Soccer Bloody Soccer), broadcasting on radio and television programs in the languages of all the major ethnic communities, the Adult Migrant Education Programme, and further facilities for migrants, were established, including translation services, and English classes.

Migrants who were Muslims however, identified themselves not only by their ethnicities, but were concerned to establish themselves as faith communities of Muslims, and sense of identity and the voice these various communities of Muslims, in their richness and diversity have gained, has likewise been facilitated by the policy of Multiculturalism. There is a distribution of Muslims across a wide range of professions and fields of employment, with varying levels of education, and opportunities and drive for upward mobility.

Ethnic loyalties however continue to be real and productive. It is a part of the nature of Islam that religious commitment is expressed through strong local loyalties and cultural forms, representing a fusion between the universal forms and doctrines of Islam with local beliefs and life-styles. This need not be understood in a chauvinistic sense, but it does emphasize that ethnicity is an important element in the composition of the Muslim *umma* in Australia, and at times may be a source of inter-Muslim community friction.

Difficulties faced by Muslims

All migrants to a new country with a largely unrelated culture face problems of adjustment and adaptation. Each group and social class faces its own problems. All need recognition, acceptance and support, and all have their own responses to the challenges this presents.

Among Australia's Muslims, there is the trauma of leaving home, family, language, social structure, familiar climate and religious environment. It is difficult to exaggerate the culture shock encountered by many of them on arriving in Australia, and the initial sense of bewilderment and disorientation they experienced in a land where the local way of life seemed colourless, sterile, boring and empty, and family relationships and kinship structures attenuated, and the great cycle of annual celebrations that mark the progress of the Muslim year, were little known and attracted next to no interest. In some cases there was the additional trauma of war and bereavement. It was not simply a case of moving from majority to minority status, although this was one consequence of migration. It was moving from an environment in which their religion is part of the air they breathed, which gave shape to every rite of passage and was an assumed, a given in every day discourse, and family and interpersonal relationships. From a ritual point of view, if misfortune struck, if a death occurred, everyone around them knew what was required, and how to respond.

They were in an environment in which neither state or local community could give them support, let alone offer recognition of the faith that was the bedrock of their view of the world or the rituals that identified them as a community. These were largely a matter of indifference in a secular state, in which the only formal official lip service to religion in the recitation of the Lord's prayer recited, at times by an agnostic with sufficiently ecumenical tendencies at the opening of sessions of parliament. For Muslims, even to find a place to pray at work was difficult (especially for women).

An Asian religion such as Buddhism might be intellectually chic, but Islam was looked on with a certain *hauteur,* notwithstanding Muslims bore a faith and a salvation history in many respects closely related to that of the Judaeo-Christian heritage of the society into which they came.

The public flaunting of sexual freedom in Australia, and its prominence in the media, for some confirmed their worst fears of the moral perils lurking in the new environment, and heightened the perception of a need for security behind the sturdy walls of their own communities.

For many, a rigorous interpretation of the prohibition of alcohol denied them entry to any building or attendance at any

139

function at which alcohol was served. But even assuming that this was not a problem of conscience, the social encounter and the relationship between colleagues, workmates on the factory floor or friends, of betting on the dogs or horses, or 'drinking together' in the local was largely excluded. Relaxation in a hotel with the atmosphere heavy with the smell of beer, disturbed by the occasional maudlin or aggressive drunk had little appeal, even as a temptation. So participation in social occasions such as the celebration of a football victory was closed to them, and even the celebration of Christmas and Easter as secular holidays.

But over and against, dwarfing even such personal problems there loomed a much greater challenge: how to survive, and how to establish the institutions that would give a corporate presence and stability to Muslim life in the new country.

Australian attitudes to Islam and Muslims

There are elements in the public profession and practise of Islam that tends to set the teeth of Anglo-Australians on edge. There are a number of reasons for this. One is that for Euro-Australians, especially those of Anglo-Saxon heritage, there is an innate reticence in speaking about religious faith, or performing religious rituals in public. One recalls how Sir Humphrey set in train his plot to derail the appointment of a highly competent and honest candidate to the Chairmanship of the Bank of England by alluding to his religiosity with the phrase: Oh, the lay preacher! The fact that Islam is a religion that requires visible signs of commitment, may itself be disconcerting. In particular women's wearing of the veil may be resented because it is felt as an ostentatious intrusion of religion into public life. Ostentatious, it is often forgotten, is a culture bound word.

Another is the lack of appreciation of the Qur'an as a revealed book. Although a recitation of the Arabic by a great reciter can hold even a non-Muslim audience spellbound, the sense, the power and incredible richness of the book are largely inaccessible through an English translation. Few make the effort to read it, and know little of its content apart from the punishments it prescribes for certain crimes, and at best that it contains stories of prophetic figures that at a superficial level, appear to be better told in the Bible.

The inherited image in Western folklore of Islam as a religion of violence and the sword is alive and well. It is enhanced by emphasis in the media on acts of violence in which Muslims are involved, such as the hijack of the Air India Airbus, the Abu Sayyaf kidnappings from Sabah, acts which has no justification in Islamic Law, and the sectarian violence in Nigeria and East Indonesia.

The press coverage of these events is dramatic. To take reports of demonstrations in the streets of Jakarta prompted by sectarian violence in Ambon as an example: There are the reports of speeches by Indonesian political figures demanding an Islamic Revolution and the abolition of the Pancasila (the Indonesian national state philosophy). The illustrations show groups of frenzied Muslim men, with bared teeth, and faces contorted with rage.[4] one of them bearing a huge banner under the national monument bearing the words 'Tolerance is nonsense, Slaughter Christians'. The SBS TV news at 6.30 on 6 January included a pan shot of a Muslim mob, one demonstrator holding up a cross with a rabbit crucified on it.

Current affairs television programmes when presenting social problems in Muslim countries attribute such problems more to Islam than to specific social-economic conditions and local tradition. The programme *Correspondent's Report* (2 May) presented a segment on honour killings of women in Pakistan. Technically, it was competent and convincing.

It showed how a woman suspected of sexual misconduct might be murdered by her husband, and he go unpunished if his wife's family, feeling that its honour too had been sullied, opted to pardon him.

The reporter regarded the practice as justified by Islamic law, unaware that a diabolical casuistry was involved in the confounding of two separate issues to justify tribal custom. One is that sexual misconduct must be proved by due process. The other is that there is a strong Qur'anic recommendation that one wronged should pardon the perpetrator of that wrong. The programme,

---

4   *The Canberra Times*, Saturday 8 January, p. 11.

however, thanks to the authority it enjoys, gives a radically false impression of Islamic social values and Islamic.

Political commentators, even in the quality press, highlight a potential for violence in Islam. Greg Sheridan, in an article prompted by the success of PAS in the Malaysian elections, self-consciously parodying the opening of the Communist Manifesto, writes, 'There is a fire burning in South East Asia, and that fire is Islam.'[5] But later remarks in a patronising tone, 'Islam in Malaysia is a much gentler creed than it is in much of the Middle East'.

In a more recent article,[6] under the headline: 'Extremely worrying symptoms: Beware the Islamic dominoes', he writes, 'Islamic extremism, or, more accurately, extremism that expresses itself in Islamic terms—is developing as the most dangerous organizational challenge to governments in South-East Asia'. It is not surprising that Muslims feel that in the West, Islam is perceived as the new enemy after the collapse of Marxism.

He goes through the motions of distinguishing between Islam and extremism, writing in a patronizing tone, 'Let's not get too paranoid. Islam is, above all, one of the world's great monotheistic religions and deserves to be treated much more respectfully in the West' Hmmmm! But the patronising tone continues, 'The overwhelming majority of South-East Asia's Muslims are law-abiding folks who pose no threat to anyone.'

While perhaps well intended, the unuttered 'despite being Muslims' seems to be suggested, with the sub-text, 'unlike the "real" Muslims in the Middle East'.

He concludes, 'We need to know much more about the dynamics of Asian Islam'. There is of course no such thing as an Asian Islam.

Interestingly, the only substantial, appreciative comment on Islamic affairs I have come across in the daily press is a report on Islamic Finance, under the headline, 'Goodwill banking—Arab Bank is about to put a whole new spin on borrowing.'[7]

Tim Boreham reports on an interview with Mohammed

---

[5] *The Weekend Australian*, 19-20 February 2000, p. 30.

[6] *The Australian*, Friday 19 May 2000, p. 11.

[7] *The Australian*, Friday 7 April 2000, p. 34.

Nasser Abdel-Hakim, founder of the Moslem Community Co-operative of Australia now in the throes of upgrading its status by becoming a credit union.

He continues, 'In Australia, Islamic Banking has had only a modest presence, but this is about to change as the local arm of the Arab Bank plans to start an Islamic banking operation in a matter of months. An online Islamic banking site launched last month will also be available locally'.

He quotes James Harb, a solicitor concerned with these matters to the effect that Islamic banking is widely used by Malaysia and Indonesia, Australia's two main trading partners. A number of Western and Asian companies, including General Motors, Alcatel, IBM and Daewoo, have done deals using Islamic finance, and concludes 'There is a tremendous amount of goodwill towards Islamic banking.'

The article is illustrated by an appealing picture of Mohammed Nasser together with an attractive lady, wearing black neck and headscarf.

It seems that devotees of Mammon are more ready to accept pluralism than the general populace.

In such news reports, (apart from the last) the question as to what constitutes the authentic norms of Islamic behaviour is not even asked. So no opportunity is given for an answer setting out basic principles of Islamic life such as social responsibility, hospitality and recognition of a transcendent source of morality above utilitarianism and economic rationalism, and not to be explained away by post-modernism. Rather any act of violence by Muslims is likely to prompt the comment, 'Now they are showing themselves in their true colours!' For the media, acts of terror by Muslims are perpetrated by *Islamic* terrorists, not *terrorists*.

Such a constant barrage of headlines and illustrations reinforces a latent resentment towards Islam and Muslims, and renders it even more difficult, even for those of good will, to take the moral, the social, and theological dimensions of Islam seriously. This is reflected in a number of incidents.

One which occurred during the Gulf War attracted international attention. Australia sailors, on ships stationed in the Persian Gulf, were seen mimicking the movements and postures of

Muslims performing the ritual prayer. Video clips swiftly passed round the world. During the same period a number of individuals of vaguely Middle East appearance were attacked in the streets of Sydney.

There have been occasions on which local councils have disallowed the building of mosques because of fears of the inconvenience worshippers might cause to the flow of traffic, and the disturbance to the tranquillity of the early morning hours by the dawn call to prayer. A recent case with a satisfactory outcome involved the proposed conversion of a disused Presbyterian church in the Sydney suburb of Bankstown for use as a mosque by the Bangladesh Islamic Centre although the semantic convolutions exercised were intriguing. The Islamic Centre bought the church in 1995. The Bankstown Council, which had given permission for the church to be built in 1954, opposed its use as a mosque. In 1998, the matter went to the Land and Environment Court which denied permission, ruling that a 'mosque, while a place of worship, is not a church, which is a place of worship in the Christian tradition ...'

This ruling was successfully challenged on the grounds that the judge giving it had failed to give effect to broader dictionary definitions of the word 'church', which could encompass a mosque or a temple in their meanings. The appeal judge commented that the term 'church' referred to a place of worship rather than a physical structure, and as such the mosque fitted this description, and could not be excluded.[8]

A recent decision by the Australian Federal Government to appoint four church charity organizations, The Wesley Mission, Mission Australia, Salvation Army and Centre Care as employment agencies, revealed varying levels of intolerance, if you will lack of compassion, in their attitudes to the hiring of non-Christians to carry out this work.

The narrowest view was that of the Wesleyan Mission which insisted that the staff it employed were expected to speak and behave in accord with Christian standards, and set an example by joining in appropriate worship services and such devotional acts as a Centre may be conducting.[9] A TV interview with a representative of this

---

[8] *The Sydney Morning Herald*, Friday 17 March 2000, p. 5.
[9] *The Sydney Morning Herald*, Wednesday 29 December, p. 2, under headline, 'Christianity a job "asset"'.

organization (ABC 7 p.m. news the same day) stressed that employees should have Christian values. When the interviewer put it to him that in a number of the areas in which it worked there were considerable communities of Muslims and Buddhist Vietnamese, and that members of these communities might well have a positive role in helping to place individuals in employment, the spokesman replied that such individuals would not feel comfortable in an organization with these (i.e. Christian) principles.

The other three had more nuanced views: 'The Christian ethos was not an essential criterion for an applicant, but highly desirable' (Mission Australia); prospective employees would need to demonstrate a commitment to the culture and vision of the Salvation Army Employment Plus and to state that they understood the work of the Salvation Army to be and how they saw themselves working within it' (The Salvation Army); the organization's policy was that an individual would be hired on the basis of qualifications, regardless of religion, as long as the ethos of the organization was understood (Centacare).

None, with the possible exception of the fourth, appeared to recognize the personal and human values in faith communities outside the Christian tradition. There seemed to be a tacit refusal to recognize that Muslims and Buddhists might share equally and fully the human values that were at issue, or might even exemplify them in their lives better than some of the self-professed Christians who believed they held a monopoly of them.

It takes little compassion to share in the hurt that these images and attitudes cause to Muslims in Australia who lead exemplary lives, and know too well that such violence is not an authentic part of Islam, and that as Muslims they too have a keen sense of social justice.

Muslims in a new environment: first responses

In such an environment, the first challenge for Muslim communities was to devise strategies for survival and effective community building. Up to the end of the 60s, the numbers of Muslims in Australia did not add up to a sufficient critical mass to establish the institutions that might serve as the basis of Islamic community life. From its earliest days however, Islam has had its own built-in devices to transform groups of individual Muslims into communities, and provide these communities with structures that make it possible for them either to govern themselves, or to establish a recognized place in a wider non-Muslim community, even as subjects of a non-Muslim state. The ingrained discipline of the daily ritual prayers, the sharing of the Fast, the celebration and emotional impact of the two great festivals—that of the end of the Fast, with its local family and community emphasis, and that of the Sacrifice (during the Hajj), with its universalistic dimension were strong centripetal factors. Together with the spirituality of the Qur'an and Hadith, and the authority of the Law under the guidance of the *'ulama'*, they created a determination to establish places of learning and worship, a school and a mosque. To them could be added family and ethnic, *madhhab* and sometimes *tariqa* (brotherhood) networks. All these elements, and other forms of association, served to define and sustain a sense of identity. Once they had coalesced, however sparse the external supports available, a familiar environment was assured for later arrivals who otherwise would find no language community, no relatives, no friends, and scant facilities for the expression and practice of their faith and its transmission to a new generation.

The policy of multiculturalism facilitated the process. But support in implementing it also came from overseas, for the building of prayer facilities, the provision of Imams, and the provision of education facilities for Muslim children. Fortuitously, this coincided with the time when there was an explosion of oil prices, and so-called petro-dollars for charitable projects from the Arab countries were plentiful, and the various Muslim communities took full advantage of these opportunities.

From small-scale activities, with perhaps no more than a single room for prayers, and Qur'an classes, the idea to build a mosque could develop. A mosque once established has a core role in the prayer life and social organization of a Muslim community. It serves as a centre for worship, and the expression, interpretation, inculcation and celebration of Muslim belief and practice. It is a community reference point, and provides the means for self-identification in the new homeland.

It was a comparable situation that faced the earliest groups of Muslim traders when they settled at focal points and trading centres in the Muslim world to Australia's north at coastal town in Sumatra and Java, centuries earlier, and the same inner resources that served as a basis for their organisation into communities of common ethnicities.

Gary Bouma in his book *Mosques and Muslim settlement in Australia* gives a lucid and sympathetic account of mosques in Australia,[10] although since it was published back in 1994, further progress has been made. At the time of writing, there were fifty-seven mosques in Australia. Two already referred to, that built outside Adelaide in 1889 by the Afghans, and still in service; and the first in New South Wales about 1891 in Broken Hill, now a museum, are over a hundred years old. More recently, there is the Canberra mosque, built to meet the needs of diplomats from Muslim countries, and numbers of Colombo Plan students, opened in January 1960. The first mosque in Sydney was built in the late 1960s, and in Sydney and New South Wales today there are upwards of twenty mosques, the majority of them built since 1968. Of these, the largest and for some the most beautiful, is the Imam Ali Mosque at Lakemba. Another major mosque is the King Faisal Mosque, built by the Islamic Society of New South Wales, and the imposing Gallipoli Mosque at Auburn inaugurated in 1999.

In Melbourne there are upwards of twenty-five mosques. The largest in Victoria is in Preston (where Shaikh Fahmi is Imam). It includes an administrative section, classrooms, library and catering area.

It was opened in 1976 by the Assistant Secretary General of the World Muslim League in the presence of a personal representative of the then Prime-Minister Malcolm Fraser, the Leader of the Opposition, then Gough Whitlam, and local religious leaders, including the Catholic Archbishop of Melbourne.

Such an occasion is symbolic importance, for it shows how within 8 years of the signing of the migration agreement with Turkey,

---

[10] Gary D Bouma, *Mosques and Muslim Settlement in Australia*, BIPR Commonwealth of Australia, 1995.

and six years after the abolition of the White Australia policy, Islam had been recognized as a faith community significant in the development of Australia as a nation, and at an official, macro-level, was welcomed by government, the older established religions in the country, and the community at large.

There are mosques in all the other capital cities each with its own story to tell, and others continue to be built. These mosques are now largely the result of support by local communities, although in some cases supported by the governments of Muslim states.

An idea of the success and vitality of the Muslim community, and the role of one of the best known Australian mosques in it can be seen from Hanifa Deen's description of celebration of the Eid al-Adha in Lakemba in 1994. She writes:

> Never had I participated in an Eid gathering as big as the Lakemba celebration. I was stunned by the size of the crowd, the sounds, the buzz in the air. The scene tapped many buried memories. I had an awkward rush of nostalgia as thoughts of my youth rose up. I savoured the ritual of prayer and the emotional charge that always lingered from its strange blend of vulnerability, submission and solidarity. People had been gathering since dawn ... By 7 a.m. Wangee Road was jammed with an excited, happy throng. People spilled into front gardens and on to balconies or perched on walls. All wanted to be together for Eid ul-Adha. The next day, newspapers reported that more than 7000 people had attended the Lakemba mosque. ... I was spell bound. From my vantage point opposite the mosque, I could see over people's heads. The scene was far different from anything I had imagined. Inside the mosque, the religious and political aspects of Lakemba life were unfolding. Dignitaries, community leaders and politicians were paying their respects (and being seen paying them), and there were dignified prayers and speeches. But outside it was a festival—an unofficial youth festival with wave after wave of laughing,

chattering young people. The allure and sheer magnetism of the occasion were irresistible.'[11]

During the 1970s and 80s, the communities of migrant Muslims, continued to grow. Alongside the building of mosques, Islamic societies mushroomed, some but by no means all centred around a mosque or prayer facility, and the motivation for each being stimulated by perceived need or issue of concern to particular communities.

Alongside mosques and schools, one would expect *tariqa* to play a role in Australia, but it is difficult to uncover detailed information about them. Certainly there are Sufis among Australian Muslims, and an Australian Centre for Sufism was established in Sydney in 1999, with its mission 'to promote the message and the beauty of Sufism and Islam in Australia through raising the awareness of God in day to day life using the teachings of Sufism to define the journey of life'. But there is a cornucopia of other organisations, a number of them *ad hoc*, to meet various needs in the community serve to bind it together, and are an expression of its vitality. They include a moon-sighting committee to announce the beginning and ending of the Fasting Month,[12] and others to ensure that *halal* food is available. An example of the success of this concern is to be seen in Brunswick, an inner city, working class suburb of Melbourne with Turkish clubs, restaurants, coffee houses, bakeries, all *halal*.[13] They also discuss issues of dress, and questions such as whether it is obligatory for women to wear a headscarf. There are friendship organisations, such as is the El Sadeaq (*sic*) Society based in Melbourne. It has a community centre and small mosque for its mainly Egyptian members. It functions as a surrogate family, embracing Egyptians of all ages, and is dedicated to serving their religious, educational, recreational and social needs that neither state nor society provide. There are others such as an Arabic Speaking Welfare Workers Association, and Arab Women's Solidarity Foundation and yet others dedicated to social welfare, community

---

[11] Deen, *Caravansarai*, p. 121-122.
[12] Deen, *Caravansarai*, p. 63.
[13] Deen, *Caravansarai*, p. 15.

support and matters of community concern throughout the various communities.

At first, these societies, given their pioneering nature, were uncertain in their organization, but by the 1980s, many were well established, and had an effective presence. Organisation was at State level. In each state Islamic councils were established, each council devising its own agenda of activities and emphases, including welfare, educational and religious facilities, coordination of state-wide community-related functions. The Islamic Council of Victoria, for example, has a board of Imams, with mechanisms to represent Muslims at State government level. Its activities include inter-faith dialogue. The development of special interest organizations has continued apace.

Of the various organizations, some have a wider role than others, and address themselves to important issues in a new way. One, of particular significance because of its innovative character, is the Canberra Islamic Centre. It is an independent organisation of Muslims, and any Muslim of any tradition, *madhhab* or ethnicity may become a member, and provisions built into its Constitution ensure that no ethnic group can dominate it.

It was established by a group of concerned Muslims as a centre for Muslim activities. It is not a mosque, although it has prayer facilities, and does not compete with the Canberra mosque. It has a number of distinctive features. Central among them is its independence. It does not depend on any of the Muslim Embassies in Canberra for financial support, rather it aims to be self-funding, and for this purpose is registered as a charity, and is the first Islamic institution in Australia to which donations are tax deductible. It is not a member of the Australian Federation of Islamic Councils (AFIC), although it has contacts with it. It is designed to provide social and cultural activities consonant with an Islamic life style, and liaise on behalf of Muslims with the Australian government and Muslim countries represented by Embassies in Canberra. It was incorporated in December 1993. The ACT government recognized it as a community organization and granted it a prime site of land for the complex of buildings that it intends to erect. Plans have been drawn up that in a modest but individual way express its Islamic character, and construction is well advanced.

Among the recreational facilities planned is a swimming pool for women, and among its cultural resources, an Australian National Islamic Library. This project has attracted the sympathetic interest of the governor-general, and in 1997, he addressed an inaugural meeting at the Hyatt Hotel. One hundred thousand books have already been collected.

The centre holds monthly meetings, issues a monthly newsletter, and has upward of a thousand members. Given that there may be no more than 3,500 Muslims in Canberra, this is a striking achievement.

There are Muslim organisations of one kind or another in all the States and Territories of Australia, some stressing more the ethnic component of the association, others a trans-ethnic orientation, including a number of convert support groups. Among them are educational institutions of greater or lesser scope, such as the Foundation of Islamic Studies and Information at Arncliffe in Sydney. Some of these have associations with Travel Agencies run by Arabic Australians, which among other activities organise groups visiting the Holy Land, either to perform the 'Umra or the Hajj. Equally, there are very many women's organizations, whether for devotional purposes, or to function as Women's Friendship and Support Groups, organising courses and lectures to assist women in issues they face in Australia. Significantly, there is a Muslim Women's National Network of Australia, which publishes a regular news letter distributed to 16 women's organisations in New South Wales, and six in the other states and territories with membership ranging from 20 to 300.

The organizations in the various states are represented at state councils, and the state councils at the Federal level have been represented since the 1970s by the Australian Federation of Islamic Councils (AFIC), an umbrella organisation for all Australian Muslims. It has been funded by support from the local communities, from oil-rich Muslim countries, by revenue generated by the issuing of *halal* certificates indicating that animals had been slaughtered for consumption as food according to the correct rituals, and as its capital resources increased, from its own investments. Utilising these funds, AFIC has been able to provide funds to support the varied activities of the Muslim community, both at local and national levels,

151

and make contributions towards the building new mosques, providing prayer facilities, and prayer facilities, the appointment of imams, and arranging educational facilities for Muslim children. It has weathered the storm caused in the late 1980s by the decline in world oil prices and the subsequent reduction in petrol dollars available for the 'propagation of Islam' worldwide, thanks to the buffer provided by the generous support in the previous decade, and was therefore able to maintain these activities. In all this work, the Saudi Kingdom played a special role.

Muslims in New Zealand

The growth of Muslim communities in New Zealand in some respects follows the same lines of development as those in Australia, but according to a different rhythm and inevitably on a smaller scale. There is no point that can be mythologized into a grand beginning, comparable to the arrival of Afghans and their camels in Australia in 1866 to explore a vast and arid continent. The origins are much more low key.

They can be traced back to a number of Gujaratis who migrated to Auckland unaccompanied by their families early in the 20th century, and worked as shopkeepers. Some of them are known by name. Among them was Ahmed Ismail Bhikhoo, who arrived in 1911, leaving his wife and family in the Gujarat. In the following years he brought out six sons, one of them Ibrahim Musa, who arrived in 1917. Father and sons were active in various Indian associations that were formed in the 1920s, during this period primary self-definition being by land of origin. In 1936 the Ibrahim Musa referred to above brought out a wife, Bai Bibi. Three years later they had a son, thereby forming the first Muslim nuclear family in New Zealand on record.

The number of Muslims, however, remained small. According to the 1945 census there were only 67 Muslims in New Zealand, 59 men and 8 women—one of whom was Bai Bibi. It was only after partition that these Gujarati men began to bring out their families. In due course they were followed by others.

A new stage was marked in 1950 that Suleiman I Bhikhoo,

oldest son of the Ismail Ahmed Bhikhoo who had arrived in 1911 celebrated the end of Fast festival with about 25 other Muslims, the first time such a celebration had been held in New Zealand. Three months later, on the Festival of the Sacrifice, the group established the New Zealand Muslim Association (NZMA), to the development of which they would henceforth devote all their energies. For the community it meant that their self-identification was no longer as Indians, but as Muslims.

This bonding as Muslims was put to the test in 1951 (a year later) when a group of central European refugees from communism landed in Wellington. Among them were fifty Muslims from the then Yugoslavia and Albania. The majority of these made their way to Auckland, and were welcomed by the Indian Muslims who had founded the NZMA. (It was not until the 1960s that their wives and children were allowed to join them after international negotiations).

In 1956 an enlarged NZMA, now a genuinely multi-ethnic body, comprising Gujaratis, Albanians, Kosovars and Bosnians, held its first Muslim Congress. They elected an executive committee to plan and built a mosque, and by 1957 had raised enough money to buy a small house to serve as a centre for prayers, and for the education of children.

The ideal of building a mosque was not quickly realized. The community grew gradually. It was not until 1978 that a mosque plan designed by a New Zealand convert to Islam, the project having gained support from Saudi Arabia, was submitted to the City Council in the suburb of Ponsonby. The dome was in place in July 1980, and in 1982, the main prayer hall was complete. From concept in 1956 to fulfilment in 1982, a period of 26 years, is a remarkable achievement considering how few was the number of Muslims to support it. Even in 1976, there were only 644 Muslims in Auckland, and during the 80s, the congregation for the Friday Prayer ranged between 50-200. The mosque maintained its multi-ethnic character, English being the common language uniting Bosnian, Albanian and Gujarati members of the community, Fijian Indians, and a number of Pakeha converts. The first Imam had been a Gujarati. His successor in 1986 was a Ugandan, who is 1989 was succeeded by a Syrian.

Muslim communities were not limited to Auckland, although

Auckland has almost half of the total population of New Zealand's Muslims. There are a number of other communities in the North Island, in Hamilton, Palmerston North, and Wellington. In the South island there are communities in Christchurch and in Dunedin. They reflect the same dynamics as led to the development of the Auckland community, and in particular the mosque at Ponsonby. Alongside the NZMA there are a number of other Muslim associations, concerned with education and social issues. All make efforts to interact appeal with the wider New Zealand community, to create an interest in Islam and even to win converts. Converts in fact make up 5 percent of the total New Zealand Muslim population according to Shafiq Khan, Secretary General of The Federation of Islamic Associations of New Zealand.[14]

There is at the same time a willingness to association with other religions, and a Council of Christians and Muslims was formed in Auckland in 1998. It meets four times a year, on one occasion holding a joint meeting with the Council of Christians and Jews. In Wellington there are at least two inter-faith groups which discuss theological topics, one sponsored by the Anglican, church, the other a joint venture between the Iranian Embassy and the Council of Churches.[15] The Muslim community has made a significant contribution to the New Zealand economy, by opening the door to the export of *halal* meat carcases to the Middle East from 1975.

In the 1990s there was a striking growth in numbers leading to a community of 10,000, partly in the wake of the coup in Fiji in 1987, and the break up of Yugoslavia in 1992, and war and famine in the Horn of Africa and Iraq.

The New Zealand government accepted many refugees, and refugees from Bosnian concentration camps, victims of ethnic cleansing, were shown on New Zealand Television, praying in this Ponsonby Mosque.

The same dynamic may be observed as was at work in Australia. The active elements bringing the Muslims together are

---

[14] In a personal letter dated 1 March 2000.
[15] I am indebted to Mr Shafiq Khan, Secretary General of the Federation of Islamic Associations of New Zealand (Inc), and Mr Abdullah Drury, Communications Officer of the Federation for making available to me the material on which this section is based, including an as yet unpublished paper by Dr William Shepard.

the discipline of the ritual prayer, the sharing of the fast, and the festival following it, the celebration of the festival of the sacrifice, and the emotional impact of both, combining to inspire a determination to build a community, and for that community to build schools to teach religion to the coming generation, and mosques as a place of worship by which Muslims could be identified as a community of faith.

The total Muslim population in New Zealand now numbers perhaps 20,000, and this may have contributed to the success of a multi-ethnic Muslim community as the norm for New Zealand, as opposed to the ethnic based mosque communities in Australia. Muslims have faced much the same problems of social and religious acceptance as in Australia and there have been instances of protests against the building of mosques, and on one occasion, in Hamilton, a mosque was burnt down.

Everything is on a smaller scale than in Australia, and this lends the processes involved rather less accessible to investigation than those across the Tasman. This does not suggest that they are of less interest, or less significant as examples of the ways in which faith communities get to know, accept and even support each other. But in the context of this talk, it is unfortunately not practical to discuss the New Zealand component of Australasia in more detail.

Movement in Australian attitudes to Islam

Reference has already been made to the latent resentment of Islam among many Australians and the reasons for it. The general attitude to religious diversity however is changing. This is not only in relation to Islam, it is part of a broader current in Australian society. Up until the 1960s, Australian Christians were divided by sectarian rivalries. Catholics would rarely go into a Protestant church, let alone 'take part in the services or prayers of a false religion', as the prevalent mode of discourse then expressed it. In the 1950s, Archbishop Mannix of Melbourne did not feel able to enter an Anglican Cathedral for the funeral service of an Anglican archbishop, a personal friend, but waited outside in his car, to join the funeral cortege after the service.

By the end of the 60s however, the ecumenical movement was bearing its first fruits, and Christian relations with Judaism too were showing positive aspects. All this, though commendable, was still within the Judaeo-Christian family, but at least the first steps towards inter-religious tolerance had been taken.

But from the beginning of the 70s with new emigration protocols, there was a marked forward movement in the number of unrelated faith communities that were establishing themselves in Australia, and becoming a positive, productive and identifiable part of the mosaic of Australian society and institutional life in Australia. However, just as Catholics, Protestants and Jews in Australia were learning to make peace with one another, they were faced with a new challenge: How to come to terms with the truth claims of other faith communities that had developed outside their largely European tradition. An old problem had been presented in a new form. There was another hard road that willy nilly had to be followed.

The process of adjustment has been and continues to be painful and complex. It can be followed at different levels and from various perspectives. At an intellectual level, there are Australian scholars contributing to an exploration of the spiritual and intellectual traditions of Islam. Much work has been done in the phenomenological appreciation of Islam. Australian scholars such as the Jesuit, Paul Jackson, in his English translation of *The Hundred Letters of Sharafuddin Maneri* (1980),[16] have contributed in their way to a wider awareness of the richness and diversity of Islamic spirituality.

In some ways, this is the easy part. Somehow 'Sufism' has been regarded as exempted from the less attractive connotations of Islam in western discourse, and can be appreciated at a cultural level, one at which for some, Islam is even an optional extra. The Sufi movement, and its treasury of religious literature can be studied and appreciated in its own right, without necessarily raising the problem of religious diversity. A more difficult challenge is to recognise the values embodied in every-day living among Muslims,

---

[16] Paul Jackson S.J., *Sharafuddin Maneri-The Hundred Letters, Translation, Introduction and Notes,* Classics of Western Spirituality, Paulist Press, New York, Ramsey, Toronto, 1980.

those are not spiritual virtuosos or write great works of religious literature. Nevertheless, a study of the high culture of 'Sufism'—and this term is a European coinage—has its value, for it may at least serve as a preparation for a positive appreciation of Islam as it is lived in daily life.

At the theoretical, intellectual level, significant effort has gone into facing the problem of religious diversity. The results are interesting, even if in many respects, Australian Christian scholars have had to take as a starting point some of the theoretical work pioneered in Europe and America. For some at least, there has been a move beyond the exclusivism of Karl Barth and Hendrik Kraemer. They have learnt from the writings of Karl Rahner and Raimundo Pannikar and responded to the insights of Thomas Merton, and Bede Griffiths, and tried to take them further.

Our concern here, naturally, is with the work of thinkers with a personal commitment to one or another of the mainstream traditions of Christianity, who, as matter of conscience, are driven to seek an intellectual and theological explanation for religious diversity without down grading the faith community of which they are full practising members, and to which they have a personal commitment. Thus I avoid reference to scholars such as John Hick and others like him who adopt a theoretical, privileged position outside any specific faith community, and elaborate a general structure of religious 'truth' that can provide a space for every religious tradition, but which no one believes in.

The *Australian Religions Studies Review* (the organ of the Australian Association for the Study of Religions, AASR) recently devoted a recent issue to the topic with the title 'Managing Religious Diversity: From Threat to Promise'.[17] It includes four major papers on Religions diversity in Social Theory and Philosophy. The motivation is twofold: to find a theological meaning for this diversity, and to have an intellectual basis for compassion. The paper by Max Charlesworth, 'Religion and Religions', sets out a draft Credo for the religious believer in the light of the plurality of religions:

---

[17] In 'Religion and Religions', *Australian Religion Studies Review*, Volume 12 No. 2, Spring 1999, Special Edition, 'Managing Religious Diversity: From Threat to Promise', Gary D Bouma (ed.), p. 44.,

1.   I believe that 'God' wills that all should be saved or achieve enlightenment and that all human beings have access to the means of salvation or enlightenment through some mode of revelation.

2.   I believe (as a Christian, or a Jew, or a Muslim, or a Hindu or Buddhist etc.) that my religious tradition has a privileged and paradigmatic status, and that 'God' has revealed himself most completely—even if not exclusively—in that tradition.

3.   I believe that certain authentic religious values which are implicit or latent within my tradition, but which have not actually been developed within that tradition, may be manifested or expressed in other religious traditions.

4.   I believe that there is also the possibility of authentic religious revelations, complementary to the paradigmatic revelation of my tradition but 'outside' my own tradition and, in a sense incommensurable with it.

5.   I believe that religious diversity is in some sense willed by 'God' and has its own intrinsic meaning and purpose, and is not merely the result of sin and ignorance.

6.   I believe that respect for, openness to, and dialogue with, other religions traditions, must be part of any authentic religious tradition.

Efforts are also made by church leaders at a pastoral level, sometimes at the cost of pain, misunderstanding and rejection. The newly elected Anglican Primate of Australia, Archbishop Peter Carnley of Perth, in attempting to broader the horizon of religious tolerance, spoke positively of other religious traditions and their salvific value, and the limited cultural context of early Christianity. He pointed out that St Paul, in addressing the Greeks, knew nothing of the Buddhist tradition in the Indian sub-continent, and remarked that Muhammad, who was to present a radical new synthesis of Judaism and Christianity, was yet to be born. His efforts led to some members of his Anglican community being absent from his enthronement, although others welcomed his initiative, one correspondent from Australia to *The Tablet* suggesting appropriate newspaper headlines to announce his ideas, 'New Primate brings fresh hope to Australian Anglicans', and 'Refreshing wind of change blows for Anglican Church'.[18]

In worship many Christian congregations, are learning to recognise Muslims as representing the third strand of the monotheistic Abrahamic community just as they have learnt to recognize the continuity of the divine covenant with Judaism as the religion of a people of God. Thus from time to time, Muslims are specifically mentioned as among the people of God in the so-called bidding prayers of a Sunday liturgy, as communities on whom God's blessing is specifically invoked.

The local broadcasting of religious events from overseas has its contribution to make to religious pluralism in Australia. For example when the ABC News 5 December 1999 broadcast a report of Yasser Arafat inaugurating Christmas celebrations in Bethlehem at Manger Square, it added the detail that when the Muslim call to prayer occurred during the singing of Christmas carols, the Christian Patriarch remarked, 'Two modes of praising the same God'.

More recently, there was a complimentary reference to the Muslim faith of Mrs Samira Pratt, wife of the Australian Aid worker imprisoned by Milosovec, sustaining her during the period of separation from him, while he was in jail.

There have been a number of educational enterprises and conferences to bring Muslims and Christians together to hear and share the theology and spiritual dimensions of Islam presented by Muslim and Christian scholars. A pioneering example is the conference on Islam and Christianity held at Mannix College, Monash University in 1979, addressed by scholars from Egypt and Saudi Arabia as well as local Muslim and Christian academics.

St Mark's Institute of Theology in Canberra offers from time to time an intensive course on Islam and Islamic beliefs, not by way of setting up straw-men to be knocked down, but approaching Muslims as fellow pilgrims on a common journey. The students are taken to the mosque, to meet the Imam, to

---

[18] *The Tablet*, 3 June 2000, p. 754.

listen to the call to prayer. In all these encounters, the learning is reciprocal. Such approaches go far beyond the 'us' and 'them' attitudes of earlier years, when a lecturer could introduce his material with words such as 'Now another heresy is ...,' 'now another false religion is ...'

There has been an important change in the teaching of religion at the high school level. Religious studies has become an academic discipline, taking a neutral position on the truth claims of various traditions, but attempting to understand them from within, and develop a positive response to the values they enshrine.[19] A report in *The Australian* observes that enrolments in religion courses are 60 times higher than in 1990.[20] While no figures are given to provide an order of magnitude, the growth is impressive, and the position seems to be religious education out, religious studies in. It takes students directly into the religious pluralism around them. The result can be seen in the regular visits of groups of school students to mosques. The effectiveness of such courses may further be judged by the pastoral care some schools exercise to ensure that Muslim students know what foods to avoid in the tuck-shop, and to provide facilities to pray for those who wish to perform the *zuhr* prayer. Such schools regularly ask advice from visiting lecturers for information helpful in meeting their responsibilities to Muslim students.

There are now a number of organisations which are dedicated to the goal of mutual religious understanding, and thereby giving Muslims a sense of belonging in Australia. Among them is the *World Conference on Religion and Peace* (WCRP) which has a pioneering role in stimulating support groups for new migrants. It has arranged a number of conferences and issued various booklets laying the groundwork for inter-religious understanding and mutual respect in practical matters, for example assisting the settlement of people, and examining the adequacy of government provision for new comers. The titles of their publications are indication enough of their goals. They include such titles as *With Other Faiths—A*

---

[19] A recent such text book is David Parnham (ed.), *Exploring Religion*, OUP, Melbourne, 2nd Edition, 2000.
[20] *The Australian*, Friday 7 January 2000, p. 3.

Guide to Living with Other Religions, Religious Pluralism in a Liberal Society, Faith to Faith—Belief in a Pluralist Society and *Guidelines on Dialogue with People of Living Faiths.*[21]

The first booklet gives an account of two local initiatives, one of them having to do with community relations in the city of Springvale, near Melbourne. A gathering of Faith Leaders organized a number of meetings, one for a day of Prayer, and another to coincide with the annual mayoral induction. These initiatives led to regular monthly meetings. The other was a series of discussion programs hosted at the Preston mosque in Melbourne. One, led by a Muslim and a Christian, was on the theme Religious Understandings of Human Dignity. The mosque leadership and local clergy and members of their congregations together made a commitment to support these meetings. The Imam at the Preston mosque, Shaikh Fahmi is one of the best known and widely respected Islamic leaders in Australia.[22]

There are other examples of such cooperation, of reciprocal activities. In New South Wales and Victoria there are biennial meetings of the heads of faith communities discussing local issues. In NSW there is a working group looking to redress racism and racial vilification, and in Victoria working on a common approach to euthanasia. Interfaith groups on behalf of Unicef are working on issues relating to children in the Pacific and Southeast Asia. About three years ago, the WCRP invited Professor Chandra Muzaffar to Australia to address meetings on 'Religious and Human Dignity: Rights and Responsibilities'.

These organizations have made joint appeals for an end to sectarian bloodshed in Indonesia. At a rally in Martin Place, community and religious leaders and the Indonesian Consul General appealed to Muslims and Christians to work together for peace, and prayed together on the occasion of the anniversary of the outbreak of violence in the eastern Indonesian province of Maluku.

The Australian Federation of Islamic Councils and the National Council of Churches in Australia (NCCA) joined in a similar

---

[21] See *With other Faiths: A Guide to Living with Other Religions*, John Baldock, World conference on Religion and Peace, 'Religion in Australia Series—Number 4, Melbourne, 1995.

[22] Baldock, *With other Faiths*, pp. 25-26, and 34-35.

appeal, the first time the two organizations had joined forces to issue a public statement, organising a rally to appeal for peace in Ambon.[23] On 19 January, in response to Muslim attack on churches and Christian homes in Lombok, purportedly in revenge for Muslims killed in Ambon, Christian and Muslims leaders in Sydney jointly appealed for peace, each declaring that neither religion justified the use of violence.

Yet another perspective is provided by the re-creation of Muslim literary motifs into the imaginative world of Australian writers, some of the themes and motifs of Islamic spiritual and Sufi literature. A recent example is Anne Fairbairn's *An Australian Conference of the Birds.*[24] She takes a motif from Farid al-Din 'Attar's (d. 1220) classic Sufi poem in Persian, 'The Conference of the Birds', and transcreates it into an Australian poem, with Australian birds as the dramatis personae. The spinifex Pigeon responds to the call of Solomon's Hoopoe (*Hudhud*) bird from distant Nishapur 'Through shadow drifting veils of time and distance', and assembles the birds of Australia under her leadership. She tells them of the spiritual journey they are called on to undertake together in faith, beating their wings as one,

> flying in our hearts towards the Light
> seeking for our darkest sins and sorrows
> with quiet resolution
>
> from the scorching and sullen swamps
> of this vast forbidding land; from the seas,
> rivers, relentless skies and steely trees.

'Attar's account of the Hoopoe bird has shown them the way they are to follow, and in a relay they take to his tomb as a gift 'a wisp of softest lamb's wool' carried by a crested hawk, across

> our starlit heart of dust
> over scrub and bony Eucalypts;
> Then by a Sea Eagle who flew north

---

[23] *The Catholic Weekly*, Sunday 30 January 2000. p. 2.
[24] Anne Fairbairn, *An Australian Conference of the Birds*, Black Pepper, Melbourne, 1995.

high over the rhythm of rolling oceans
winging his way through storm-inked monsoon clouds
split by fire, winds and hurricanes to Hormuz.

And then by the golden eagle who takes it to Nishapur to 'Attar's tomb—a gift of softest wool to the great Sufi poet, whose words inspired them, as a token of love and respect from Australia to one of the great spiritual masters of humankind.

At a more basic level another aspect of a growing familiarization with Islamic peoples is the growing popularity of Lebanese, Arab and Turkish restaurants. This is an index of a broader acceptance of pluralism. A marked extension of the days when to go Chinese for a meal was an event. Going Chinese broadened to include Vietnamese, Indonesian and Malaysian, Thai and Indian. Going Middle Eastern—at least Turkish and Lebanese, goes deeper into Islamic cuisine, and marks a further step in pluralism, if not globalisation.

It is a reminder that there is such a thing as Muslim humanism, that welcomes the celebration of joyful occasions with feasting, singing and music. I am reminded by a remark from a colleague in Malaysia of what he calls McDialogue. The multinational phenomenon of MacDonalds in which everything served is *halal*, provides a place for every race and every religious tradition in Malaysia to meet on human terms, in an environment in which all feel comfortable—and modern!

Responses among Muslims

The first concern of Muslims in Australia was community survival, and considerable effort has gone into establishing the institutions crucial to this. But the effort has not been limited to institutions for their own sake. It has been accompanied by a wide range of personal and pastoral responses to life in Australia, reflecting a realisation that institutions alone are not enough, and that it is necessary to think and go further.

Among them is adherence to a conservative understanding of the obligations of faithfulness to the Islamic tradition. It is exemplified by the views of Mr Mohamed Suwayti, by birth a

Palestinian from near Hebron, Imam of the Canberra mosque. In an interview on 14 May 2000, he made the following observations on his community.

The mosque is to serve Muslims in Canberra, whom he reckons as numbering about 3000. Because of a large transitory component, he is not able to generalise about the ethnic mix. Among his concerns for the moral health of the community is the changing temperament of the new generation. They are less patient and in more of a hurry than their elders. In consequence, they are more likely to divorce.

He has a special care for the teaching of children. Numbers are too great for the physical resources available, and he can accept no more than one hundred. Small groups are organised by ability not by age, in effect the *halaqa* method. He has a strong sense responsibility for the children's welfare, and personally ensures that they are re-united with their parents before leaving the mosque grounds.

The atmosphere within the courtyard as the class dispersed shortly after my arrival was filled with personal warmth and community feeling among the adults.

Dietary rules are a major problem facing Muslims wishing to integrate into Australian social life, but he regards any compromise as unacceptable. His view is that Muslims are forbidden to go to places or to take part in functions where alcohol is served, even if they themselves do not partake of alcohol. Thus he would not attend even an Embassy function if alcohol were served there. He regards it as inappropriate that Muslims should enter a church building, even as guests at a wedding, or mourners at a funeral.

His association with leaders of other faith communities is limited to giving information about Islam when requested. He is always ready to welcome groups coming to the mosque to learn about Islam. Occasionally parties of students come to the mosque as part of the syllabus for courses in Religious Studies. He does not see this necessarily as motivated by more than a need to meet curricular requirements.

It is necessary in Canberra for Muslims to accept support from the social services provided by local government social services, since the Muslim community is small. He feels however, that in the larger metropolitan centres such as Sydney or Melbourne, Muslim communities could or perhaps even should be self-sufficient. He is always ready to visit local hospitals to speak about Islam, and the care of Muslim patients.

There have been a number of converts to Islam, but this varies from year to year, and no pattern is discernible. In the previous year there had been two Euro-Australian married couples who spontaneously decided to embrace Islam. From time to time there was a Euro-Australian male who wished to marry a Muslim woman, and was prepared to study, and accept Islam with sincerity as a pre-condition for marriage. He stressed that the marriage of a male non-Muslim to a female Muslim could never be accepted.

To sum up, his views represent an exclusivist understanding of Islam, dominated by a concern that the community needs support and protection in a markedly secular environment.

As a postscript it may be noted that not every Muslim ethnic group attends the Canberra mosque. The Indonesian community, for example has its own religious programme: for Friday prayers, for *tarawih* devotions during the Fasting Month and for the public prayers on the occasion of the two festivals. There is an Indonesian community Religious Study Circle which meets monthly for a meal followed by the night prayer and a lecture, sometimes with guest speakers coming from Indonesia. There are several possible reasons for this independence: language and culture, the Indonesian community having a critical mass sufficient to sustain its own programmes of religious devotions; disagreement with the understanding of Islam presented by the Imam or possibly a difference of *madhhab*, Indonesians being Shafi'i, not Hanafi; or simply that the mosque, built in 1960 is not large enough for every ethnic community now in Canberra, particularly on festival days, and that for one group to opt out is a welcome relief of pressure on limited resources.

*   *   *

A differently nuanced attitude was presented by Mr Mehmet Osalp, the director for non-Turkish and non-Muslim relations at the NSW Turkish Islamic Centre associated with the Gallipoli Mosque at Auburn, in a telephone conversation on 5 June 2000.

The mosque serves a large and vigorous Muslim

community. The congregation at the Friday Juma' prayer is around 2000. The number performing the five daily prayers at the mosque is 300, with perhaps 60-100 at each *salat*. The Centre is outward looking, and aims to play a community role on equal terms with other strategic groupings in society.

There has been a generational change in the Turkish community that it serves. The first generation, the migrants who arrived in 1968 and those immediately following was inward-looking, due to culture-shock in the new environment and problems with English. The new generation, which he, aged 31 represents, is concerned to look outwards and share in the non-Turkish and non-Islamic life around them.

The Cultural Centre and the Mosque welcomes visitors. He hopes the mosque will be recognized as an integral part of the wider community in which it is set. He recognizes the symbolic value of the Gallipoli name. Auburn is a neighbouring suburb of Homebush, the site of the Olympics, and he hopes the mosque will attract interest as a local feature. He is considering open days to bring the general community to the mosque and to meet Muslims, and is planning a newsletter. It already welcomes visitors, and readily provides information for school students who come to visit it as part of their courses in religious studies. One may note that this interest is another example of positive results from the new programmes of religious studies in the school system referred to earlier.

He regards inter-religious contacts as important for all communities, and regularly visits and talks with the clergy of Christian denominations.

He speaks warmly of, and takes as a role model a Turkish pioneer in inter-faith dialogue, Fethullah Gulen, a prominent religious leader who has met the Orthodox Patriarch Bartholomeus, who has had an audience with the Pope, and is one of the first in Turkey to take inter-faith dialogue seriously. Fethullah is an inspiration to him to take part in inter-religious dialogue in Auburn.

*   *   *

Not all Muslim activities are centred round a mosque. The Canberra

Islamic Centre mentioned earlier has an imaginative, creative approach to the indigenisation of Islam in Australia. It is determined to learn from the difficulties faced by other Muslim organizations in Australia, and to function within the framework and institutions of Australia as a civil society.

Mr Asmi Wood, a Torres Strait Islander convert to Islam, spoke of it in an interview on 20 January 2000.

The membership is currently around 1,000, of whom about 50 are associated with various sub-committees. He hopes that membership will have risen to 2,000 by the year 2001. The 1996 Census of Population and Housing gave the Muslim population of Canberra as 2,000. He suggests 3,500 may be a more accurate figure. One reason for the disparity is cultural. Many Muslims are from countries with a natural fear of giving more information on government forms than is legally required. Since an answer to the question on the form relating to religion is optional, the space is left blank, due to concern that the information may be somehow used against them.

The centre he sees as having a number of functions. One is to provide an environment in which all ethnicities can feel comfortable. To ensure this, the constitution has excluded the possibility of any ethnic group dominating the executive committee, by limiting the number of ethnic representatives to two of any one group. He acknowledges the strength of ethnic feeling in some groups, and mentioned that some of Sunni Lebanese insisted on marriage within their own ethnicity. The centre does its best to ensure that overseas conflicts are not brought into the new country, and provides counselling for Serbs in mixed marriages.

It takes care to avoid disagreements over matters of detail. It gives parity of esteem to variations in ritual observance between the various traditions of Islam. There are, for example, minor variants in the breaking of the Fast. The Shi'a breaking it a little later than the Sunnis, and the Hanafis set the *imsak* later than the Shafi'is. Issues such as whether women should 'cover', are left to the conscience of the individual.

It works with refugees from as far afield as Iraq, Eritraea and Indonesia. It provides them with moral support, and makes accessible to them information about the legal avenues accessible to them. It does not however coach individuals in the preparation of their cases.

It is concerned with the problems of youth in the community. These are of the same kind as afflicts the broader community: drugs, underage drinking, pre-marital sex and unplanned pregnancies. It sees such problems not so much as an expression of revolt, but as misguided attempts by young people to discover themselves in a new and unstable environment, and gain a sense of identity in a new country.

It has established good relations with the police. If an underage drinker is caught intoxicated in a nightclub, the police turn a blind eye to the legal aspects of the matter, and contact the centre. The centre sends a representative to take the delinquent home. Asmi went to pick up one offender, who said to him tipsily, '*Salam alaikum*. I want another beer.' He replied, 'You've had too many beers already, how about a coffee? Let's go home!' He replied, 'How can I go home, my father will kill me?'

The centre co-operates with the police in the control of demonstrations by Muslim groups, helping to choreographing the event, discreetly limiting the area in which events are to take place, providing flags to be burnt, but also having fire-extinguishers ready in case of emergency.

The path it follows has not always been easy, and it has worked its way through disagreements, some of them serious. One concerned the participation of the Australian Capital Territory electoral office in administering the centre's elections. Some members objected on the grounds that this was tantamount to non-Muslims taking part in Muslim affairs. The matter came to a court case. A few members resigned from the centre in protest, but a clear majority accepted that the issue was a procedural, not a religious matter. The decision is significant because it indicates the centre's acceptance of the instrumentalities of a civil society in running its affairs.

Another issue arose when some of members objected to the election of women to the executive council. Those objecting were outvoted, and again a few resigned in protest.

There was disagreement over a project to collect cassettes and disks of the music of the many Islamic cultures represented in the centre. After debate, the project went ahead.

At one time, language was an issue. Some members wished to give Arabic a central position. This was rejected on practical grounds, given the linguistic diversity of the membership. The centre now recognises five languages, English, Turkish, French, Urdu and Arabic.

In these and other matters, it has shown considerable skill in accommodating differences of view between members.

It circulates a well-structured and informative monthly newsletter via the internet, which keeps members in touch with its activities, and the progress of the new building. It includes interesting, and often courageous articles, in the April issue reprinting an essay by an English convert to Islam, complaining about the suspicion with which he was often treated when attending a mosque, and the petty matters of detail on which he was questioned to assess whether or not he was a sincere Muslim, leading him to expostulate: Islam, Yes! Muslims, No![25]

It has an interest in world events. It is deeply moved by political and religious strife, especially the tragedy in Ambon. On 19 January 2000, there was a joint meeting of Muslims and Christians organised by Christian and Muslim leaders in Melbourne, which went unreported in the national press. The centre chairman, Mr Sultan Bhimani went to Melbourne to attend it.

Its concerns extend to secular activities. When the Pakistan cricket test team visited Canberra, it invited them to a community centre it had hired, and gave all members of the Muslim community an opportunity to meet them.[26]

The centre has now made itself a respected institution on the Canberra scene, and as it grows, its membership of diverse backgrounds is evolving culturally in two ways: one, by the gradual but continuing acculturation of its members in an Australian environment, and by new blood brought into the organization by converts. While no figures are given, these converts are largely Anglo-Celts, Chinese and East Europeans. Aboriginals are very few. Of interest, is that eight out of ten converts are women.

A new development planned on the site is a private school, to be known as the ANZAC School, financed by Turkish

---

[25] *CIC Newsletter*, April 2000.
[26] *CIC Newletter*, 11/12 January 2000.

businessmen to be built next to the centre complex. It is to be a secular school, but with an Islamic ethos, and special facilities for Muslim students. All in all, everything to do with the Centre points to an integration of Muslims of various ethnic backgrounds as functioning, recognized, recognizable and respected components with a place in Australian society.

*   *   *

There is further a distinctive feminine element playing a creative role in the development of Muslim communities in Australia. This feminine dimension of Muslim living and women's reflections on their religion is often overlooked. In most western societies, including Australia, knowledge of this area goes no further than concern with two issues, female circumcision and the wearing of the veil. A moving account of a feminine, female perception of Islam is given by Leila Ahmed, Professor of Women's Studies in Religion at the Harvard Divinity School in a recent book.[27] Some extracts under the inspired title 'The Heard Word: Passing on the message of Islam, woman to woman,' are published in the Harvard Divinity Bulletin.[28]

For her, women have their own understanding of Islam, one different from man's Islam, 'official' Islam. Of her childhood she writes,

> 'Although in those days it was only grandmother who performed all the regular formal prayers for the women of the house, religion was an essential part of how they made sense of and understood their own lives. It was through religion that one pondered the things that happened, and what one should make of them, how one should take them.
>
> 'Islam, as I got it from them, was gentle, generous, pacifist, inclusive, and somewhat mystical— just as they themselves were.'

---

[27] *A Border Passage: From Cairo to America—A Woman's Journey*, Farrar, Straus and Giroux, 1999.
[28] Volume 28 1999, No. 2/3, pp. 13/14.

Since women were not obliged to attend the Friday congregational prayer, they were largely insulated from the influence of a male orthodoxy, with its aggressive, dominating emphases. Thus she understood Islam, as it was passed to her aurally from her foremothers, and the fruit of her listening to the Qur'an over a lifetime is her memories of its most recurring themes, ideas, words and permeating spirit, reappearing now in this passage, now in that: mercy justice, peace compassion humanity, fairness, kindness, truthfulness, charity, mercy, justice. (Though she concedes that some women, such as Zeinab al-Ghazali, have been contaminated by the macho-Islam of their males relatives!)

The attitude, the tone, and authenticity of the emphases in her understanding of Islam will strike a chord to anyone who has lived in Muslim societies (and women do not have a monopoly of it). It is expressed in many of the numerous Muslim women's groups and organizations across Australia. These organisations are linked by the Muslim Women's National Network of Australia INC. referred to earlier. Its aims include the following:

- To bring together Muslim women of different age groups, different ethnic backgrounds and different education in order to break down any false barriers of age, ethnicity and education.
- To work for the strengthening of the family.
- To form bridges and dialogue with non-Muslim Australians for the positive understanding of Islam and Muslims in general.
- To offer a support system for new Muslim women without a family, women in distress, the aged and orphans.

It is not afraid to be self-critical:

- To campaign for a more positive attitude towards community needs rather than the existing complacent attitude in the Muslim community.
- To be actively involved in setting an Islamic example of unity and integrity in guiding, advising, planning,

> criticising and if need be correcting Islamic practices, activities and attitudes in our community.

It produces a regular newsletter. The fact that it is in English, has an Australia wide distribution, and serves organizations of different ethnicities, underlines its character as aiming to establish an Australian Muslim identity.

Its tone is irenic, it is educational, it presents an international dimension to women's concerns and women's issues, as well as news of activities and issues in various regions of Australia. Unpretentious in format and clearly written, it is directed to the general reader. It does not claim to be high culture. Its articles are not ones that would be listed on the conventional university c.v. They are something that in the context of human relations is rather more important: issues of everyday living, and the problems and uncertainties that Muslim women and their families face in a non-Muslim environment.

It is open to the wider community of which it sees itself part. Thus it gave full front page treatment to an inter-faith gathering of Islamic, Buddhist Hindu, Indigenous, Baha'i and Jewish faith communities, hosted by Cardinal Clancy, to discuss and explore hopes for the new millennium in Australia. It quoted part of the address of the Chairman of the Bishop's Committee for the great Jubilee, speaking of Australia's unique position to further inter-faith relations, offering a way of establishing peaceful working relationships.

It reported the responses of each of these different religious groups to the bishop's speech, quoting a representative of the Islamic Council of New South Wales, who expressed the hope that such dialogue would continue, 'It is promoting an essential message of the Qur'an: We are all from a single origin, and as the Qur'an states, the diversity that we have is a sign of the greatness of the creator, and that this diversity is there so that we can get to know one another.' An illustration shows a group of Catholic, Muslim and Jewish representatives at a coffee table, with members of the Network.[29] The article is testimony to a warmth, sincerity, generosity, and openness to other religious communities.

---

[29] *MWNNA Newsletter*, November 1999, p. 1.

This openness is also shown in a readiness to draw on examples of Christian piety to serve as a model to Muslims reported in an earlier issue in which under the headline 'Teaching Children to Pray', is a quotation from Mother Theresa: 'Prayer is needed for children. Whatever religion we are, we must pray together'. It is followed by the advice remark, the Christians have a saying, 'The family that prays together stays together.'[30]

It includes reports on visits overseas, and includes an opinion that it is only a matter of time before women are allowed to drive in Saudi Arabia, it is safer to allow a woman to drive than to put her in the care of a male chauffeur.[31]

It gives an extended report of a seminar on Islamic finance and banking at UTS, opened by the Minister for Immigration and Multicultural Affairs, at which a number of papers set out the principles of Islamic business ethics.[32]

It handles special concerns of women. In one issue it takes up the complaint of a number of women that they had not been allowed to enter the Auburn, now the Gallipoli Mosque for the celebration of the 'Id on the grounds 'it was not customary' for Turkish women to go to the mosque. As an organisation it wrote to the mosque officials, seeking an assurance that women not be excluded from the building in the future.[33]

It gives self-protection hints to women to protect themselves from assault, what words to use (I couldn't repeat them here) and what to do with feet, hands, and anything available as a weapon, including a toothbrush to repel an attempted assault.[34]

It advises on ritual issues. It reported on one occasion women had been forbidden to hold meetings in a mosque in case some of them might be menstruating. It argues that menstruating women may enter a mosque, and may touch and recite the Qur'an.[35]

It includes an agony column for girls in which advice is given by an 'Aunt Fatima'. Some of the problems it receives reflect

---

[30] *MWNNA Newsletter*, March 1998, p. 10.

[31] *MWNNA Newsletter*, March 2000, pp. 4-5.

[32] *MWNNA Newsletter*, March 2000, pp. 6-7.

[33] *MWNNA Newsletter*, March 1998, p. 2.

[34] *MWNNA Newsletter*, March 1998, p. 7.

[35] *MWNNA Newsletter*, March 1998, p. 11.

inter-generational conflict between first generation migrant parents, and their daughters growing up in Australia, who attempt to establish friendships with Australian girls. It is a common problem. One problem addressed is that of a Muslim adolescent girl refused by her parents' permission to go to non-Muslim girls' homes to celebrate birthdays or to take part in end of year parties.

The worries of parents from a rural background for their daughters entering the alien world of non-Muslims possibly closed to the mother due to a lack of English, and associating with non-Muslims can be readily understood. There are concerns for the integrity of faith, culture, morality, and there may even be a fear of racism on the Australian side. The advice in the reply is irenic. Invite the girl who invited you to visit you with her mother at your home and meet your mother. It concludes with a word to Muslim parents in general, 'Many non-Muslim Australians have similar ethics, moral values and close family ties [like ourselves]—make the effort—find out.'[36]

It tells, non-judgementally, of an unhappy love story in Malaysia when a Malay woman wished to marry a Christian, forbidden by Malaysian law, and the couple fled to Thailand.[37]

The problems caused by the possibility of such marriages is inevitably a real one in Australia as it must be in Britain. From one perspective it strikes at the heart of the structure of the Muslim family as traditionally understood. I have not seen this issue raised in the Network Newsletter. However it is referred to in Hanifa Deen's *Caravanserai* referred to earlier. In one chapter she gives an account of a conference of Australian Muslim Women held in Sydney. At one of the sessions, a delegate spoke of women marrying outside the faith. She said, 'I know I shouldn't be saying this, but if it was me, I couldn't stand by and watch my daughter mentally and emotionally disintegrate in front of me, or worse still, take her own life. 'If it came to that', she had quietly uttered to a hushed audience, 'I would be forced, reluctantly, to accept her marrying a non-Muslim rather than lose her for ever.' She paused, while ripples mostly of

---

[36] *MWNNA Newsletter*, March 1998, p. 6.
[37] *MWNNA Newsletter*, March 1998, p. 4.

shock, a few of understanding—passed through the hall. 'Five years ago, I would not have said this; five years ago, I would have insisted that she not do this, but I've seen what happens.'[38]

*   *   *

At yet another level, there is the intellectual challenge of re-examining the Islamic tradition in order to separate out what is intrinsic to the revelation, and what has been conditioned by the changing circumstances and cultural experience of Muslims over the centuries. It is, in a phrase, a search for essential values. The task is difficult and painful as many issues are involved, some relating to formulations of Islamic jurisprudence, so time honoured, that individuals may cling to them as though they were part of the faith. Yet they go beyond this. They concern the very acceptance of a civil society, relations between men and women, the acceptance of a woman's right to marriage that goes beyond even the Hanafi position, legal adoption, interest on investments, speculating on the stock exchange, employment in industries that have to do with products and goods traditionally regarded as prohibited to Muslims, and in the widest sense, inter-faith relations. Can for example, conversions, whether from or to Islam, be regarded as simply an occupational risk, something that goes with the territory in a plural society, and in this matter, the primacy of conscience be accepted and respected, in whatever direction it leads. These are issues that challenge Muslim intellectuals in Australia, and the task, in Australia at least, is one that has begun.

In brief, it is a mistake to think of Muslims in Australasia as intellectually passive, erecting a fortress mentality behind which to shelter. There is a continuous movement in community understanding of Islam and modes of self-identification in Australasia, just as there are in Europe, where the mix is enriched by the writings of Western converts to Islam of high intellectual stature, such as Garaudy and Murad W Hofmann, telling of their experience of religion and Islam, as they follow in the footsteps of

---

[38] Deen,*Caravanserai*, p. 160.

Marmaduke Pickthall and Leopold Weiss, who belonged to an earlier generation.

They face the challenge of living in a plural changing world in which little is constant. Since there is no large and stable community supported by a state structure behind which to shelter, they are mercilessly exposed to a variety of confrontations: the need for a rethinking of the application of the rules of *fiqh*; the need to distinguish between what in their traditions is cultural heritage, and what is essential to the integrity of an honest commitment to Islam as a revealed religion. They need to be ready to endure the pain that confronting such issues involves.

The potential for meeting these challenges has always been present in both religions, before the gates of economic cultural and political differences between Christians and Muslims swung shut, more tightly in some places and at some times, than others. Now, they are being forced back open.

Conclusion

In a presentation of this kind it is not possible to be exhaustive, let alone to be sure how representative or valid any view or aspiration may be.

From one standpoint the theme of this presentation appears straightforward: how to rediscover compassion in inter-religious relations. But in fact there never is or has been a situation in which one can speak simply of Muslims and Christians. A Muslim is never simply a Muslim, just as a Christian is never simply a Christian. Neither religion exists in a pure state, without the impedimenta of culture and history. One needs always to ask: What Muslims, what Christians? When and Where? What is the self perception of each community, and its perception of the other, among other others. There are issues of ethnicity, of history, of cultural traditions, of cultural relationships, of environment. The possible combinations are almost without limit. It is not simply a case of one encountering the other in a plural society. There are relationships of power, class and gender. There are tendencies and emphases, and intrinsic qualities. There is alas a macho-Christianity, exemplified by the

Maronite warlords in Lebanon, alongside a kinder, feminine (but not feminist) perspective of Faith, just as there is a macho-Islam of the kind deplored by Leila Ahmed.

Two examples may show the distance travelled since 1960, each of which shows compassion in the sense that we seek it. One is in New Zealand.

A serious anti-Muslim incident took place in Hamilton in 1998. There had been opposition to the building of a mosque in 1997, and about six months after it was opened, it was burnt down in an arson attack. The event shocked public opinion. The whole community rallied round in support of the Muslim community. The City Council provided accommodation for prayers while the mosque was being rebuilt, and a number of church groups and the local Jewish congregation organised donations to enable them to build a protective fence, and install a security system. A manifestation of Compassion indeed. But it was no more than that displayed by the Muslim leader who commented that the event showed the Muslim community how many friends they had.[39]

The other is in Australia. It is the formal inauguration of the Gallipoli Mosque at Auburn on 28 November 1999. This is an event rich in symbolism for the progress of both the Turkish community and the establishment of Islam as a religion in and of Australia.

The antecedents go back to 1977, replicating the pattern that can been seen in many new Muslim communities, not only in Australia, when Turkish migrants established the Qur'an course of the Auburn Islamic Cultural Centre less than ten years after their first arrival.

The success of this Qur'an course in meeting social, educational and religious needs provided the inspiration for the Mosque. Construction began in 1986 (less than 20 years after the founding of the community) funded largely by contributions from the wider Muslim community in Australia, but also by funding from Turkey, Saudi Arabia, the United Arab Emirates and Malaysia.

Alongside the building of the mosque, the Qur'an course of the Auburn Islamic Cultural Centre which had inspired it

---

[39] William Shepard, unpublished paper. See fn 14.

developed into the NSW Auburn Turkish Cultural Centre. This serves the needs of the community in both in its heritage and ethnic aspects, and its religious needs. It organises giving lessons in Turkish to second and now third generation members of the community to maintain a link with their past, and develops their religious knowledge by providing lessons in Arabic. It serves the community in other ways: providing celebrants to conduct marriages and funerals, and offering help, guidance and counselling in family and social matters.

The name Gallipoli has a special resonance. It is a word that has had a key role in the development of an Australian national consciousness, and evokes the memory of the military encounter between Australians and Turks in 1915. Historically, it took place in the geo-political context of World War I. But it has wider resonances. At one level the conflict was political, between Britain, France and their allies and Germany. At another it was inter-racial, between Anglo-Celts and the Turkic peoples of Central Asia. But at yet another, though not often construed in these terms, on a personal level, it was between Australian soldiers who were by and large Christians, and Turkish soldiers, defending their homeland, who were by and large Muslims.

Despite the horror of the fighting, there was a mutual respect between Turks and Australians as soldiers. It was shown by both sides despite the barriers of language, during periods of cease fire; it was shown in the care both sides gave for each other's dead and wounded.[40] It was commemorated in the immortal and inspired words of Ataturk addressing the ANZAC war dead, 'Heroes, who shed their blood and lost their lives, you are now lying in the soil of a friendly country. Therefore, rest in peace. There is no difference between the Johnnies and the Mehmets to us where they lie side by side here in this country of ours ... having lost their lives on this land, they have become our sons as well'[41]—words that perhaps express the ultimate in compassion.

The inauguration of the mosque then is symbolic in that it

---

[40] Major General Peter R Phillips, National President, Returned and Services League of Australia 1999 in *ATAM Australian-Turkish Assembly Magazine*, Volume 1, Issue 1, p. 22.

[41] *Ibid.*

calls to mind this crucial engagement between Turks and Australians in 1915, with a symbolism clearly present in the ceremony itself— in the performance of the Turkish and Australian National Anthems, in the recitation of the Qur'an, and a rendering of the verses recited in English, and in the mix of guests and speakers representing senior members of the Turkish local and diplomatic communities, and of the State of New South Wales and the Australian Commonwealth government. Notable was the presence and speech of the State President of the NSW branch of the RSL giving a generous welcome to a non-Anglo-Celtic community in Australia, and the establishment of a public sign of the faith community of Islam declaring Australia its home. To anyone familiar with Australia in 1960, it shows how the RSL had evolved from a xenophobic right wing organisation, into a willing participant in a pluralist nation. But beyond this, alongside consecrating a fellowship between Turks and Australians born in the Dardanelles in 1915, the ceremony may be seen as symbolizing the burying of ancient hostilities between Muslims and Christians.

It is up to theologians to devise ways and means of justifying mutual respect between religious traditions whose core formulations draw lines that set them apart as mutually exclusive. Theologians need to write with extreme care, particularly those in an authoritarian tradition of Christianity, lest they be misunderstood, like the unfortunate Peter Carnley. Sometimes, with such care as has been said of Karl Rahner's particularly opaque German, that they cannot be understood at all.

But ordinary folk do not need theologians to enable them to recognise that in both religious traditions, the God they worship is not a god of the philosophers, but the God of Abraham Isaac and Jacob. Without compromising the differing understanding each tradition has of the person of Christ and the vocation of Muhammad, there are radiant theological principles shared, though hidden by cultural veils. Both believe in the forgiveness of sin, the resurrection of the dead, and life ever lasting. How many Christians are aware that the greatest opposition and scorn that Muhammad encountered from his fellow Meccans was provoked by the Qur'anic proclamation of a day of resurrection and Judgement, and its demands for social justice. Indeed the key values for social behaviour that are shared between both traditions derive their ultimate authority from beyond time. Once this is recognized, it is possible to move beyond tolerance—which if truth be told is a rather patronizing and unsatisfactory state of mind—beyond acceptance, to sharing.

Can there be any sharing that goes beyond the verses from Surat al-Rum, often recited at Muslim weddings, and sometimes read in a churches when there are Muslim guests, as a sign of beliefs and values that are shared:

In the name of God the Merciful the Compassionate

17   Glorify God then, when you come to the
     declining day, and when you reach its dawning

18   —to Him be praise in the heavens and on earth
     —when you come to its noontide, and at the
     approach of night

19   He brings the living from the dead,
     and the dead from the living,
     He brings the dry earth back to life
     after its death [in drought]
     just as you will be brought forth.

20   Among the signs [He can do this]
     is that He fashioned you from dust,
     then behold you were humankind
     dispersed [over the face of the earth].

21   Among His signs is that he fashioned from you
     the spouses with whom you dwell,
     and set between you tenderness and love.
     In this indeed are signs for a people who reflect.

22   Among His signs is the fashioning
     of the heavens and the earth,
     and the diversity in your languages
     and complexions

In this indeed are signs for those who
understand.

23   Among His signs is your rest at night
and during the noon-day heat,
and in your seeking of His bounty.
In this indeed are signs for a people who pay
heed

24   Among His signs is that He shows you the
lightening
it causes fear, it brings hope
He will send to you rain from the heavens
by it to revive the dry earth after its death [in
drought].
In this indeed are signs for a people who reflect.

25   Among His signs is that the heavens and the
earth
stand firm at His command.
So then, when He summons you from the earth,
behold, you will come forth.

26   To Him belongs everything in the heavens and
on earth,
all are subject to Him.

27   It is He who originates humankind
then will restore it [at the resurrection].
This is simple for Him.

28   Of Him is the loftiest that can be said
In the heavens and on earth
[—there is no god but He!—]
       He is the mighty, the wise.

God the Almighty speaks truly.

CHRISTIAN-MUSLIM RELATIONS IN BRITAIN:
BETWEEN THE LOCAL AND THE GLOBAL
Phillip Lewis

In Britain, Christian-Muslim relations cannot be isolated from a context of religious diversity, which encompasses both the oldest religious minority—the Jews—and Sikh and Hindu communities formed since the Second World War, part of that larger flow of migrants from former British colonies invited to fill labour shortages. As we will see, much of the institutionalisation of Christian-Muslim relations is part of this larger reality. Britain's religious minorities vary in size and socio-economic profile. Extrapolations from the 1991 census suggest that Hindus number 400,000, Muslims 1 million, 75 per cent of whom originate from South Asia, Sikhs 400,000 and Jews who number 300,000. Demographic projections indicate that by 2011 Hindu and Sikh communities will increase to half a million each while Muslims will probably double (this in a population numbering some 54 million).

These communities are overwhelmingly concentrated in urban areas, and most especially in London, the industrial cities of the Midlands, and the textile towns of Yorkshire and Lancashire. Each city has a different mix of communities; Wolverhampton has a majority of Sikhs, Leicester a majority of Hindus and Bradford a majority of Muslims. As with Hindus and Sikhs, the formation of significant Muslim communities in Britain is recent. Bradford, home to the third largest concentration of Muslims after London and Birmingham, exemplifies just how recent the formation of such communities has been. In 1961 the Muslim component of the population was 3,000, in 1991 50,000. This figure is projected to increase to 110,000 in 2011, one fifth of the residents in the Metropolitan District.

In Britain today, there is an array of Muslim communities, bearers of different nationalities, languages, regional identities and migration histories, embodying an equally diverse set of cultural practices. Arab elites in London—recently dubbed 'Beirut on Thames' by journalists—often have little in common with the large South Asian communities in East London (Tower Hamlets), Birmingham or Bradford, many of whom are one generation away from rural peasantry.

While the Hindus and Sikhs are outperforming the ethnic majority on most indicators, the Bangladeshi Muslims are languishing far behind all other communities, in part because they entered Britain last, at a time of rapid restructuring and recession in the national economy. As with wider society, Pakistani and Bangladeshi communities are increasingly polarised into those who are economically successful and those at the very base of the social pyramid whose lot has worsened. Political commentators worry that we are seeing the emergence of a British Pakistani underclass in many of our cities: recent riots (May 2001) in two northern cities—Oldham and Bradford—suggests that such fears are not entirely misplaced. Such anxieties are also shaping a changing agenda for Christian-Muslim relations.

Assets for accommodating British Muslims

To understand Christian-Muslim relations in Britain we also need to locate them within a wider political, institutional and historical context. Britain enjoys major assets in seeking to accommodate its Muslim communities: rights of citizenship; since 1976, legislative protection against racial discrimination; an established Church which allows 'religion' public space and which has facilitated a constructive dialogue across religious traditions; finally, Britain's historic and commercial links with the Muslim world.

It is worth expanding on each briefly. Because migrants from Pakistan and the Commonwealth enjoy rights of citizenship and local government still enjoys some, if diminished, influence, this means that wherever significant Muslim communities have settled this translates into elected councillors able to influence the local state. There are now over 160 Muslim councillors across the country.[1] In

[1] See K Purdam, 'The Political Identities of Muslim Local Councillors in Britain', *Local Government Studies*, 2000, vol. 26, pp. 47-64.

1997 the first Muslim Member of Parliament from these communities was returned. The government has also elevated three Muslims to the House of Lords, each of South Asian ancestry: a Pakistani, a Bengali (woman) and an Indian.

Legislative protection against racial discrimination has recently been strengthened as a result of the Macpherson Inquiry—published in February 1999—into the racist murder of the black teenager Stephen Lawrence. The recommendations of the inquiry, although focusing on the Metropolitan Police, were not confined to them and argued that 'collective failure is apparent in many [institutions and organisations], including the criminal justice system. It is incumbent upon every institution to examine their policies and practices to guard against disadvantaging any section of our communities' (para 46. 27). Such recommendations have now been given legislative form in the Race Relations (Amendment) Act 2000.

With the Runnymede Trust report—*Islamophobia, a challenge to us all* (1997)—the term 'Islamophobia' has now entered public discourse. This is part of a wider public acknowledgement of the importance of religion in identity, as evidenced in the recently published Parekh Report, *The Future of Multi-Ethnic Britain* (2000). It includes a chapter on 'religion and belief' where it notes that:

> The historic commitment of religious traditions to race equality are reflected in the work of ... the Churches Commission for Racial Justice (CCRI), the Islamic Human Rights Commission and the Jewish Council for Racial Equality ... However, most race equality organisations are broadly secular, not religious. It is perhaps for this reason that they frequently appear insensitive to forms of racism that target aspects of religious identity. For example, they are widely perceived by British Muslims to be insensitive to distinctive Muslim concerns, by Jewish people to be uninterested in antisemitism, and by Irish people to be indifferent to sectarianism and anti-Catholicism ... there is little recognition ... of the work and importance of black-majority churches (p. 237).

In Britain, civil society includes civic religion with government funded chaplaincies to parliament, the armed forces and wherever people are vulnerable, whether in prison or hospital. The use of Church of England personnel and buildings on the occasion of state rituals of celebration and mourning remains largely unquestioned. Public service broadcasting continues to include religion.

All state schools must teach religious education and taxpayers fund students to study non-denominational theology at university level, so the discipline is not confined to confessional colleges and must maintain a conversation with academic life in all its diversity. As part of the general culture, such study can act as a brake on irrational and intolerant expressions of Christianity. The state also funds religious schools which educate over 20 per cent of all pupils—the majority belong to Christian denominations but there are also Jewish and Sikh schools. The private sector—'public schools'—include many prestigious Christian foundations.

One peculiarity of English Christianity is that the existence of an Anglican establishment does not preclude public space for other Christian denominations. Ecumenism and a continuing public role for Christianity is a vital safeguard against nostalgia for unitary notions of Church and state, a Christian variant of 'religious nationalism' now sweeping the globe.[2] Their historic experience of coming to terms with plurality within Christianity has prepared the Churches for engagement with religious diversity. They contribute to developing a 'religious literacy' amongst policy makers. In Britain it is unlikely that a Home Secretary would say with his French opposite number that 'delinquency' among Muslim youth is 'more preferable in France' than 'fundamentalism/integrisme'.[3]

Because churches are themselves multi-ethnic in composition and part of transnational communities, they can act as an antidote to a 'Little Englander' sentiment which favours narrow and exclusive definitions of national identity. As public and civic life is permeated by Christian influence, it is proving increasingly hospitable to Muslim concerns. Civic religion now includes members of other faiths: the

---

[2] See M Juergensmeyer, *The New Cold War? Religious Nationalism Confronts the Secular State*, University of California Press, 1993.

[3] T Ramadan, *Muslims in France, the Way Towards Co-existence*, The Islamic Foundation, Leicester, 1999, p. 9.

annual ceremony at the Cenotaph to remember those who died in two world wars now incorporates representatives from all faiths.

All new religious education syllabi used in schools have to reflect religious diversity and can no longer simply teach about Christianity. Many university departments of theology include religious studies. Islamic studies can now be studied at postgraduate level at sixteen universities. A growing number of academics teaching such courses are themselves Muslim. Thus, Islam is being embedded in British academic life. Finally, in 1992 the Inner Cities Religious Council (ICRC) was established, a bold initiative on the part of the government and the Archbishop of Canterbury, intended to create a mechanism for consulting all religious traditions and involving them in economic and social regeneration in deprived urban areas.

Muslims and the politics of social inclusion

The historic and commercial links with the Muslim world, not least the presence of an Arab elite in London, can create a context within which the British state has to be seen to be treating its Muslim citizens fairly. Arab economic influence was clear in an address delivered by Iqbal Ahmed Khan of HSBC to a British Council conference held in London in April 1999—*Mutualities: Britain and Islam*. He pointed out that Britain had benefited enormously from the oil boom of the last twenty years: 'Petrol dollar surpluses [have found] safe havens in British funds ... some thirty six Arab banks operate in London alongside more than a hundred Muslim-owned financial institutions ... [most hold] their gold reserves in the Bank of England. Analysts believed that the real estate held by Muslim investors in London property in 1998 and the first quarter of 1999 amounted to well over twenty per cent of the market ... Britain is also host to several Arabic newspapers and four Arab television stations based in London' (conference report).

The present Labour government has committed itself to policies targeting the socially excluded, spearheaded by a social exclusion unit located in the Cabinet Office. The unit has published many reports—the latest 'Minority Ethnic Issues in Social Exclusion and Neighbourhood Renewal' (June 2000)—and its activities are evident in a raft of initiatives impacting on all communities, especially disaffected and disenfranchised youth between 18 and 24 years old, aimed to increase their skills and get them into work. Further, a range of policies and decisions have been taken to meet long term concerns specific to Muslim communities: in 1998, after a ten year struggle, they won the battle for state funded schools hitherto only enjoyed by Christians and Jews; in September 1999 the Prison Service appointed the first Muslim adviser and there are now a handful of Muslim hospital chaplains; a religious affiliation question is to be included in the 2001 census in England after strenuous lobbying by Muslims, who won the support of many Christians and Jews. The Home Office also commissioned research to determine the extent of religious discrimination, an issue which has exercised many Muslims since the publication of the Islamophobia report.

While some of these measures are more symbolic than substantive, cumulatively they signal that British Muslims do not have to render invisible their religious identity as a precondition to participate in public and civic life. Finally, the Prime Minister's active advocacy of military intervention to support the Kosovars has begun to challenge the widely held Muslim view that British foreign policy is necessarily anti-Muslim. Certainly, this was the view of Iqbal Sacranie, the previous General Secretary of the Muslim Council of Britain (MCB). In a recent conversation, he told me that, as a member of the ICRC 'it [had] pleasantly surprised all of us [whether Hindu, Jewish, Muslim, Sikh or Christian] how members of different communities can sit at one table, able to discuss key issues affecting society, whether inner city regeneration, homelessness, poverty ... We have different perspectives but at the end of the day we feel there is a consensus that emerges on many issues ... [Moreover] there is now an open door to government—Home Office and Foreign Office—and the Archbishop of Canterbury's office ...'

The dynamics of Christian-Muslim relations
1) a Christian perspective

The main motor for interest in Islam and Muslims within the mainline Churches was undoubtedly pastoral. A secondary consideration was mission. The Anglican Church's parish system which covers the entire country means that every parish priest takes the whole parish as his area of responsibility, even when parishioners include members of other faiths such as Muslims. Further, Anglican schools with their inclusive ethos, have also continued to serve the whole parish which includes a readiness to admit pupils from non-Christian backgrounds.

With the consolidation of religious minorities in Britain— especially from South Asia—priests with missionary experience and possessing the linguistic and cultural skills to relate to these new communities were actively sought by diocesan bishops to fill such livings. As the religious minorities grew so bishops began to appoint diocesan community relations chaplains/advisers on inter-faith issues to resource local congregations and the hierarchy. In Bradford the bishop appointed the first community relations chaplain in 1973, a priest who had worked in Bangladesh and so had the appropriate linguistic and cultural skills.

Parallel with such developments, the city created a Community Relations Council in 1966. The first chairman was the Anglican bishop, who persuaded a retired local policeman—well respected in all the local communities and an active churchman—to become its first community relations officer. Since their inception such organisations have changed in emphasis and membership. Initially, an organization concerned with the welfare needs of the black and South Asian settlers, they passed through a phase of emphasizing mutual understanding and the removal of friction points between communities, to becoming a vehicle for addressing racial equality. Christians have been active at all these phases, insisting that the religious component of minority community identity be acknowledged and their religious needs addressed.

The interplay between these two sets of initiatives is clear in the following example. The Community Relations Chaplain in Bradford established the first bi-lateral dialogue between Christians and Muslims in May 1973, the theme 'Islam in the Parish'. This led to an ongoing panel which met around the themes of 'The family in Islam and Christianity' in May 1974, and 'Worship and Prayer in Islam and Christianity' in May 1975—the proceedings of which were published by the CRC and the Community Relations Officer.[4]

---

[4] For this paragraph I have drawn on material from A Siddiqui, 'Issues in Co-existence

At the same time as some Christians were active within congregational and civic initiatives to relate to Muslims, so inter-faith groups emerged in large cities with newly formed minority communities. These were usually informal fellowships including individuals from all local religious traditions, who typically would meet monthly to get to know one another and to discuss issues of common concern. The oldest such groups were created in Leeds, Birmingham and Wolverhampton in the mid-1970s. They were subsequently organised into a national body in 1987—the Inter-Faith Network for the UK.

The Network now links some 70 organisations including local inter-faith groups, representatives from Britain's nine major faith communities, academic institutions and organisations concerned with multi-faith education. One of its co-chairs has usually been a London bishop. The network acts as a central information and contact point for statutory and voluntary bodies wanting information or advice on inter-faith affairs or local faith community contacts. It fosters local inter-faith groups and initiatives and provides a national forum for discussion of key issues. In 1993 it published an important consultative document entitled *Mission, Dialogue and Inter Religious Encounter*, which included a 'code of conduct' which offered a shared ethic of inter religious encounter.

One additional resource for Christian-Muslim relations merits particular mention. In 1976 Professor David Kerr set up the Centre for the Study of Islam and Christian-Muslim Relations (CSIC) in Selly Oak in Birmingham, now associated institutionally with the University of Birmingham. This was a genuinely collaborative venture involving Christians and Muslims at advisory level and as staff and students. It has served its joint constituency well with high quality publications, popular and scholarly.

The institutionalisation of Christian-Muslim relations at national level was late and still remains a part of the larger inter-faith concern. For a time the Anglican Church was happy to work exclusively within ecumenical structures and discuss issues raised, initially, by the World Council of Churches (WCC). The WCC set up a sub-unit on dialogue in 1971. The British Council of Churches (BCC) in concert

---

and Dialogue: Muslims and Christians in Britain', in J Waardenburg (ed), *Muslim-Christian Perceptions of Dialogue Today: experiences and expectations*, Peeters, Leuven, 2000.

with the Conference on Missionary Societies in Great Britain and Ireland (CBMS) set up an 'Advisory group on the presence of Islam' in the mid-1970s under the chairmanship of the Bishop of Guildford, Rt Revd David Brown. They produced their report, *A New Threshold: Guidelines for the Churches in their relations with Muslim Communities* in 1976, serendipitously the same year as the Festival of Islam in London had generated considerable interest in such a topic.

Unfortunately, this advisory group did not form the nucleus of a separate group within the BCC. Rather, the BCC set up a sub-committee, the Committee for Relations with People of Other Faiths (CRPOF) in 1978—renamed the Churches Commission on Inter-faith Relations (CCIFR) in 1992. To date the only bi-lateral group is the *Council of Christians and Jews* (CCJ). CCJ was founded in 1942 with the Archbishop of Canterbury and all leaders of the country's major denominations and the Chief Rabbi as joint presidents and was rooted in the desire to combat religious and racial intolerance and foster co-operation between Jews and Christians in study and service directed to post-war reconstruction. Of course, Christian-Jewish relations have a unique character rooted in a century of shared biblical scholarship and shared anguish to understand the roots of the holocaust.

A separate Anglican group—the Inter-Faith Consultative Group (IFCG)—was only established in 1980, when it became clear that a range of issues was emerging which directly touched the established Church. It produced a series of reports for debate and discussion within the General Synod which, with the exception of *Towards a Theology for Inter-faith Dialogue*, were responses to practical and pastoral issues: the disposal and use of church buildings by other faiths, the issue of mixed marriage and whether or not something construed as 'multi-faith worship' was acceptable. Issues of religious education, worship and curriculum for church schools seeking to accommodate pupils admitted from other faiths fell to the Board of Education and its specialist bodies.

Academic theology in general, and Anglican theologians in particular, have been slower to address the issues thrown up by the presence of a plurality of religious communities in Britain. Even where departments of theology have been pluralised to include the study of (non-Christian) religions, it is not uncommon to find specialists in each discipline pursuing their specific tasks with little regard to each other. Theologians seem more preoccupied with seeking to bridge the gap between New Testament studies and theology, and theology and 'secular' society than between theology and religious studies. This only began to change in the 1990s as *mainstream* academic theologians began to respond to the questions posed by other faiths. Illustrative of this development is the work of Keith Ward, Regius Professor of divinity at Oxford University. His excellent *Religion and Community* (2000) is his fourth work on major religious themes studied in comparative perspective.

Historically, it is the mission societies—particularly Church Mission Society [CMS] —which have not only provided personnel to resource the Church in its encounter with Muslims but have also generated innovative theological reflection on the relationship between Christianity and other faiths. Thus, Canon Max Warren (1904-1977) as general secretary of CMS pioneered the notion of Christian presence and commissioned a series of exemplary studies including Bishop Kenneth Cragg's *Sandals at the Mosque: Christian Presence amid Islam* (1959) which includes Warren's celebrated comment in its introduction:

> Our first task in approaching another people, another culture, another religion is to take off our shoes for the place we are approaching is holy. Else we may find ourselves treading on men's dreams ... to be 'present' with them.[5]

A new generation of CMS personnel continue to have a considerable influence on dialogical practice and principles. Bishop Michael Nazir-Ali, before taking up his appointment as Bishop of Rochester, was General Secretary of CMS. His background as a Pakistani bishop and his experience of the world church as general-secretary of CMS has given him a major role in Christian-Muslim relations. He was author of an important discussion document which went to all the Anglican bishops who met for the ten yearly Lambeth Conference in 1998, *Embassy, Hospitality and Dialogue, Christians and People of Other Faiths.*

---

[5] K A Cragg, *Sandals at the Mosque: Christian Presence and Islam*, London, 1959, p. 10.

2) a Muslim perspective [6]

For the newly formed Muslim communities in Britain meeting with Christians and reflection on Christianity has to compete with far more pressing demands. These range from developing appropriate institutions which can relate to the state, addressing Islamophobia, worrying about the emergence of a Muslim underclass in inner cities, developing an Islamic jurisprudence appropriate for minority status, networking groups of professionals within the legal and educational system, to organising Islamic aid to help Muslim groups across the world, suffering from oppression and natural disasters. In such a situation, the frank supersessionism written into the Islamic tradition vis-à-vis Christianity, leaves little need or energy for 'curiosity' about 'the otherness of the other'.[7]

Not only is there little curiosity about Christians—and for Muslims coming from majority Muslim countries often little experience of living with Christians—there is suspicion that dialogue is but a subtle ploy to convert them or subvert Islam. This needs to be located within the wider context that saw Christians launch in January 1991 a 'Decade of Evangelism'—while this was mainly addressed to nominal Christians, some careless remarks wrongly suggested that Muslims might be targeted. Such developments occurred in the wake of the 1988 an Education Reform Act which seemed to suggest a retreat from teaching a diversity of faiths in religious education in favour of privileging Christianity.

Such developments heightened a sense of insecurity generated by the furore that erupted around Muslims in Britain attendant on *The Satanic Verses* affair, which saw British Muslims burning the novel in Bradford on 14 January 1989. With the intervention of the Iranian spiritual leader a month later with his notorious *fatwa*, Muslims felt themselves a beleaguered minority. Throughout the 1990s international politics further deepened their sense of being under close scrutiny and set them apart from wider

---

[6] I have found two articles by Dr Ataullah Siddiqui particularly helpful in writing this section—'Issues in Co-existence …' and his 'Fifty years of Christian-Muslim Relations: exploring and engaging in a new relationship' in *Islamochristiana*, vol. 26, 2000, pp. 51-77.

[7] A Siddiqui, *Christian-Muslim Dialogue in the Twentieth Century*, Macmillan, London, 1997, p. 196.

society. The Gulf crisis, Bosnia, the ongoing Kashmiri tragedy, the Algerian Civil War, the Palestinian *Intifada*, the Chechen crisis could all feed the perception spread abroad by Muslim radical organisations that the West and the world of Islam where locked into a new round of the crusades, with Westerners either directly undermining Muslim governments or indirectly through support for oppressive regimes.

Within self-consciously Sunni Islamic institutions and organisations within Britain there were broadly four responses to Christianity and Christians.[8] For most Islamic *madaris* ('seminaries') in Britain, Christianity is simply invisible, part of non-Muslim society often painted in lurid colours as irredeemably corrupt. Institutions committed to *da'wa* (invitation to Islam) often draw on and develop a rich anti-Christian polemical tradition. Radical Muslim groups have developed a rejectionist stance of all things Western/Christian, for which the term 'occidentalism' has been coined.[9]

Finally, a disparate group of organisations is beginning to respond to and create forums for those Muslim professionals and academics—some active in inter-faith movements—who want to co-operate with Christians on a range of pressing social issues. Such pragmatic engagement is beginning to generate a more informed and Islamically serious encounter with Christianity in its particularity and 'otherness'.

This latter group are the most significant new voice amongst Muslims in Britain. Within this group there is a genuine concern that the American academic, Professor Samuel Huntington's much discussed and controversial thesis that the main threat to world peace comes from the clash between the Western and Islamic worlds—developed in his *The Clash of Civilizations and the Remaking of the World Order* (1996)— should be challenged. A new journal—*Encounters: Journal of Inter-Cultural Perspectives* (1995)—produced by The Islamic Foundation in Leicester is one of a number of important Muslim initiatives made in the 1990s

---

8 For reasons of space I have confined my remarks to the majority Sunni communities. Such Shi'ite organisations as the Al-Khoei Foundation in London produce an excellent journal devoted to dialogue. Further, a new initiative, entitled *Discourse* began publication in 2000.

9 I have drawn these observations from my contribution—'Depictions of "Christianity" within British Islamic institutions'—to Lloyd Ridgeon (ed), *Islamic Interpretations of Christianity*, Curzon, London, 2001.

to offer a self-consciously Islamic voice to the burgeoning concern for inter-faith and inter-civilizational dialogue.

British converts to Islam are also finding a voice. One example will have to suffice. Tim Winter is an example of an English convert to Islam who has studied both at Cambridge (Arabic) and at Al-Azhar and is active in translating key Islamic texts into English. He is thus in an ideal position to interpret mainstream Islam to a British audience. At present he lectures in Islamic Studies at Cambridge University. Winter's work is extensive and appears on the internet.[10] I want to draw attention to three of his recent articles, 'The Trinity: a Muslim Perspective', 'Islamic Spirituality, the Forgotten Revolution' and 'British and Muslim', the first was first delivered to a group of Christians and the third was presented at a conference of British converts.

Winter's lectures—not least that on the Trinity—are a model of courteous and religiously serious reflection by a Muslim thinker. His willingness to engage with Christians directly in discussion of their central beliefs represents a welcome development in British Islamic reflection on Christianity.

Peering into the future

One of the most promising initiatives in recent years in Christian-Muslim relations has been the development of the 'Faith and Society' process between Christians and Muslims. It started life in a conference in London in November 1997 entitled 'Faith and Power' where some 200 Christians and Muslims met to reflect on issues of law, education, media, local government and family. This was initially organised by evangelical Christians who realised that Muslims were understandably concerned with such issues. This is a new and welcome departure for many evangelical Churches which, historically, if they have thought of Muslims at all, did so in terms of debate and evangelism.

Since 1997 the 'Faith and Society' network has developed to include Christians and Muslims in its planning and attract Christians from outside the evangelical tradition: each year there is an annual

---

[10] On the internet he writes under the Muslim name Abdal Hakim Murad.

conference either at a Muslim or Christian centre, drawing on delegates from across the country. There are also some regional meetings to reflect on the five areas of concern identified and discussed in the original London conference. This dawning recognition of shared concerns in public life is timely and accords with the government's desire to work more closely with faith groups on inner city regeneration.

A second priority has been to address the question of appropriate religious formation for Christian and Muslim leaders for this new and bewildering context of religious plurality. Dialogue with other faith communities in parts of the world can often be a matter of life and death and has assumed an even greater urgency with the collapse of communism. The demise of a bi-polar world of superpower politics has seen a proliferation of religious and ethnic conflicts. In a lecture to Muslim scholars at Al-Azhar University in Cairo in October 1995 Dr George Carey, the Archbishop of Canterbury, remarked: 'It is extraordinary how ignorant we are of one another. Yet ignorance is the most terrible of cultural diseases for from it stem fear, misunderstanding and intolerance.' The archbishop went on to repeat a hope he had voiced in a lecture delivered earlier in the year in Madras: 'I long for the day when all those studying their own faith in depth will also be required to examine the life and teachings of two other faiths as well.'[11]

At the moment this remains an aspiration rather than a reality. But the fact that a leader of one of the mainstream Christian denominations in the country has articulated such a need, is itself encouraging. A well-informed Muslim commentator recently remarked that in Europe he was 'not aware of any *madrasa* which is in the business of training *ulama* … teaching even the basic concepts and ideas about Judaeo-Christian traditions, which are an important component of the West. Furthermore, there is an urgent need to introduce the intellectual and cultural trends of Western society into Muslim seminaries' syllabi.'[12] Clearly, if the proliferation of meetings and consultations on Christian-Muslim relations are to have any impact

---

[11] George Carey, 'The Challenges Facing Christian-Muslim Dialogue', *Islam & Christian-Muslim* Relations, 1996, 7: 1, p. 98.

[12] Siddiqui, 'Fifty years of Christian-Muslim relations …', p. 73.

on ordinary mosque and church-goers this issue will need to be addressed with some urgency.

The time is also right for the establishment of a bi-lateral council for Christian-Muslim relations. The Council for Christians and Jews (CCJ) emerged at a critical moment in Christian-Jewish relations. In Britain and in Europe we are at a similar critical moment with regard to Islam: Islamophobia is rife across Europe and sections of the Muslim communities are in danger of becoming the new underclass. The issue of equitable treatment of Muslim minorities in Europe and Christian minorities in parts of the Muslim world is perhaps the most pressing concern threatening to sour relations between Muslims and Christians.

Let me return, finally, to Tim Winter, whose remarks on the culture war between *sufi* and *salafi* Muslims worldwide at the conference in London in 1999—*Mutualities: Britain and Islam*—reminds us that relations of Muslims and Christians can never be divorced from wider geo-political and intra-Muslim tensions. In his address, Winter worried that Saudi oil wealth was systematically being used to drown out the voices of mainstream Islam with many Islamic publishing houses in Cairo and Beirut being subsidised by Wahhabi organisations. This, he claimed, prevented them from publishing traditional works on Sufism, and saw them remove passages in other works unacceptable to Wahhabist doctrine.

Such influence is not confined to Egypt and Lebanon. A recent study documenting the relationship between the West and the Arab elite noted Saudi Arabia's financial control of the extensive London Arabic-language newspapers and magazines. This includes some forty or fifty daily and weekly publications, more than the number of published in Cairo, Beirut or the whole of Saudi Arabia, and includes the television station MBC and the BBC's World Television Arabic Service. 'Because the Saudis want to use Beirut-in-Thames to monopolise Islamic teachings and advance their version of Islam, they have banned the independent Islamic magazine *Al 'Alam* and this publication also receives no advertising'.[13]

If British Muslims are allowed to develop their own agenda,

---

[13] See S K Aburish, *A Brutal Friendship, The West and the Arab Elite* , Indigo, London, 1998, p. 361.

without petrol dollars keeping a previous generation's polemic artificially alive, the foundations are being laid for an encounter between Christians and Muslims which has few parallels in Western history: a dialogue which moves beyond ill-informed and dismissive caricature—the lingering legacy of mutual incomprehension, conflict and colonialism—conducted by a Muslim minority not enjoying political power in a language other than Arabic. Because such a meeting would be conducted in English it could have a much wider impact, not least in Muslim majority areas.

THE COLLAPSE OF COMPASSION: THE AFRICAN EXPERIENCE
Matthew Hassan Kukah

Setting the scene

Compassion has a certain kind of resonance. In a world that has become so violent and Darwinian—where only the strong survive—nowhere does this find greater expression than in Africa. Yet, we must be careful because this subject and theme are very delicate. There are many institutions of human concern that have taken over the work of compassion to the point that the religious motive is far from being the primary concern. In many respects, we live today in a world that is prepared to go to any lengths to protect the so-called endangered animal species, from whales to the rarest baboon. Yet, we live in a world that has refused to contemplate embarking on more aggressive pursuits to end war, hunger and cruel diseases such as AIDS etc. We have refused to wage a war to preserve human kind, created in the image and likeness of God and have rather chosen to domesticate and worship other species of God's creation. It is obvious that the obsession with 'animal kind' rather than 'human kind' flies in the face of God's plans for the place of the human person in His creation. As a Christian, I am convinced that if our *compassion* is not anchored on the fact that the human person is created in the image and likeness of God and is the apex of creation, if it is not propelled by the teachings of the Sacred Scriptures, then we can easily lapse into secular humanism and deism. My concern in this paper is not to trace the theology of compassion. I am aware of the fact that our discourse has more to do with the present global situation more than anything else and that will be the focus of our attention now.

The fall of Communism in 1989 left the rest of the world in a certain sense rudderless. The certainty of the Cold War created an ideological divide in the image and likeness of the cowboy world where there are the Good Guys on the one hand and the Bad Guys on the other. Thanks to Western and American propaganda, there was almost no need to look further as to who the Baddies and Goodies were. From Churchill's famous 'Iron Curtain' speech through Kennedy's 'Let the Wall Come Down' speech to Ronald Reagan's characterisation of Soviet Union as the Evil Empire, the over forty years of the Cold War witnessed thinly veiled and aggressive propaganda. In the end, the Iron Curtain and the Wall came tumbling down and the evil empire was killed. Or at least so we thought. Thanks to the CNNisation of world, we watched from our sitting rooms as the walls came tumbling down and saw the prices of pieces of brick from the Berlin Wall floated from the floors of the London Stock Exchange to Wall Street. It might be suggested that I exaggerate—for that I apologise. However, no one who was around Europe could easily forget the excitement on the streets and everywhere else. With the death of the devil, the logic seemed rather straightforward, namely that Paradise would follow immediately. Things did not turn out that way.

In 1989, when the Wall fell, Francis Fukuyama, the American policy analyst with the Rand Corporation, fired the first shot by calling the momentous events the *End of History*. The politicians burst into celebration arguing that the end of history was to be sequentially followed by the birth of the *New World Order*. This New World Order was to be sustained by the ideals of Western liberal democracy and capitalism. It was taken for granted that the birth of this New World Order was to be midwifed by the United States of America which had baptised itself the only superpower and the world's new policeman. With the United States boasting superlatively about being the world's most powerful democracy, running the most powerful economy, presided over by the most powerful leader of the free world, it was evident that the United States had clearly assigned to itself the duty of supervising this world on behalf of God Almighty Himself. The rest of the world was now to aspire to become of one sheepfold, under one shepherd—America!

However, Mr Fukuyama's highly plausible thesis was soon challenged by the American professor, Samuel Huntington, who argued that contrary to what Fukuyama and other ideologues of liberal capitalism and democracy thought, the world was indeed going to face a *clash of civilisations* instead. Professor Huntington believed that Islam was capable of giving the New World Order a moral challenge while countries like India and China, due to sheer population and cultural complexity, would definitely challenge these assumptions in many respects.

In the 90s, a wind of democratic struggles swept through Africa as we can witness from the upsurge of the democratic impulse across the continent: 250 political associations in Zaire, 100 in Congo, 68 in Cameroon, 30 in Senegal and so on. Yet, all of these did not bring democracy any closer to the continent. The descendants of Harold Macmillan, the former British Prime Minister, must have felt proud that the old man's prophesy about the wind of 'change' (democracy) sweeping through Africa in the 60s, after thirty years of gestation, was now bearing fruit. There were so many possibilities across the world in the first two years after the fall of the wall. Nelson Mandela, the world's most famous prisoner, walked out of prison on 11 February 1991, thus marking the first major cracks in the walls of *apartheid*. The Solidarity Movement in Poland was already signalling to other political associations across the former Soviet Union that new democracies could emerge from the rubble of the old empire. Then all of a sudden, the world had a rude awakening: Saddam Hussein rolled his tanks into Kuwait, war broke out in the former Yugoslavia, forcing Europe and America to rethink their assumptions about the likely consequences of the end of history and the context and content of the New World Order.

In Africa, the winds of democracy suddenly turned into a tornado as Rwanda went ablaze. The genocide in Rwanda turned out to be Africa's rite of initiation into the New World Order and the beginning of its own history and preparation to welcome the new millennium. Against this background therefore, where does Africa stand in the faced of a globalised world? To address these issues, I wish to divide this paper into three sections and a conclusion. Section 1 will attempt to look at where Africa is coming from by looking very briefly at the social, moral and political consequences of independence for Africa. Section 2 will try to look at the consequences of moral failure and the manifestation of the collapse of compassion in Africa. Section 3 will attempt to address the issue of the challenges facing Islam, Christianity and traditional religion in shaping the moral future of Africa. By way of conclusion, Section 4 will try to make some projections as to the nature of the challenges facing Islam and Christianity in Africa.

1 Africa in the eyes of a globalised world

Although the popular mantra is that no one has any choices regarding globalisation and that indeed, poor nations have a lot to benefit from globalisation, African students and Africans must address their minds to very concrete realities and not allow themselves to be carried away by emotions and romantic assumptions about either the past or even the future. The 1980s were years of intense challenges as the rest of the world sought to rescue Africa from itself by seemingly fighting *apartheid*, disease, famine and war. At the close of that decade, the West publicly announced that it was showing symptoms of what came be known as donor fatigue. The 1990s witnessed a Western world swinging between the extremes of indecision, fatalism and cynicism regarding what to do with Africa. No where does this find expression more clearly than in the way the rest of the world handled the problem of Rwanda. Those who rule the United Nations refused to do anything until that country sank into chaos, destruction and almost national suicide. What no one seemed willing to tell Africans openly was that weariness and fatigue had set in as a result of the time, energy and resources that were now being channelled into the Balkans. Charges of racism have been levied by those who have been sincere in addressing the issues of the injustice of the New World Order and the persistence of the old devils of racism.

Despite Africa being called the white man's grave, the heart of darkness and the dark continent, Europe and America did not experience fatigue in the four hundred years of slavery. Despite the plausible work of the Abolitionist Movement, I am of the view that slavery ended because it had become expensive in an industrialised Europe. The next two hundred years of imperialism and colonialism became imperative as Africa provided the West with what was required to power its new industries. This was a period for the extraction of minerals and resources needed in a new Europe. When the needs of the West changed in postcolonial Africa from cotton, beniseed, groundnuts, tin, sisal etc, to oil, gold, and diamonds, the relations again were altered, but the mission remained the same. The system became less physically brutal, but the long-time psychological impact was to remain with us. A new post-colonial elite, lacking in patriotism or discipline, became content in serving as middlemen and commission agents to multi-national corporations across the continent. The role of oil and mining companies in Africa is well known. From the murder of Ken Saro Wiwa and his kinsmen to the barbarity which has been expressed recently in the Congo and Sierra Leone, we know that the road ahead for Africa in a so-called globalised world is filled with devastating land mines!

In a recent publication of *The Economist* (London), the very influential magazine came to the conclusion that Africa had become a hopeless continent. For the remaining month of May, the deluge of angry reactions from Africans across the world over the internet testified to the feeling of treachery and betrayal that Africans felt. There were those who believed that *The Economist* cover story was a racist, uncharitable, unfair and bare-knuckled attack from white conservatives. Many of my elite friends who can afford the prestigious magazine confessed that they had to cancel their subscriptions. But when I read the story, my feelings of sadness were soon transformed when it became clear to me that, indeed, *The Economist* had merely confirmed what many of us had been saying for a long time, namely, the black man was really on his own in a dangerous world. If for nothing else, *The Economist* ought to be commended for providing us this wake-up call. Bitter as the pill may be, it is our elites that have brought us to this collective grief. Given the percentage of African leaders who have argued over the last one hundred or more years that Africa's future lies in collaborating with the West in the areas of technology transfer and other forms of exchanges in the area of culture and so on, it is now clear that we need to rethink certain assumptions we have had. In the last fifty years, Africans have murdered their heroes for standing up against foreign and local oppression and pointing out the nature of the forces arrayed against us as a people. The tombstones of the Kimathis, Lumumbas, the Diallos, the Nkrumahs, the Odingas, etc., witness against us. I will conclude this section by asking whether indeed Africa has a role to play in a globalised world. If the answer is yes, and I believe it is, the question is, what should this new role be? Given the forces arrayed against Africa and the fact that the last seven hundred years have left us a sad hybrid of a race strung between European and African culture, should we not be spending more of our energy in self discovery? Although the New World Order is hinged on the rules of the market and democracy, should Africa democratise or develop? If so, what models of development?

Against the background of devastating state failure marked by grinding poverty, industrial stagnation and political decay, it seems to be that there are too many things that we need to reconceptualise in Africa. For example, African students and African politicians (elsewhere known as the post colonial elite) spent the first thirty or more years of our independence struggling to convince us that we really did not need democracy because of the conflictual contradictions inherent in the insistence on multipartyism. African leaders insisted that they were in the main projections of the African chief who could brook no opposition. The result is that politics in Africa has largely been a zero-sum game in which the winner takes all—the loser hardly lives to tell the story. What are the implications of this for Africa? To attempt an answer, let us look at the real consequences of these development on our people.

2 Moral failure and the collapse of compassion in Africa

The state of anomie that marked the expertise of Africa with colonialism was graphically manifested in the array of literature that came out of the continent in the wake of independence. Again, we need to address the issue of how Africans expressed the sense of moral failure and the collapse of their world. This has found its most eloquent testimony in the written word. But as it has become clear, reducing African literature to the written word does injustice and hence, orature has become a vital component of African literature. (As an aside, Professor Wole Soyinka's Nobel Prize is a testament of the stature of African literature in the world today!).

In this section, I will look at a few titles that marked how Africans tried to explain their experiences with colonialism. A random sample of a few titles tells the story: *Facing Mount Kenya, Zambia Shall be Free, Things Fall Apart, No Longer at Ease, The African Child, The River Between, No Past, No Present, No Future, Cry the Beloved Country, God's Bits of Wood, Petals of Blood, Poor Christ of Bomba, King Lazarus, Tell Freedom, Mine Boy, The Beautiful Ones are Not Yet Born, Not Yet Uhuru, Morning Yet on Creation Day*, etc.

The development of orature was a very controversial issue, but it has come to stay. Orature is the compendium of African proverbs, sayings, songs, dances etc that convey its experiences and encounter with life. Covering almost every aspect of life, proverbs have been described by the Nigerian novelist, Chinua Achebe, as the palm oil with which the African eats his yam. I will take just a few proverbs and mention one or two stories that demonstrate compassion in African life.

Life has become one of the first casualties in the wake of modernisation and globalisation and nowhere is the collapse of compassion better expressed than in how life is now treated in the world. Africa is caught in the middle, with its elite mimicking Western values and seeking to present them as evidence of modernisation. Since the West planted the idea by masking its murderous and exploitative missions to Africa as civilising missions to enlighten the barbarians in the dark continent, the word has stuck among many of our people that anywhere you go, West is best. Our people have now become, to coin an expression, *westoxicated*!

Today, the thinking is that children and child-bearing is being redefined. And here, I hasten to point out that I do not expect a handshake from feminists, but I speak as a Christian based on my experience with God and His plans for the world. Children and child-bearing have now become a nuisance of sorts. Take the sticker I saw on a car: *Motherhood is Slavery!* Sex is no longer a sacred institution. The children of the free love of the sixties are now in their forties and they are claiming the freedom of their parents. So, abortion is not killing, it is just removing a nuisance on the path to joy and happiness. A foetus is merely a tissue and not an issue! Women now say, it is my body and I do what I like with it! Take the famous sticker of the sixties, *Make Love not War*. The relationship between the sexes is changing very fast. With the rise of the Gay Movement, the recognition of their marriages, their rights to adopt other people's children, it is clear again that marriage as an institution and the family as a basis for the organisation of society and its continuation is heading for the rocks. In Africa's quest for authentic values, we need to be discerning and prudent when assessing the scheme of values offered by others to us.

Old age was treasured in Africa and the old were loved for their wisdom and knowledge. Today, they too have become a nuisance and the best place for them is in a home for the elderly. The old have to be kept away so that we can find time to get on what we now consider the most important things in life: a career and an easy life! I saw a poster somewhere and it said: *Take revenge on your children: Live long!* The emergence of euthanasia as a cure for pain and suffering for the elderly and the incurably sick, its spread and prevalence today, is another pointer to how life has become very much devalued.

Let us turn our attention to values. In African traditional life, values are expressed in children, marriage, dignity, integrity, a good name, harmony, etc. A few examples will do:

> If you see your neighbour's house on fire, put water on your roof.
> The cow that has no tail, it is God that keeps away the flies for it.
> We honour those who have children, not those who have money.
> We only count chickens and not children.
> A house with foolish men and women is better than one full of lizards.
> The okro tree never grows taller than the one who planted it.
> No artist can fashion a child.

Or take an example of this song sung by a rich man who had made a fruitless search for a child and then heard that a baby had been found on the roadside. He turned his sorrow into a song, which went something like this:

People come and see, people come and see
I looked everywhere for a child, but I found none,
I prayed to every god and goddess for a child, but got
      none,
People come and see, people come and see,
I was ready to pay any amount of money to have a
      child,
But no one knew the name of the market where
      children are sold,
No one knew the amount that a child is sold for,
People come and see, people come and see,
I heard yesterday that Yata the daughter of Akama
      threw away a baby,
I asked how can the world be like this, people are
      throwing away what others are looking for,
People come and see, people come and see,
People come and hear, people come and hear.

Are these problems the result of the failure of religion or can religion solve them in Africa? To answer this question, let us look at the role of religion in Africa.

3 A trinity of challenges

In seeking to find the role of religion and politics in Africa, certain theological realities have to be underscored. In Africa, the dominant religions remain African traditional religion, Christianity and Islam. They all relate with and impact on African politics in varying degrees. African traditional religion, because it is culturally time bound, has no role in politics beyond its immediate community location. Politics requires a certain level of universalism in its appeal, in order for it to resonate among peoples of various nationalities, races, beliefs or tongues. African traditional religion on the other hand is the religious expression of the hopes, fears, anxieties and entire gamut of the cultural lives of a given society. Non-members of a given community cannot be initiated into the religion of another ethnic group, no matter how much friendship or collaboration may exist among the peoples. As such, despite being the oldest religion of the peoples of Africa, African traditional religion has had very little impact in national politics beyond serving as arrows or shields for those who appeal to its powers as a means of securing political protection or warding off the threats of real or imagined opponents. As for Christianity, many commentators have tended to go back to the dilemma between Caesar and God as a means of explaining the relation between religion and politics. They have glibly taken this to mean that Jesus categorically separated religion from politics. On the contrary, the text actually has the opposite meaning! This is because further theological analysis and investigation reveal that since both the coin and Caesar belong to God, politics should be treated as a rendering of both Caesar and his coin as an offering to God in service. However, beyond the merger created in the times of Constantine, Christianity has tended to urge the separation of Church and State especially after the 16th-century Reformation and the 18th-century French Revolution. Islam on the other hand has argued that ideologically, both the state and religion should be intertwined and one should be used to reinforce the other. The result is that religion has always been employed as a tool for political mobilisation and a basis for governance. Now, given these seemingly diametrically opposed positions, and also given the complex cultural and ethnic mix that constitutes many states in Africa, what role should religion play in African states and politics? A survey of the place of religion in African political life will show that, in the hands of an illegitimate political elite, African leaders have used religion to cause sorrow, pain and death.

In Nigeria, the sources of tensions and frictions among believers in the two universal faiths have centred on a four factors: access to power, distribution of state resources, freedom of religion, access to justice. A few examples of the sources of these tensions will be enough to demonstrate the point being made. Although Nigerians have been collectively devastated by military rule, the fact is that all but one of our military leaders have been Muslims and Northerners, and that in our civilian life only one civilian leader has been non-Muslim. All these sentiments have exacerbated the tensions within the non-Muslim population in the country. The result is that the indiscretions and misrule of these men have been attributed to their Islamic and Northern origins by many Southern commentators. Thus, there are conspiracy theories relating the plans by Muslims to Islamise Nigeria, by the North to rule Nigeria forever etc. Muslims on the other hand argue that there is a plot by Christians to undermine Islam and that non-Muslims do not see any thing good in Islam. Unfortunately, the truth is that both Christians and Muslims are victims to the excesses of military rule on the polity and its persistence in manipulating and exacerbating religious bigotry. The devastating impact of military rule and the collapse of the state in Africa have led our continent through untold pain and hardship. Military rule criminalised an entire populace, severely wounded and fractured our collective basis of harmony and existence. Muslims and Christians or worshippers of traditional religion became tools in the hands of military dictators, who, hungry for legitimacy, played and turned religion, in whatever shape or form, into a vital tool in the game of its Russian roulette. The result is that rather than playing their redemptive roles, these religions have become caught in a game of intrigues by government and its agencies. Nowhere has this tragedy been more played out than in Nigeria where the challenge to both Christians and Muslims leaders is whether they can rescue their religions from the grip of the political class who only wish to use religion to extend their political mileage. For as long as the issues of injustice, oppression, hunger, poverty and squalor exist, no one can claim to be living the true teachings of any religion, revealed or concealed. To conclude, how do we cope with the challenges of globalisation today?

4 Summary and conclusion

What is the future for both Islam and Christianity in Africa?[1] The impact of both traditional religion and the two universal religions is

---

[1] See Fr Matthew Hassan Kukah, *Religion and Politics in Northern Nigeria*, PhD thesis, School of Oriental and African Studies, University of London, 1989, published as *Religion and Politics in Northern Nigeria*, Spectrum Books, Ibadan-Lagos, 1992; M H Kukah, 'An assessment of the intellectual response of the Nigerian Ulama to the *Shari'a* debate since Independence', *Islam et Sociétés au sud du Sahara*, vol. 7, Paris, 1993, pp. 35-55; M H Kukah and Taoyin Falola, *Religious Militancy and Self-Assertion: Islam and Politics in Nigeria*, Avebury, Aldershot, 1996.

all over Africa. Yet, despite their numerical advantage, they have not been able to make the desired impact because of the disharmony between both universal religions across the continent. To be sure, there are many countries in Africa that are quick to say that there are no problems between Christians and Muslims. It normally depends on whom one is speaking with. From Algeria, Egypt, Sudan, Nigeria or Kenya and South Africa, these problems manifest themselves differently. It is a matter of numbers and access to power. However, on a general note, for both Islam and Christianity to play their roles as agents of compassion in Africa, I propose a few ideas for further reflection.

i) *Work towards a just society for all*
So far, the tensions across the continent, especially in Nigeria, have tended to be cast rather narrowly as quarrels between Muslims and Christians. The result is that many people are now wondering whether peaceful coexistence is possible at all between the two groups. Yet, we know that both religions are functioning under severe economic, social and political chaos and that the chaos is a major contributor to tensions and the rise in ethnic and religious manipulation. Africans must see themselves more as citizens of their various continents and emphasise their national identities. They must realise that it is only good citizens that can really be good Muslims or Christians.

ii) *Dialogue*
To achieve these and a lot more, dialogue is an imperative. For this dialogue to take place, a certain amount of confidence building must take place. Communities must identify areas of common interest and work hard at attaining those ideals.

iii) *Dialogue of life*
Both Christians and Muslims must help the continent pull back from the brink to which it is headed, goaded by those who preach that we have more human beings than the world can feed. It is redistributive justice that is lacking in many places not population. We must keep our people on track so that they can continue to value human life as a gift from God which must be nourished and sustained. To do this, we must define and educate our people about

family planning without resorting to dubious propaganda that tends to devalue human life or see motherhood as a burden.

iv) *Poverty eradication*

It is clear that the tensions that have manifested themselves in our society are largely on the periphery of the urban areas. As long as our people remain poor, so long will they continue to be vulnerable to messengers of salvation. This is the lesson that we ought to learn from the Kanungu tragedy in Uganda, where hundreds of people were led to their deaths.

v) *Law enforcement and good governance*

It is evident that many of those who have succeeded in perpetrating violence belong to the tribe of those who tend to take advantage of poor policing. Regulating conduct and creating an environment conducive to the legitimate pursuit of business are important.

In his book, *The Lexus and the Olive Tree*, Thomas Friedman, the American journalist with *The New York Times*, used the *Lexus* and *Car* and the *Olive Tree* as idioms for defining the challenges of globalisation. He noted that:

> Any society that wants to thrive economically today must constantly be trying to build a better Lexus and driving it out into the world. But no one should have any illusions that merely participating in the global economy will make a country healthy. If participation comes at the price of a country's identity, individuals will feel their olive tree roots crushed, or washed out by this global system, those olive tree roots will rebel. They will rise up and strangle the process ... A country without healthy olive trees will never feel rooted or secure enough to open up fully to the world and reach out to it. But a country that is only olive trees, that has only roots, and has no Lexus, will never go, or grow very far. Keeping the two in balance is a constant struggle.

As I have repeatedly said, both Presidents Thabo Mbeki and Obasanjo seem to have realised the magnitude of Africa's new challenges. While tending to our olives at home, let us not forget to dream of a new world that is not based on the beauty or sophistication of the Lexus but one that subordinates the Lexus to the betterment of the human person. Mr Mbeki's *Africa's Renaissance* and Mr Obasanjo's programme of *National Rebirth* can offer platforms for the continent to launch a moral crusade to renew its identity and prepare itself for a new role in a globalised world. So far, we have wasted energy defending the olive trees, and one believes it is time for us to face the prospects of designing our own Lexus. We have the men, women and the resources and it all depends on whether for the first time in her life, African leaders can painfully and faithfully look at their people's hopes, fear, dreams and anxieties and use them as a mirror to sincerely map out a new agenda for the millennium. Africa can and must participate in a global world, but it must seek to do so by coming to terms with the concrete realities of its history and people. In this regard, given the important role that religion has played in our quest for a just society, we as believers need to seriously re-examine its role in our new democracy. So far, the crisis created around the *Shari'a* (Islamic law) discourse threatens to send out the wrong signals that religion has the capacity to undermine democracy. This would be tragic indeed. A globalised world must be a humanised world if we are to survive. The future does not lie in blind material quest. Perhaps the two greatest human beings on this side of the 20th century are Mahatma Gandhi and Mother Theresa. It is purely accidental that both are associated with India. It is more telling that between both of them, their attire cost less than ten dollars! We should work towards a globalised world that does not vandalise the environment, a new world order that does not engender disorder but rather encompasses a new more humane world inhabited not by men and women, white, yellow, brown or black, but by one race: *the human race*. After all, Africa was the first home of the human race!

MUSLIM-CHRISTIAN RELATIONS IN INDIA

Anthony O'Mahony

In the Republic of India the vast Hindu majority, along with Muslim, Sikh, Christian and other smaller minorities, are called to strive together for a better future within the democratic, secular framework of the constitution of January 1950.[1] Both Christians and Muslims find themselves in a unique position, as minorities both sharing the challenge of living their faith tradition within a context of another dominant religious culture. The Muslim-Christian encounter and their on-going relationship in India are an important and surprisingly rich element in the history of South Asia. The engagement between Muslims and Christian has unfolded itself in a multiplicity of *témoignage*—scriptural, spirituality and political, which has in its turn given unique and a particular pattern to the overall important encounter between these two global religions: Christianity and Islam.

---

[1] What is the traditional relation of religion to politics in India? Recent scholarly debate has generated at least two divergent answers. According to one view there is a long-standing traditional opposition between religion and politics in India because its highest value (*Moksa*) is renunciatory and asocial. According to another view a separation of religion from politics is contrary to Indian ways of thinking and the present currency of such a picture is the product of various colonialist strategies. Roy W Perrett, 'Religion and Politics in India: Some Philosophical Perspectives', *Religious Studies*, Vol. 33 (1997), pp. 1-14. Modern Indian intellectuals like T N Madan and Ashis Nady have claimed that the separation of religion and politics now reflected in modern India's constitutionally guaranteed secularism is a Western-derived model alien to the Indian tradition, a product of various colonialist strategies. T N Nadan, 'Secularism in its Place', *Journal of Asian Studies*, Vol. 46 (1988), pp. 747-760 and Ashis Nandy, *An Anti-Secular Manifesto, Gandhi's Significance for Today*, (eds) John Hick and Lamont Hempel, Macmillan, London, 1989. Finally, the work of the anthropologist McKim-Marriot is often invoked in support of the view that the separation of religion and politics, or power from purity, is contrary to Indian ways of thinking: McKim-Marriott (ed), *India Through Hindu Categories*, Sage, London, 1990. See also the studies in *Les Ruses du salut. Religion et politiques dans le monde indien*, (eds) M-L Reiniche and H Stern, EHESS, Paris, 1995; A Schimmel, *Islam in the Indian Subcontinent*, Brill, Leiden, 1980.

Islam in India[2]

The link between religion and politics is central to Islam because the idea of Islamic nationhood is part and parcel of any discourse on politics. Islam contains an ethical ideal as well as guidelines for a polity. Although it must be said that Islam was not an exclusive factor in nation-building during the emergence of the Muslim states in Asia it is clearly reflected in the respective constitutions of the different Islamic countries.[3] Islamic thought and tradition considers the whole Muslim world as being fundamentally one in its concept of *umma—*

---

[2] On the early history of Islam in India see the studies by Marc Gaborieau, 'L'islamisation de l'Inde et de l'Asie orientale', *Etats, sociétés et cultures de monde musulam médieval (Xe-XVe siécle)*, PUF, Paris, 1995, pp. 431-459; 'Les Oulemas soufis dans l'inde mongole: anthropologie historique de religieux musulmans', *Annales: économies, societés, civilisation*, no. 5 (1989).

[3] Although Pakistan was created in the euphoria of Islamic triumphalism, it did not neglect a concern for minorities. In the design of the flag, Islam was represented by a green field with a star and crescent; a white stripe covering one-quarter of the area represented the minorities. This was an accurate reflection of the reality of a minority population of nearly 25 percent almost all of whom were in East Pakistan. The secession of East Pakistan in 1971 changed the numerical strength of the minorities dramatically, reducing them from 24-30 percent of the population. If the flag of the same plan were designed today, the white panel would be reduced to a barely visible thin stripe. However, communal harmony was uppermost in the minds of the founders. It was indelibly inscribed in the new polity. For example in the heat of the struggle for independence, one of Pakistan's founding members, Quaid-i-Azam—Mohammed Ali Jinnah to the Constituent Assembly in 1947 declared that Pakistan was not going to be a theocratic state. For him, the new state would be a modern democratic state with sovereignty resting with the people. All members of the new nation would have equal rights of citizenship regardless of their religion, caste or creed. He wanted a Pakistan where Muslims and non-Muslims could live together, be equal citizens and where religion was to be the private affair of the individual and not a matter of administration by the state. Although bearing in mind the rhetorical context, he emphasized that 'in the course of time Hindus would cease to be Hindus and Muslims would cease to be Muslims, not in the religious sense, because that is the personal faith of each individual but in the political sense as citizens of the state'. Although, it must be said, these ideals did not last long. Soon after independence the political forces embraced Islam as the principal doctrine of formation and articulation for the nature of the state created in Pakistan. This shift found its first expression in the Objective Resolution (1947) which incorporated the concept of God's sovereignty and stated that no law be enacted against the Qur'an and the *Sunnah*. All successive Constitutions promised that no law repugnant to Islam would be enacted and that all laws would be brought into conformity with Islam. The Objective Resolution was subsequently incorporated as part of an appendix to the Constitution of 1985, through an amendment. This changed in 1956 when Pakistan was declared to be an

ideally to be constituted as one state. Islam does not take into consideration the separation of church and state. A common acceptance of the laws of Islam is the proper basis for organizing a polity. This means that, in its ideal form, an Islamic polity calls for a single Muslim state. Islamic laws deal with an individual on the basis of his being a Muslim. The territory or the state to which he belongs

---

Islamic state. The name 'Islamic' Republic of Pakistan was adopted in the first constitution, dropped in 1962, but restored again in the Constitution of 1973 and its amended versions of 1977 and 1985. The Islamic character of the state was supported by Pakistan's rulers since and strongly enforced particularly under rule of Zia ul-Haq, with the support of the *Jama'at-i-Islami* group. Since the declaration of Pakistan as an Islamic state in 1956 the religious character of the state has been re-emphasized several times. While the Constitution pledges to safeguard the legitimate rights and interests of minorities, it requires that the president of the republic be a Muslim' and calls upon the state to take steps 'to enable Muslims to live in accordance with the fundamental principles of Islam, including the compulsory teaching of the Holy Qur'an'. Islamization in Pakistan has created problems for those outside Islamic orthodoxy, and puts a great deal of pressure on the non-Muslim citizens, who see that everything is being reduced to an Islamic way. See the following studies which set out the development of Islamic thought in Pakistan and how it influenced the political realm: Sayyid V R Nasr: *Mawdudi and the Making of Islamic Revivalism*, Oxford University Press, 1996; *id.*, *The Vanguard of the Islamic Revoluton: The Jama'at-i Islami of Pakistan*, Oxford University Press, 1994, and M Gaborieau: 'Rôles politiques de l'Islam au Pakistan', Oliver Carré (ed), *L'Islam et l'État: dans le monde d'aujourd'hui*, Presses Universitaires de France, Paris, 1982, pp. 189-203 and M Gaborieau, 'Le néo-fondamentalisme au Pakistan: Maududi et la Jama'at-i Islami', O Carré: *Radicalismes islamiques, Vol. 2: Maroc, Pakistan, Inde, Yougoslavie, Mali*, Presses Universitaires de France, Paris, 1986, pp. 33-76.

The data on minorities are approximate. Non-Muslims are a small minority in Pakistan—between 2-3 percent (about 3 million) of the total population in 1995 estimated at 128 million. The same proportions of minority size existed in the 1960s, though the absolute figures are somewhat (perhaps 4 percent) lower. The Christian population is thought to be about 1.3 million, evenly divided between Catholics and Protestants. About one million are in the Punjab; the second largest concentration is in Sindh, mostly in the city of Karachi. Although some Christians are engaged in education, business and professions, many are employed in manual labour. For the Christian experience, see *Pakistan: A Young Church in a Young Muslim Country*. Pro Mundi Vita: Dossiers: Asia and Australasia dossier 18 (1981); Achilles de Souza, 'Dialogue in the Islamic Republic of Pakistan', *Islamochristiana* (Rome), Vol. 14 (1988), pp. 211-218; and Joseph Cardinal Cordeiro, 'The Christian Minority in an Islamic State: The Case of Pakistan', *The Vatican, Islam and the Middle East*, (ed) Kail C Ellis, Syracuse University Press, 1987, pp. 277-294. For Bangladesh: 'Muslim-Christian Dialogue in Bangladesh', *Islamochristiana*, Vol. 17 (1991), pp. 131-167. See also the debate between 'Hasim Hasan Shah: Law and Religion and Michael Nazir-Ali: Law and Religion: a friend responds to Dr. Nasim Hasan Shah', *Islam and Christian-Muslim Relations*, Vol. 11 (2000), pp. 243-251.

becomes an issue only when such a territory is or is not governed by Islamic law.[4]

Wilfred Cantwell Smith in his *Islam in Modern History*[5] characterized the situation of the Muslims in the Indian Republic as unprecedented. He put forward two observations: one that Muslims living in India inherited an indigenous 'thousand-year tradition of imposing dimensions' in all walks of life and that they share citizenship in the new, secularly constituted republic with an immense number of people, most of them inheritors of a cultural and religious system that in many ways is different from, if not diametrically opposed to, that of Islam.[6] Turning to the specifically religious question, Smith writes: 'Here as elsewhere the Muslims are confronted with the general task of reconciling their faith to modernity. In addition, here they have their special minority status ... The question of political power and social organization, so central to Islam, has in the past always been considered in yes-or-no terms. Muslims have either had political power or they have not. Never before have they shared it with others'. To live with others, 'to participate in constructing a life in common', presents an unprecedented challenge to them. 'It raises the deepest issues both of the meaning of man's being and of social morality. It raises the deepest issues of the significance of revelation, truth, and the relation to other people's faith.'[7]

Islam in India thus faces a dilemma of how to live as a religious minority, albeit, an important one, in an environment of

---

[4] For a general introduction to the relationship between Islam and Politics see the following studies: Patrick Bannerman, *Islam in Perspective: a guide to Islamic society, politics and law*, Routledge, London, for the Royal Institute of International Affairs 1988; Dale F Eickelman and James Piscatori: *Muslim Politics*, Princeton University Press, 1996; John L. Esposito: *Islam and Politics*, Syracuse University Press 1987.

[5] Wilfred Cantwell Smith, *Islam in Modern History*, Mentor Books, New York, 1959. First Edition, 1957.

[6] I owe this reference, and much of my thought here, to the Jesuit scholar, Christian W Troll, 'Sharing in the Pluralistic Nation-State of India: The Views of Some Contemporary Indian Muslim Leaders and Thinkers', *Christian-Muslim Encounters*, (eds) Yvonne Y Haddad and W Haddad, University of Florida Press, Miami 1995, pp. 245-262. This valuable paper has been reprinted several times: C W Troll, 'Islam and Pluralism in India', *Dossiers de la commission pour les rapports religieux avec les musulmans (CRRM) (1995-1999): Religion et politique: un thème pour le dialogue Islamo-chrétien*, Cité du Vatican, Rome, 1999, pp. 160-177; and 'Islam and Pluralism in India', *Encounters: documents for Muslim-Christian Understanding*, (Rome) no. 220 (1995), pp. 1-22.

[7] Smith, *Islam in Modern History*, pp. 287, 289.

shared political power.[8] One commentator on contemporary Islam and Islamic thought has compared the situation of Muslims in India and Europe:

> Hinduism and Islam in India are significant for Europe in comparative terms as an object of study with regard to their capability to coexist peacefully in a political culture defined by the modern secular nation-state. Unlike the Western nation-states the Indian State does not impose its secularity on religious minorities. It is true that the constitution of India in its article 44 rules the elaboration of a secular common civil code for all Indians, regardless of their religious affiliations. This code has never come into being. Political realities as well as articles 26, 27, and 28 of the Indian constitution grant minorities the right as communities to manage their own religious affairs. The result is the legal reality of Muslim Personal Law, as based on the *shar'ia*. To be sure, *shar'ia* has two meanings: traditionally, *shar'ia* is not a political issue insofar as it focuses on civil law affairs as marriage, inheritance, and other personal affairs. Muslim Personal Law in India is based on this understanding of the *shar'ia*. The other meaning of the *shar'ia* is the one developed by contemporary Muslim fundamentalists who interpret the *shar'ia* as a political-legal body essential for their concept of the Islamic state. Indian Muslims insist on their practice of the

---

[8] Classical Islamic thought has divided the world up into two spheres, *Dar al-Islam* (The House of Islam) and *Dar al-Harb* (The House of War). In the former Muslims govern Islamic society according to its practices and in the later unbelievers reign. The presence in India, the Americas, Asia and Europe—*Dar al-Harb*—of large numbers of Muslim intellectuals articulating dissent against the rulers of many Islamic states—*Dar al-Islam*—is creating tensions within contemporary Islamic thought of how to square the circle within classical parameters. See the following two papers which attempt to understand the dilemma in historical context and contemporary reality: Maurice Borrmans, 'Future Prospects for Muslim-Christian coexistence in non-Islamic countries in the light of past experience', *Journal of the Institute for Muslim Minority Affairs*, Vol. 10, no. 1 (1989), pp. 50-62 and Bernard Lewis, 'Legal and historical reflections on the position of Muslim populations under non-Muslim rule', *Muslims in Europe*, (eds) B Lewis and D Schnapper, Pinter, London, 1994, pp. 1-18.

shar'ia as civil law, but have no political claims related to a Muslim state. Relating the communitarian rights of Indian Muslims to the immigration issue in Europe evokes the question whether it is recommendable to grant non-Western minorities—evolving as a result of immigration to Western Europe—a status similar to the one given to Indian Muslims. Despite the fact that the latter are not immigrants, their identity revolves around the issue whether it is related to the polity of India or to the *Umma*, i.e. to the worldwide Islamic community. The answer to this question depends not only on how India's identity is being determined, but also on the image, which Indian Muslims have of themselves. Muslims living in European states are exposed to a similar challenge. Are Muslim immigrants willing to identify themselves as European citizens? If India is able to dissociate its polity from Hindu culture and then rigorously be shaped along the lines of political culture of the secular nation-state, why then cannot Muslims unequivocally feel like citizens of India? Could Indian Muslims practice the *shar'ia* and—in this line—link themselves to the universalism of the Islamic *Umma* and at the same time continue to be true citizens of India? The essential concept underlying this question is the idea of citizenship.[9]

An earlier reflection on the dilemma faced by Islam in India due to the continuing growth of British power was by the Muslim

---

[9] Bassam Tibi, Islam, 'Hinduism and the Limited Secularity in India. A Model for Muslim-European Relations in the Age of Migration?', *Muslims in the Margin: Political Responses to the Presence of Islam in Western Europe*, (eds) W A R Shadid and P S Van Koningsveld, Pharos, Kampen, 1996, pp. 130-144, p. 132-133. See also Anthony O'Mahony, 'Islam in Europe', *The Way: Contemporary Christian Spirituality*, Vol. 41, no. 2 (2001), pp. 122-135. Rafiq Zakaria: *The Struggle within Islam*, Penguin, London, 1989, gives another view of the ambiguous situation of Indian Muslims caught between the two conflicting forces of secularism and fundamentalism. He states that 'no other Muslim in any part of the world is faced with such a dilemma or finds himself so confused and helpless', p. 262. For some other approaches, see Roland E Miller, 'Modern Indian Muslim Responses', *Modern Indian Responses to Religious Pluralism*, (ed) H G Coward, State University of New York Press, Albany, 1987, pp. 235-269.

theologian in Delhi, Shah 'Abd al-'Aziz (d. 1824) who implied in a *fatwa* that *shar'ia* law did not prevail, but had been supplanted by 'Christian' law. This being the case, India was now *Dar al-Harb*— literally land of war, which meant that it was no longer incumbent for Muslims to observe certain injunctions of *shar'ia* law.[10] Muslims throughout the world have lived as minorities surrounded by neighbours of other religious and political traditions, but only Muslims in South Asia have succeeded in registering successfully the claim that members of a minority Muslim culture must have their own state to protect their culture. This must be regarded as a distinctively South Asian Muslim contribution to world Islam; so too must the openness of the theological, ethical, and jurisprudential debates occurring among the Muslims of the Republic of India on how best to obey God in their present situation.[11] A further echo of this is the observation by Roger Hardy, that perhaps it is the very protean character of Islam in South Asia that constitutes its distinctive South Asian character.[12] So perhaps is the sense of disappointment and

---

[10] Aziz Ahmad: *Islamic Modernism in India and Pakistan, 1857-1964*, Oxford University Press, 1967, p. 19. There has been much debate to whether or not this *fatwa* actually declared India to be *dar al-Harb*, see P Hardy: *The Muslims of British India*, Cambridge University Press, 1972.

[11] On Indian Muslim Religious-Political thought see: Sheila McDonough, *The Authority of the Past: A Study of Three Muslim Modernists*, Yale University Press, New Haven, 1970; Peter Hardy, *Partners in Freedom and True Muslims: The Political Thought of Some Muslim Scholars in British India, 1912-1947*, Scandinavian Institute of Asian Studies, Lund, 1971. See also the *mélange* of interesting studies on Islam in India by Christian W Troll: 'Islam and Reconciliation', *Encounter: Documents for Muslim-Christian Understanding*, no. 103 (1984), pp. 1-19; 'Social Justice in Islam', *Encounter: Documents for Muslim-Christian Understanding*, no. 89 (1982), pp. 1-15; 'Islam as a Missionary Religion: Some observations with Special Reference to South and South-East Asia' *Encounter, Documents for Muslim-Christian Understanding*, no. 130 (1986), pp. 1-47; 'Modern Trends in Indian Islamic Thought: The Recent Past', *Encounter: Documents for Muslim-Christian Understanding*, no. 137-138 (1987), pp. 1-26; 'The Qur'anic View of Other Religions', *Encounter: Documents for Muslim-Christian Understanding*, no. 140 (1987), pp. 1-16; 'Islam Lived and Perceived from within a Pluralistic World: The Case of Maulana Abul Kalam Azad', *Encounter: Documents for Muslim-Christian Understanding*, no. 147 (1988), pp. 1-15; 'Mission and Dialogue: The Example of Islam', *Encounter: Documents for Muslim-Christian Understanding*, no. 189-190 (1992), pp. 1-14; and C W Troll, 'Two conceptions of *Da'wa* in India' *Jama'at-i Islami* and *Tablighi Jama'at*, *Archives de science sociale des religions*, Vol. 87 (1994), pp. 115-133.

[12] If a patterned and lively confusion is characteristic of Hinduism, so too is it characteristic of Islam in South Asia: Marc Gaborieau, 'Les Ordres mystiques dans la sous-continent indienne', *Les ordres mystiques dans l'Islam: cheminements et situation* (eds) A Popovic and G

uneasy wariness among the Muslims of the region at having, after so many centuries, some witnessing great Muslim kingdoms and empires, still to live in close proximity with a majority of neighbours whose Hindu culture can be seriously assaulted but not seriously wounded.[13] However, these negative perceptions are at the same time quite contrary to some of the earliest Muslim views and attitudes concerning Hindus and Hinduism from the 8th century, when Muslims first arrived in India. For example, the attitude of Muhammad ibn al-Qasim, who conquered the region of Sind in northwest India around the year 712 AD, was remarkably calm and accepting of the existing socio-religious structure, allowing the population to maintain their affairs in the manner they deemed appropriate.[14]

The phrase, the 'Muslim World',[15] may be applied to an area that is under Islamic rule, an area that has a majority of Muslims, an area with a significant body of Muslims or to any combinations of

Veinstein, Editions de l'Ecole des Hautes Etudes en sceince sociales, Paris, 1986, pp. 105-134; 'Les sous-continent indien', *Les voies d'Allah. Les ordres mystiques dans l'Islam des origines à aujourd'hui*, (eds) A Popovic and G Vienstein, Fayard, Paris 1996, pp. 285-295; 'Le concept de Malamat en Inde: Hétropraxie et Hiérarchi'e, *Melamis-Bayramis: Études sur trois mouvment mystiques musulmans*, (eds) N Clayer, A Popovic and Th. Zarcone, ISIS, Istanbul 1998, pp. 37-49; 'Inde', *Le culte des saints dans le monde musulman*, (eds) H Chambert-Loir and Cl. Guillot, Presses de l'École Française d'Extrême-Orient, Paris, 1995; and 'Typologie des spécialistes religieux dans le sous-continent indien: Les limits de l'islamisation', *Archives de sciences sociales des religions*, Vol. 55 (1983), pp. 29-51 and Desiderio Pinto, 'Piri-muridi and Power, Faith, Power and Violence', *Muslims and Christians in a Plural Society, Past and Present*, (eds) John J Donohue and Christian W Troll, Pontificio Istituto Orientale, Rome, 1998, pp. 241-257; *Piri-muridi Relationship: A Study of the Nizamuddin Daragh*, Manohar, New Delhi, 1995; *The Mystery of the Nizamuddin Daragh: The Accounts of pilgrims, Muslim Shrines in India: Their Character, History and Significance*, (ed) C W Troll, Oxford University Press, Delhi, 1989, pp. 112-124.

[13] Peter Hardy, 'Islam in South Asia', *Encyclopaedia of Religion*, Vol. 7, pp. 390-404. The influence of Islam and Christianity on modern Hindu religious culture and Hindu-inspired movements has always been a controversial and tricky matter to narrate. J B P More, 'Christian-Muslim Influence in Pondicherry, South India', *Islam and Christian-Muslim Relations*, Vol. 6, no. 1 (1995), pp. 63-78, and equally the question of conversion: Yohannan Friedmann, '*Qissat Shakarwati Farmad*, A Tradition Concerning the introduction of Islam to Malabar', *Israel Oriental Studies*, Vol. 5 (1975), pp. 233-258; and P Hardy, 'Modern European and Muslim Explanations of Conversion to Islam in South Asia: A Preliminary Survey of the Literature', *Conversion to Islam*,(ed) Nehemia Levtzion, Holmes & Meier, New York, 1979, pp. 68-99.

[14] Yohanan Friedman, 'The Origins and Significance of the Chach Nama', *Islam in Asia, Vol. 1: South Asia*, (ed) Y Freidmann, The Magnus Press, Jerusalem, 1984, pp. 23-35.

[15] Olivier Lacombe, 'L'Islam vu de l'Inde', *Recherches d'islamologie. Recueil d'articles offert à Georges C. Anawati et Louis Gardet par leurs collègues et amis*, Éditions Peeters, Louvain, 1977, pp. 159-170.

these. Thus India maybe considered part of the Muslim world in the sense that it contains a significant body of Muslims; in fact, it has one of the largest concentrations of Muslims resident in any nation today, even though they represent only twelve per cent of the total population of India. Moreover, in the period generally encompassed by the description 'medieval', large areas of India were also under Muslim rule and hegemony.[16] Muslims came to South Asia to trade, to conquer, to teach their religion and to seek refuge. According to tradition, within a generation of the Prophet Muhammad's death, the western coastal peoples first encountered Muslims as Arab settler-traders. In the following centuries, Arab Muslim traders were to be found in most ports on the east and west coasts of south India. By the 10th century (4th century AH), Muslim merchants had settled in the major cities of the Deccan and the North Indian plain. In the 11th century, Isma'ili missionaries from the Yemen were active in Gujarat. The Arabs conquered Sind from 711 on. Ghaznah became the Muslim headquarters in 962 and from the time of Sëbuktigin (977-997) Muslims from Central Asia were using force to penetrate the North Indian plain. Inland areas of Bengal were conquered at the beginning of the 13th century, and Muslims invaded Assam and Orissa about the same time. Muslim Turks were probably first seen in Kashmir in the 11th century, while from the 14th century Muslims from Northern India penetrated the Terai plain at the foot of the mountains of Nepal. Muslim settlements in the central and western areas of Nepal date from the 17th century.[17] Major Muslim settlement in the interior of

---

[16] Paul Jackson, 'Islam in India', *Encounters: documents for Muslim-Christian Understanding*, no. 199-200 (1993), pp. 1-24; P Jackson (ed): *The Muslims of India. Beliefs and Practices*, Islamic Studies and Assocations. Theological Publications in India, Bangalore, 1988; Augustine Thottakara (ed), *Islamic Spirituality*, Centre for Indian and Inter-religious Studies, Rome—Dharmaram Publications, Bangalore, 1993.

[17] For Islamic presence in Tibet and Nepal see: M Gaborieau: *Récit d'un voyageur musulman au Tibet (texte urdu avec traduction et notes)*, Klincksieck, Paris, 1973; 'The Life Cycle Ceremonies of Converted Muslims in Nepal and Northern India', *Islam in Asia, Vol. 1: South Asia*, (ed) Yohanan Friedmann, The Magnus Press, Jerusalem 1984, pp. 241-262; and 'Powers and Authority of Sufis among the Kashmiri Muslims in Tibet', *The Tibet Journal*, Vol. 20 (1995), pp. 21-30. The contemporary question of Islam and Christianity and religious conversion in Nepal, see the studies by M.Gaborieau, 'Une affaire d'État au Népal. Depuis deux siècles le prosèlytisme chrétien et musulman', *Archives de sceince sociales des religions*, Vol. 87, no. 3 (1994), pp. 57-72; 'La montée du prosélytisme dans sous-continent indien: introduction', *Archives de science sociales des religions*, Vol. 87, no. 3 (1994), pp. 13-33.

the Deccan and the south—as distinct from settlement of resident traders—began with raids by the forces of the sultan of Delhi between 1295-1323. There are traditional accounts of the penetration of parts of Bengal and Bijapour by Muslim saints before the main Muslim military thrusts occurred in those regions, but there is no clear consensus that such traditions represent actual historical events.

At the time of the partition of India and Pakistan in 1947, Muslims comprised about one quarter of the population of the subcontinent. In a number of respects, the Muslim experience in India has been different from that of the Muslims elsewhere. Since the 10th century, as outlined above, Muslims have been actively coming into India from Iran, Afghanistan, and Central Asia. The Muslims who came into India found themselves involved with the majority population of Hindus. For several centuries, differing forms of accommodation had evolved in relation to the majority population. Finally, events took a different turn when the British arrived in the 16th century and gradually came to dominate Indian life.[18] In the 19th century, the Muslims were beginning to discover that their status was becoming increasingly insecure. It has been pointed out that a Muslim from this relatively insecure milieu, Sayyid Abu l-A'la Mawdudi, who, in the mid-20th century, articulated for Muslims of the sub-continent the most influential version of their dilemma within the framework of a stark neo-traditionalist perspective.[19] The partition of the Indian sub-continent was an event whose consequences cannot be overestimated. The partition of 1947 drastically decreased Muslim

---

[18] Sheila McDonough, 'The Muslims of South Asia (1857-1947)', *Muslim Perceptions of Other Religions: A Historical Survey*, (ed) Jacques Waardenburg, Oxford University Press, 1999, pp. 250-262.

[19] Emilio Platti, 'La théologie de Abu l-A'laMawdudi', *Philsophy and Arts in the Islamic World*, (eds) U Vermeulen and D de Smet, Peeters, Louvain, 1998, pp. 243-251. Germane to our story here is the figure of A R Cornelius, the Catholic Chief Justice of Pakistan. Of the fifty-five states which declared themselves to be constitutively Islamic, Pakistan alone has had a non-Muslim at the pinnacle of its judicial system. Other Muslims polities such as Egypt, Jordan and Iraq—Lebanon is an exception as it can rightly be called a Christian-Muslim political expression—have had non-Muslims in important juridical posts, although usually for short periods. Sénegal's president for twenty years was Léopold Senghor, a Catholic (see the important biography by the French Catholic scholar of West Africa Fr. Joseph-Roger de Benoist, *Léopold Sédar Senghor. Témoignage de Cheikh Hamidou Kane*, Beauchesne, Paris, 1998, who outlines Léopold Senghor's understanding of Islam and Christianity polity). But none has had a non-Muslim in the judiciary for over a period of

influences in politics, culture and society within the new Indian Republic. The Muslims of India lost their eminence as well as their leadership. They became, moreover, suspect in the eyes of the majority community, especially when prominent Indian Muslims were switching their allegiance to Pakistan right into the 1950s. This in turn has resulted in the re-emergence of a largely inward-looking leadership with pietistic leanings and the weakening of a more confident and dynamic face of Islam in India.[20]

The Indian Muslim population makes up some twelve percent of the total population of India. However, except for the state of Jammu and Kashmir, where Muslims make up approximately 65 percent of the population they are a minority in all other Indian states. The greatest concentration of Muslims is in the Kashmir valley, where they constitute 95 percent of the population and in a district of Mallapuram in Kerala

---

two unbroken decades. A R Cornelius, a Catholic, had a distinguished legal career from the establishment of Pakistan in 1947 to his resignation as law minister in the Yahya Khan cabinet in 1971. For seventeen years of this period he served on the Supreme Court. From 1960 until his retirement in 1968, he was Chief Justice. The legal community has held few jurists in high esteem, nor has anyone had greater influence on Pakistan's constitutional development. It is remarkable that in a country as self-consciously Muslim as Pakistan, the question of religion was muted if not ignored. Except for one brief incident in 1970, it was never a serious political issue. Cornelius developed a profound admiration for Islam which deepened towards the end of his life. Cornelius was brought up a Presbyterian and became a Catholic Christian after his marriage in 1931 to Ione Francis, a devout Catholic. He died in 1991 at the age of 88. As a self-described 'Neo-Thomist' he synthesized Christian and Islamic values through the medium of natural law. This synthesis is a case study in the compatibility of Islam and Christianity developed not on theological grounds but within the context of jurisprudence. It was his belief that 'the religious way of life carries the highest measure of hope for the living of the perfect life … This belief can also be found in a well recognized philosophy in Christianity which commenced with the well-known saint, St Thomas Aquinas'. The notion of infusing Western structures with Pakistani, hence Islamic, norms was carried a step further when Cornelius advocated translating the Fundamental Rights Legislation in Pakistan into Arabic, the language of the Qur'an. They—Fundamental Rights—would thus be 'invested with overtones of undeniable obligation … and their assimilation into the public conscience … greatly enhanced'. See Ralph Braibanti, *Chief Justice Cornelius of Pakistan. An analysis with letters and speeches*, Oxford University Press, 1999; and 'Cornelius of Pakistan: Catholic Chief Justice of a Muslim State', *Islam and Christian-Muslim Relations*, Vol. 10, no. 2 (1999), pp. 117-157.

[20] A study of the post-independence situation of Indian Muslims is found in Mushirul Hasan: *Legacy of a Divided Nation: India's Muslims since Independence*, Hurst, London, 1997; Peter Hardy, 'Islam and Muslims in South Asia', *The Crescent in the East: Islam in Asia Minor*, (ed) Raphael Israel, Curzon, London, 1982, pp. 36-61.

in southern India where they form a majority.[21] In some towns and cities of the largest and politically important State of Uttar Pradesh Muslims form a significant part of the population. There is an urban bias in the composition of the Muslim population: 30 per cent are town-dwellers as compared to the overall proportion of 12 per cent of the total Indian population. The overwhelming majority of Indian Muslims are Sunni (85-90 per cent). The Barelwi group is the largest, although the Deobandis have enjoyed greater prestige with the Indian government because of the support they gave to the Congress movement during the struggle against British rule.[22]

When the British put an end to the Muslim Mughal state, a period of the gradual decline of the Muslim community set in. The Muslims not only lost their power and prestige but also their glory and dignity. During the early stages of British rule the Muslims, who might be described as more conservative than the Hindu community, failed to understand and to appreciate the Western liberal model that was gradually prevailing on the subcontinent. From being rulers the Muslims became a minority community. A combination of all these factors made the Muslim suspicious of British intentions and of the Hindus who in political matters were led by the Indian National Congress. In 1882, because of an ever-growing opposition to their rule, the British embarked upon reforms leading to self-government through, among other things, the liberalization and expansion of the legislative councils at the provincial level. When the Muslim community became aware of this plan, they sent a delegation to explain the problems and the grievances of the Muslim community. Indeed, it is reported that the delegation promised Muslim cooperation and loyalty to British rule in exchange for separate representation in the councils and other rights and privileges for their community. The Muslims felt that, if there was no separate representation on the basis of the communities, they would be swept aside in the legislative councils by

[21] Roland E Miller: *The Mappila Muslims of Kerala—A Study in Islamic Trends*, Orient Longman, Madras 1976; rev. ed., Sangam Books, London, 1992, and J B P More, 'Muslim Evolution and Conversions in Karikal, South India', *Islam and Christian-Muslim Relations*, Vol. 4, no. 1 (1993), pp. 67-82.

[22] Barbara Daly Metcalf, *Islamic Revival in British India: the Deobandi 'ulama, 1860-1900*, Princeton University Press, 1982. See also Aziz Ahmad, *Studies in Islamic culture in the Indian environment*, Clarendon Press, Oxford, 1964, and *An Intellectual History of Islam in India*, Edinburgh University Press, 1969.

the great Hindu majority. Up to then many Muslims had supported the Indian National Congress, but now the need was felt for a separate political organization. Thus on 30 December 1906 at a meeting of the All-Indian Mohammedan Educational Conference, the All-India Muslim League was created. The League's objectives were to promote feelings of loyalty towards the British government; to protect political and other rights of the Muslims; to bring their needs and aspirations to the attention of the government; and to promote cordial relations between Muslims and Hindus. The emergence of the Muslim League indicated that the political aspirations of the Hindus and those of the Muslims were poles apart. In 1909, the Muslim community and the Muslim League fought for a separate electorate, something, which was strongly opposed by the Indian National Congress. The existence of two distinct political organizations, respectively representing the Hindus and Muslims, gave rise to disharmony, bitterness, and growing tensions between the two communities. The British made a number of proposals in an attempt to solve the problem of self-government between the communities, but without success. The leaders of the two movements continued growing apart and became increasingly hostile to one another.

The Muslim League's ideology was based on the idea that the Muslims of India constitute a distinct nation, separate from the Hindus. According to this view, known as 'the two nations theory— *do qawmi nazariyya*'—very sharp differences exist between the Muslims and the other communities of India. Moreover, these differences are not restricted to the spiritual or religious sphere, since Islam and Hinduism are not merely religions. Each has its own notion of society, and each draws its inspiration from different historical roots. Hinduism is based on a caste system, is diametrically opposed to the egalitarian Islam and considers all Muslims as untouchables. Hindus and Muslims do not intermarry, their social customs are very different. In India's history, Hinduism was always the enemy of Islam. Muslim victories were often defeats for Hinduism. Muslim heroes frequently displayed their courage in wars against the Hindus. Islam and Hinduism are, therefore, two different cultures; the Muslims and the Hindus are two distinct nations, which are no more similar to each other than the various nations of Europe, and cannot possibly be united, in one political framework. The Muslim League's conclusion was that a separate political entity—Pakistan—should be established for the Muslims in the areas where they constitute a majority. The League's leaders claimed that the failure to achieve this goal and the establishment of a united India would be a disaster for Islam and for the Indian Muslims. The 'two nations theory' forbade the Muslims to assimilate into their Indian environment, and demanded that they establish a political framework in which they could safeguard their cultural uniqueness and live in accordance with their Islamic ideals.[23]

As a result the Muslim League made it clear to the British that only a 'separate homeland' would be acceptable to Muslims. On 3 June 1947, the last viceroy, Lord Mountbatten, proposed a plan for the partition of the subcontinent, which was accepted by both the Indian National Congress and the Muslim League. This partition was perhaps one of the most tragic events in the recent history of peoples who had struggled for national independence and the end of colonialism. As the 'Quit India Movement' against the British gained momentum, the frenzy between Hindus and Muslims too reached a peak. On the one hand, the Hindus were bitter because the Muslim demand for a separate homeland meant the division of *Bharat Mata* ('Mother India'). On the other hand, the Muslims, fearing the domination of the large Hindu majority in all spheres of life, insisted that there was no other solution. Muhammad Ali Jinnah, the leader of the Pakistan movement, stated that Hindus and Muslims could not live together peacefully: both are distinct communities that practice different religions and have different social traditions and cultural heritages. When the partition went into effect, it gave rise to much violence. In a fit of madness and religious fanaticism Hindus and Muslims turned against one another. The results were up to a million dead and many millions homeless—as result of the ensuing mass migrations of peoples from one state to the other.

The creation of Pakistan as a separate Muslim state was a

---

[23] Yohannan Friedmann, 'The Attitude of the *Jam'iyyat-i 'Ulama-i Hind* to the Indian National Movement and the Establishment of Pakistan', *Asian and African Studies*, Vol. 7 (1971), pp. 157-180. See also the studies by Violette Graff on Islam in India and its political role: 'Les musulmans de l'Inde', *L'Islam et l'Etat dans le monde aujourd'hui*, (ed) O Carré, Presses Universitaires de France, Paris, 1982, pp. 205-228; 'La Jamaat-e-islami hind', *Radicalismes Islamiques, Vol. 2. Maroc, Pakistan, Inde, Yougoslavie, Mali*, (eds) O Carré and Paul Dumont, L'Harmattan, Paris, 1986), pp. 77-99; 'L'islam dans le sous-continent indien', *Hérodote: reuve de géographie et de géopolitique*, Vol. 35 (1984), pp. 80-110.

devastating blow to the overall position of Muslims who stayed behind in India. It greatly angered the Hindus for whom the whole subcontinent was an indivisible cultural whole wherein were located their ancient roots. Moreover, Muslim entrepreneurs and the intelligentsia of northern India migrated to Pakistan leaving a largely poor and uneducated Muslim population behind. In recent years everyday Muslim-Hindu relations have undergone numerous particularly violent challenges to co-existence; Hindu nationalists have sought to highlight the alleged wrongs done against the Hindu community and its religion by the Muslims between the 13th and 19th centuries.[24] The classic allegation is that in 1528 the founder of the Mughal empire, Zahiruddin Babur, had a mosque built at Ayodhya in northern India on the exact spot where the god Rama is believed to have been born some thousands of years ago. The campaign to dismantle the mosque began in real earnest in the mid-1980s. The Hindu nationalists, however, intensified their campaign for the destruction of the mosque. It culminated in hundreds of thousands of extremists from different parts of the country coming to Ayodhya in early December 1992. They easily overpowered the small police force, climbed onto the mosque and demolished it in a few hours. Suddenly India was in the midst of perhaps the most serious communal conflict between Hindu and Muslims since the partition. Given the exposed and vulnerable nature of the Indian Muslim community, any apparent sign of Muslim strength can antagonise Hindu nationalists. There is a widespread popular belief in India that the Muslim population is increasing more rapidly than others, because of early marriage. Indian Muslims have also had some advantage in finding employment in the Arabian-Persian Gulf Region. Both Iran and Saudi Arabia have taken a keen interest in the affairs of the Muslim community in India. Substantial economic aid is given to Muslim religious organizations for the building of study centres, Qur'an schools and the upkeep of mosques. Such aid, given mainly to *ulama* and groups supportive of these countries, has helped bolster the

---

[24] C Jaffrelot: *Les nationalistes hindous. Idéologie, implantation et mobilisation des années 1920 aux années 1990*, Presses de la Fondation nationale des Sciences politiques, Paris, 1993; Jackie Assayag, 'Action rituelle ou reaction politique? L'invention des processions du nationalisme hindou dans les années 1980 en Inde', *Annales: économies, sociétés, civilisation*, Vol. 52 (1997), pp. 853-879.

position of conservative Muslims *vis-à-vis* modernist Muslims. Hindu parties have perceived these changes as threats.[25]

To begin any consideration of Muslim-Christian relations in India, one must underline the complexity of Indian religious history, involving interaction among Hindu, Jain, Buddhist, Christian, Muslim Sikh and other religious traditions.[26] The Christian presence in India is now woven throughout the tapestry of India life. Syrian, Catholic and Protestant traditions, each in their own way having made a notable impact. The Christian population of India, however, is relatively small some three to five per cent of the total.[27] It is Hinduism that represents the dominant motif in the Indian religious fabric of society. There

---

[25] P Jackson, 'L'Islam en Inde après la destruction de la mosquée d'Ayodhya', *Se Comprendre*, no. 93 (1993), pp. 1-22. The destruction of the Babri Masjid at Ayodhya on 6 December 1992, was undoubtedly a landmark event in the recent political and religious history of South Asia. The Ayodyha attack and its aftermath gave India's Hindu majority, as well as the subcontinents Muslim, Sikh and Christian communities, a dramatic display of the power of a recently revitalised Hindu activist religion, 'allied to claims of territorial exclusion and conquest'. The 'victory' of the Hindu militants at the Babri Masjid is likely to encourage self-styled purifiers and holy warriors in many other parts of South Asia (the destruction of Buddhist shrines in Afghanistan in 2001 might be cited as an example), where local conflicts over territory and resources have interlocked with wider campaigns to seize shrines and expel those of rival faiths from contested terrain. The demolition of this approximately five century year old mosque by some two hundred thousand self-professed 'servants' or *Kar sevaks* of the Hindu god Ram provoked Hindu-Muslim violence in almost every region in the subcontinent. These are though to have been South Asia's worst intercommunal riots since the violence that accompanied the Partition of India in 1947-1948. See Susan Bayly, 'Christians and Competing Fundamentalisms in South Indian Society', *op. cit.*, 757-763 and Roger Friedland and Richard Hecht, 'The Bodies of Nations: A Comparative Study of Religious Violence—Jerusalem and Ayodhya', *History of Religions*, Vol. 38, no. 2 (1998), pp. 101-149.

[26] For a regionally description of the multi-dimensional encounter between Hindus-Christians-Muslim in India see the studies by Roland E Miller on the religious situation in Kerala: 'The Dynamics of Religious Coexistence in Kerala: Religious Interaction in Kerala with Special Reference to the Impact of European Medieval Christianity', *Conversion and Continuity: Indigenous Christian Communities in Islamic Lands. Eighth to Eighteenth Centuries*, (eds) Michael Gervers and Ramzi Jibran Bikhazi, Pontifical Institute of Medieval Studies, Toronto, 1989, pp. 437-448 and 'The Dynamics of Religious Coexistence in Kerala: Muslims, Christians and Hindus', *Christian-Muslim Encounters*, (eds) Yvonne Y Haddad and W Haddad, University of Florida Press, Miami 1995, pp. 263-284.

[27] See the description of Christian India in Charles Pye-Smith, *Rebels and Outcasts. A journey through Christian India*, Viking, London, 1997. For the standard history of Christianity in India, see Stephen Neil, *A History of Christianity in India, I: The Beginnings to A.D. 1707*, Cambridge University Press, 1984, and *A History of Christianity in India, II: 1707-1858*, Cambridge University Press, 1985.

are even those who continue to posit that India is essentially and properly a Hindu land and nation, and that all other religious must be viewed as foreign accretions, even though the term 'Hinduism' is itself a modern construct.[28] At another level of observation, it is agreed that Hinduism provides the cultural context within which other religious traditions and communities in India must understand their way of life and their mutual relationships. In describing the encounter between Hinduism and Islam, R Morton Smith writes:

> Islam and Hinduism, are well made for mutual non-appreciation' (p. 307); 'It might be well to explain why Islam had so little appeal to the thought of traditional India. Its great message is the unity, uniqueness, power and mercy of God: Hinduism is unsympathetic to all of these. The brahman might tolerate Allah as an ethnic Brahma, but Allah was not to continue as a monopoly of the invaders, and even if he should so continue by the suspension of conversion, Allah is active and arbitrary—the very continuance of the world is an exhibition of his power, Brahma however is neither active nor arbitrary, for even if the next cycle of emanation could be different, *Karma* has taken hold on this. Allah cares, Brahma exists. Allah is a personal and ethical God, just and merciful; damnation is not far away, and Allah could rightly damn, but he is merciful. But Hindu damnation is more life, not destruction' (p. 310); 'Technical effects of the Islamic conquest seem

---

[28] Thus for example Gerald Larson claims that the notion of 'religion' in South Asia derives largely from Islamic and Christian traditions and has no precise analogue in South Asia prior to the coming of Islam. Moreover, the linkage of the notion of 'religion' with the notion of 'Hindu' is also problematic. He continues that he is 'inclined to agree that notions such as the 'Hindu majority', Hindu religion and 'Hinduism' are largely an 'artifact of categorization' that have generated a variety of conceptual muddles and have tended to direct our studies into 'trackless deserts of nonsense'. Gerald James Larson, 'Discourse about "Religion"', *Colonial and Postcolonial India, Ethical and Political Dilemmas of Modern India,* (eds) Ninian Smart and Shivesh Thakur, Macmillan, London, 1993, p. 181; see also, Robert Eric Frykenberg, 'The Emergence of Modern "Hinduism" as a Concept and as an Institution: A Reappraisal with Special Reference to South India', *Hindusism Reconsidered,* (eds) G D Sontheimer and H Kulke, Manohar, Delhi, 1991.

to be long delayed: technology is not a brahman interest. In some things India was the teacher, e.g., in medicine, astronomy, mathematics: but Indian thought influenced Islam rather as part of Persian, wither its export of pre-Sasanid, and in the translation from the ethic of the thinking to the fighting class it is not likely to be unchanged, e.g., the assertion of the self as the universe, static in India, must be dynamic outside, hence personalized. We should remember that Buddhism was in Iranian lands for 800 years before Islam, and even if not institutionalised in the west, it should not be expected to have had no effect. We suggest Sufism owes something in this way, and it may be that the dervish does Siva's cosmic dance unknowing. But Islam did not come to India to learn, nor can it be said that the brahman was ever eager to teach outsiders his secret lore: his high philosophy was for very few; the popular philosophy of the Epic/MahaBharata might have been more accessible to invaders, but it is not particularly impressive. The ordinary Muslim had no reason to be dissatisfied with his own religion, or therefore to learn— the idea that everybody else is as good as ourselves if not better is one of our modern Western advances. But the teaching impulse seems to have been early exhausted, and certainly did not find a willing pupil in the brahman. He or his substitute, the heretic monk, has no reason to want to learn about a world he has transcended, and indeed he never has learned from another culture without having to (as today Western science is a necessity), e.g., there is no trace of the influence from East Asia despite all the pilgrims of Buddhism, including many very intelligent men. Of social effects of Islam the most important were the introduction of purdah, and a more secular system of taxation—the Muslim ruler was not bound to observe the rules of Manu in this matter. Islam does influence the Indian feeling, its triumph is incomplete, e.g., the basic inequality of man remains untouched, even if

Lingayat Saivas theoretically hold men and women equal; the idol remains, and there is no thought of a Muslim India (p. 323).[29]

Christianity in India

Compared to the Muslims the Christians in India form a much smaller minority, approximately 3-5 per cent of the population. They are even less evenly spread over the country than the Muslims. They are concentrated in the southern States, especially Kerala and Goa, and reach higher numbers in some of the larger urban centres (e.g. Bombay, Madras, Poona, Hyderabad and Calcutta) as well as in tribal areas, for instance, those of North-Eastern India. The Indian Christians as a community were hardly affected by partition. Whereas most of them had not on the whole participated actively in the struggle for independence from Britain, they did not oppose it actively either. As compared with the Muslims, there was less of a problem for them in accepting the democratic and secular character of the Indian Republic as outlined in the constitution. Furthermore, the status of being a minority is not in itself as problematic for a group of Christians as it is for a group of Muslims. The history of Christianity, especially that of its formative period, of the first three hundred years, provides an accepted model of dynamic Christian life of faith in community without the support of a 'Christian' political structure or state. As has been outlined, the case of Islam is totally different.

The principal endeavour of Indian Christianity in the decades since Independence has been to strengthen its sense of community, its coherence and identity.[30] To this end it has tried to shed the traces of its colonial and foreign dependence, to indigenise Church

---

[29] R Morton Smith, 'Meeting of Opposites: Islam and Hinduism', *Logos Islamikos: Studia Islamica in honorem Georgii Michaelis Wickens*, (eds) Roger R Savoury and Dionisius A Agius, Pontifical Institute of Medieval Studies, Toronto, 1984, pp. 307-324. See also the interesting theological reflection by Arij A Roest Crollius, *The Word in the Experience of Revelation in the Qur'an and Hindu Scriptures*, Editrice Pontificia Università Gregoriana, Rome, 1974.

[30] A M Mundadam: *Indian Christians Search for Identity and Struggle for Autonomy*, Dharmaram, Bangalore, 1984, and J H Beaglehole, 'The Indian Christian: a study of a minority', *Modern Asian Studies*, Vol. 1, no. 1 (1967). See also the interesting work by Catherine Clémentin-Ohja, Le christianisme indien dans le regard hindou', *Revue de l'Institut catholique de Paris*,

personnel, to indianize Christian life, expression and thought, to strengthen the community by educational and social services and to witness to their Christian faith not only by the word of preaching but by service, especially in the educational, medical and social field.

Significant new membership of the Church has been won during those decades among the tribal peoples, the 'Harijans' and Hindu low-caste people. To the 'untouchables' and tribals, Christianity was not merely a religious event but a means of re-adapting themselves to the changed situation. In the latter half of the nineteenth and early-20th century, caste movements among the 'low castes' took a religious turn: there were mass conversions to the groups that preached equality. Untouchables and tribals joined religions like Islam, Sikhism, Arya Samaj, Christianity and others, which gave them hope of liberation from their state of oppression. It was also the age of social movements and rebellions among the tribals, the Kol (1832), Santal (1855-57), Sardar Larai (1885) and the Birsa Movement (1895) being the main ones.[31] In the context of contemporary India, there are groups of Hindu nationalists whose avowed aim is of 'reclaiming' such people for Hinduism, and its commitment to fight off further 'incursions' by the churches among the tribal and low-caste groups, has been a source of conflict in the northeast, and has been observed with alarm in south India, the country's only other zone of large-scale Christian population. There are close parallels with campaigns of *shuddhi* or 'reconversion' of Christians by militant Hindus in north India in the late 19th century. The tour of Pope John Paul II to India

no. 38 (1991); 'Indianisation et enracinement: les enjeux de l'inculturation en Inde', *Bulletin de l'École française d'Extrême-Orient*, Vol. 80 (1993), pp. 107-137; 'Des Indiens en quête leur indianité: inculturation et formation des jésuites à Patna (Bihar)', *Altérité et identité. Islam et christianisme en Inde*, (eds) Jackie Assayag and Gilles Tarabout, Editions de l'École des Hautes Etudes en science sociales, Paris, 1997, and 'La formation du clergé indigène en Inde: les débuts de l'indianisation (1925-1965)', *Les cadres locaux et les ministères consacrés dans les jeunes Églises XIX-XXe siècle*, Collection du CREDIC, 13 (1998), Lyon, pp. 241-269; and the debate in the French Jesuit review *Études*, Michael Amaladoss, 'Être chrétien en Inde', *Études*, Vol. 388 (1998), pp. 637-644; Micahel Fédou, 'Débats théologiques en Inde', *Études*, Vol. 383 (1995), pp. 661-671; Catherine Clémentin-Ohja, 'Retour sur les débates théologiques en Inde', *Études*, No. 3843 (1996), pp. 387-390.

[31] *Christians of Scheduled Caste Origin*, Pro Muni Vita: Dossiers (1982); Asia-Australasia Dossier 22; Geneviere Lemercinier, 'The Effect of the Caste System on conversion to Christianity in Tamil Nadu', *Social Compass*, Vol. 28, nos. 2-3 (1981), pp. 237-268; C J Fuller, 'Kerala Christians and the Caste System', *Man*, Vol. 11, no. 1 (1976), pp. 53-70.

in 1986 was portrayed by Hindu militant organizations as yet another incursion into the 'Hindu homeland'. They claimed that *darshan* (the Hindu concept of sanctified sighting) of the pope would 'induce' Hindus to convert to Christianity.[32]

The powerful Protestant movement during the 19th and 20th century had led to conversions from Islam. In many Protestant Churches,[33] therefore, we find to this day a substantial element of Urdu culture and the cherishing of other important elements of Indian Muslim heritage. With regard to Islam, and in contrast to a couple of lone Catholic pioneers, the Protestant churches in India can look back to a great continuing tradition of outreach to Muslims and engagement with Islam, from the beginnings of Serampore College at the end of the 18th century and Henry Martyn onwards. This outreach is characterized by an approach that aimed primarily at conversion and Church expansion. The Catholic Church in India,[34] after the end of the Jesuit mission at the Mughal court, had no such tradition of a determined evangelical outreach to Islam. Catholic missionary activity and thinking during the 19th and 20th century was predominantly concerned either in the tradition of Roberto de Nobili (1577-1656),[35]

---

[32] See Susan Bayly, 'Christians and Competing Fundamentalisms in South Indian Society', *Accounting for Fundamentalisms. The Dynamic Character of the Movements*, (eds) Martin E Marty and R Scott Appleby, The University of Chicago Press, 1994, pp. 726-769, and Catherine Clémentin-Ohja 'La "Suddhi" de l'Arya Samaj ou l'invention d'un rituel de (re)-conversion à l'hindouisme', *Archives de science sociales des religions*, Vol. 67, no. 4 (1994), pp. 99-114. See also A Sharma (ed), *Neo-Hindu Views of Christianity*, E J Brill, Leiden, 1988, and Daniel Gold, 'Organized Hinduisms', *Fundamentalisms Observed*, (eds) Martin E Marty and R Scott Appleby, University of Chicago Press, 1991, pp. 531-593.

[33] For the Protestant churches see the work of Geoffrey A Oddie: *Hindu and Christian in South-East India*, Curzon, London 1991; *Social Protest in India. British Protestant Missionaries and Social Reforms, 1850-1900 Religion in South Asia*, Delhi, 1979, *Religious Conversion and Revival Movements in South Asia in Medieval and Modern Times*, Delhi, 1977.

[34] *The Indian Catholic Community: Its peoples and institutions in interaction with the Indian Situation today*, Pro Mundi Vita: Dossiers (1980): Asia-Australasia 12-13, and Kenneth Ballhatchet, *Caste, Class and Catholicism in India, 1789-1914*, Curzon, London, 1998.

[35] Roberto de Nobili (1577-1656) was an Italian Jesuit who came to India in 1605, reached the city of Madurai in South India in November 1606, and for the most of the next forty years lived and worked as a missionary there. De Nobili is best remembered and admired for his willingness to adopt Indian customs of dress, food and manner of living; he was determined to show that the Christian faith could be lived in a way not entirely bound by European cultural values. He was also an important thinker and writer; though not the first Jesuit (even in his generation) to study Hinduism seriously, he was a remarkable and creative thinker outstanding for the detail, energy, and intellectual rigour of his writings,

with conversions from upper-caste Hinduism, or from the scheduled Hindu castes and the Adivasi population.

The Indian Church is a complex phenomenon. One primary question is what was the consequence for Indian Christians of Indian independence; for many, political freedom was not a total break from the past, but represented continuity with change. Many actions of the

---

particularly in the Tamil vernacular. A talented linguist, he was one of the first Europeans to learn Tamil and perhaps the first to write theological treatises in that or any Indian language. See the studies by F X Clooney, 'Robert de Nobili's *Dialogue on Eternal Life* and an Early Jesuit Evaluation of Religion in South India', *The Jesuits: Cultures, Sciences and the Arts, 1540-1773*, (eds) John W O'Malley, SJ, Gauvin Alexander Bailey, Steven Harris and T Frank Kennedy, SJ, University of Toronto Press, 1999, pp. 402-417; Roberto de Nobili, 'Adaptation, and the Reasonable Interpretation of Religion', *Missiology*, Vol. 18 (1990), pp. 25-36; 'Religious Memory and the Pluralism of Readings: Reflections on Roberto de Nobili and the Taittiriya Upanisad', *Sophia*, Vol. 34 (1995), pp. 204-225, 'Christ as the Divine Guru in the Theology of Roberto de Nobili', *Boston Theological Society Series*, (ed) Ruy Costa, Orbis Press, Vol. 2 (1988), pp. 24-40; 'Roberto de Nobili's response to India and Hinduism, in theory and practice', *Third Millennium*, Vol. 1, no. 2 (1998), pp. 72-80. The modern day interpreter of De Nobili, the American Jesuit, Francis X Clooney, has written a number of studies reflecting a similar theological endeavour 'In Ten Thousand Places, in Every Blade of Grass. Uneventful but True Confession about Finding God in India, and Here Too', *Studies in the Spirituality of the Jesuits*, Vol. 28, no. 3 (1996), pp. 1-45; *Seeing Through Texts: Doing Theology among the Srivaisnavas of South India*, State University of New York Press, Albany, 1996; *Hindu Wisdom for All God's Children*, Orbis, Maryknoll, 1998; *Theology after Vedanta. An Experiment in Comparative Theology*, State University of New York Press, Albany, 1993; and very interestingly, 'Obligation, Experience and Tradition: A Possible Hindu Contribution to the Christian Understanding of the Motives for Eucharistic Participation', *Studia Liturgica*, Vol. 29, no. 2 (1999), pp. 129-145.

More germane to our purposes here and within the context of Muslim-Christian relations in India, the Australian Jesuit and longtime resident in India, Paul Jackson has made comparative studies in the spiritual affinity between Sharafuddin Ahmad bin Yahya Maneri (1290-1381 AD) and the founder of the Jesuits and Spanish-Basque saint, Ignatius of Loyola. It is this type of theology combined with the history of religion which will allow for a different type of dialogue to emerge between Christians and Muslims outside the traditional areas of difference and polemic: P Jackson, 'Maneri in an Ignation Perspective', *Encounter: Documents for Muslim-Christian Understanding*, no. 188 (1992), pp. 1-16; 'Sufism and Jesuit in Bihar', *Ignis*, Vol. 25, no. 4 (1996), pp. 53-60; 'Sheikh Shrafuddin Maneri as spiritual master', *Studia Missionalia*, Vol. 36 (1987), pp. 127-146; 'Spiritual Guidance in Islam: A Case Study—Sharafuddin Maneri', *The Way: Contemporary Christian Spirituality* (1987), pp. 144-152; 'Sheikh Sharafuddin Maneri's vision of Muhammad', *Vidyajyoti: Journal of Theological Reflection*, Vol. XLVI, no. 8 (1982), pp. 380-392; and the edited version of Maneri's theological and spiritual letters by P Jackson, *Sharafuddin Maneri: The Hundred Letters*, Paulist Press, New York, 1980). Fr Desiderio Pinto, the Director of the Department for Islamic Studies at Vidyajyoti, has also attempted to look at the concept of spiritual and religious life in both Christianity and Islam: 'Religious Life in Islam', *Vidyajyoti: Journal of Theological Reflection*, Vol. LVII, (1993), pp. 420-429.

post-1947 Christian community are an outcome of attitudes built up in the colonial era and during the independence struggle. The Indian Christian leaders have always declared the 'good of the Church' to be their main aim. Its formulation has taken forms such as 'freedom of religion' or 'defending the rights of the minority', but throughout the years, the decision-makers have made this the criterion of their actions, and have explained and justified their deeds according to this goal. The main discussion during this period was centred on the right to propagate one's faith and the right to run educational institutions. These controversies have influenced post-independence and non-Christian attitudes. Again another variation of this theme, the post-independence Christian community has often viewed itself as a minority whose interests need to be safeguarded against possible encroachment by what it has often considered a hostile Hindu majority, Many of its decisions are conditioned by this perception. With the growth of a Hindu militancy which has often been aimed at, and has taken a violent turn against, many Christians communities and targeted Christian institutions have felt much insecurity. How this increasingly hostile environment will play out within religious and theological character of the Christian community is difficult to read at present, but one consequence is that the various Christians communities are finding joint character and texture to their collective vulnerability.[36] Very little understanding existed between Catholics and Protestants in pre-independence India, or for

---

[36] For example catholic schools in the archdioceses of Bombay were closed on 13 August 2001 as a protest against the killing of a nun and an attack which left a priest injured in two separate incidents. In Ujjain, a central Indian town, a nun was shot at point-blank range and killed; in Bombay a priest, Fr Oscar Mendonca, was attacked by a mob and injured. The local Bishop of Indore Diocese had called for a judicial inquiry after the killing of Sr Leena near Ujjain. The shooting follows the murder of Sr Rani Maria in 1995 and the rape of a community of nuns in Jhabua in 1998. Cardinal Ivan Dias, Archbishop of Bombay, said of the attack on Fr Mendonca: 'I want to emphasize the serious nature of the incident, which must be considered much more sacrilegious than any attack on a church, temple or mosque, for it was a premeditated assault on a priest.' What the archbishop seemed to be indicating was that attacks have moved firmly from property to people. The attack apparently took place when 25 people, after a meeting to mourn a member of the Hindu extremist organization RSS slain at Tripura in the northeast, went to St John the Baptist Church nearby and attacked the priest. In another incident, two Christian schools in the western state of Gujarat were reported to have been target by a Hindu extremist group. The cause of the attack was alleged to have been a directive issued by the school management forbidding teachers and students from putting on *bindis*, or caste marks, on their foreheads. *The Tablet* (London), 18 August 2001.

that matter, for over a decade of the Indian Republic. The situation has changed considerably due to the post-Vatican II ecumenical atmosphere, and the need of all Christians to 'defend their rights'. The two sides had come together on specific issues such as the anti-government agitation in Kerala in 1959. In the mid-1960s one notices the two trying to coordinate their activities much more than before, also during the State of Emergency period, 1975-1977.[37] The Church-related institutions formed the All- India Association of Christian Higher Education (AIACHE). Some academic and development associations have also been formed. There is now an All-India Christian Council (AICC), which tries to speak up for Christian interests in Indian society. And as has already been indicated, attention to the recent Hindu radicalism which has been directed at many Christian communities and Christian institutions across India, has also focused the attention of all the Christians of India as a collective body. In the four southern states of Tamil Nadu, Kerala, Karnataka, and Andhra Pradesh, they have become a critical reference point for large-scale pan-Indian assertive Hindu groups such as—Rashtriya Swayamsevak Sangh (RSS) and Visva Hindu Parishad (VHP). The south has also been the focus for expansive Islamising campaigns. These developments have had a profound effect on the numerous and dynamic forms of Christianity which have their home in the southern states, especially in Tamil Nadu and Kerala, which contain a disproportionately large number of India's professing Christians. The Christians of the south have also started to assert themselves. For Christians as well as other groups in south India, the leading hallmark of the new radicalism is a commitment to campaigns of public activism which are generated out of local disputes and the recast to take on a larger pan-regional and pan-Indian dimension. A solitary and exclusiveness is also characteristic. This has involved an emotive move toward the heightening of corporate identity. In the case of the Christian populations of the south, fellow believers are encouraged to rally around symbols of 'true' Christianity, and to repudiate emblems and forms of worship which express common ground with Hindusism and Islam in the same densely populated sacred landscapes. In this shift towards exclusiveness and a strengthening of previously loose and fluid communal boundaries, the fact of interaction,

---

[37] *Christians and the Emergency in India*, Pro Mundi Vita: Dossiers (1980): Asia-Australasia 14.

of being spurred to assertive behaviour by the example of others, has been a crucial element in the rise of organised radicalism in the southern states, among Christians, Muslims and Hindus.[38]

Muslim-Christian relations in India

Muslim-Christian relations in India are varied in historical context and their contemporary frameworks are intensely diverse. They cover a large an engagement, to include religion and politics and state relations, intellectual and faith encounters, to deep spiritual levels of friendship and mysticism. We have only selected a couple of engagements from this vast itinerary to give some form and context for this all important and unique unfolding engagement between Christians and Muslims.

Some early encounters

Christianity in India as a minority community has a greater preoccupation with and interest in relating itself in dialogue with the majority Hindu and minority Muslim worlds. However, the push for dialogue does not in fact come from its minority sentiment or status, but on the contrary from its consciousness of belonging to the largest global religious community—Christianity. This consciousness is sufficiently strong among Christians to assert themselves on the national level in religious questions. This consciousness is set against an on going dialogue of interreligious encounter between Christianity and other faith traditions in India.[39]

For the modern chapter in the history of Muslim-Christian relations in India we must start our story at the opening of the 19th century. Henry Martyn (1781-1812), the pioneer Protestant missionary among the Muslims of India and Iran, became famous for his

---

[38] My account here is greatly indebted to Susan Bayly, 'Christians and Competing Fundamentalisms in South Indian Society', *Accounting for Fundamentalisms. The Dynamic Character of the Movements*, (eds) Martin E Marty and R Scott Appleby, The University of Chicago Press, 1994. See also S Bayly, *Saints, Goddeses and Kings: Muslims and Christians in South Indian Society, 1700-1900*, Cambridge University Press, 1989.

[39] For an overview of Christian-Hindu relations, see Anand Nayak, *Hindu-Christian Dialogue in India*, Pro Mundi Vita Bulletin, 88 (1982).

Controversial Tracts, prepared for the disputations with Muslim scholars. Yet his overall approach to Muslims was much broader than is evinced by the tracts. He had strong reservations as to the aptness of disputations and controversies for conveying the Christian message. At best, he thought, they would arouse a spirit of inquiry. By contrast, he felt that personal conversations or dialogues with a small group or circle of interested Muslims produced what he called 'mutually responsive notes'. He purposely set out to appreciate whatever was best in his Muslim acquaintances and ascribe such to the activity of God. He stressed the need to direct attention to the sacred scriptures of Islam and Christianity themselves rather than to later, scholastic elaboration and insisted on the need for fostering lasting friendship with the inquirer. He stressed the centrality of God's work in the souls of men and women and consequent respect for those souls.[40]

Sometime later in April 1854 we find ourselves in the schoolroom of the British Church Missionary Society (CMS) in Agra, among several hundred Muslims and Europeans, mostly Christian missionaries, but also a few government officials of the British colonial power. They are all gathered in order to listen to the public debate initiated by the Muslim community in Agra. The debate was carried out between the German missionary, Karl Gottlieb Pfander (1803-1865), coming out of the pietistic movement in Württemberg and an Indian Muslim Shi 'a theologian, Rahmatullah Ibn Khalil al-'Uthmani al-Kairanawi (1818-1891). Despite the fact that this debate took place nearly hundred and fifty years ago, both opponents are still well remembered in the India Muslim world today. The subject of discussion at the public debate, which lasted for two days, was the

---

[40] C W Troll, 'Christian-Muslim Relations in India: a critical survey', *Islamochristiana*, Vol. 5 (1979), pp. 119-145. The Henry Martyn Institute of Islamic Studies which was founded in 1930 as a school preparing missionaries to work with Muslims, has become a pioneer in the field of Christian-Muslim relations in India. Based in Hyderabad, it has today become a centre for the study of Islam and Christian-Muslim relations with a clearly defined focus on the ministry of reconciliation. Its main task is to help the church in India to become an instrument of mediation in situations of conflict, particularly between religious communities. Besides giving short and long courses in various seminaries and colleges. The Henry Martyn Institute of Islamic Studies became the Henry Martyn Institute in 1959 and its English language quarterly became known since 1960 as *The Bulletin of the Henry Martyn Institute of Islamic Studies*, which publishes research articles, Islam and Christian-Muslim relations and other interfaith concerns, while the Urdu quarterly *Al-Basheer*, is meant mainly for Muslims and Urdu-speaking Christians.

question of Christian scripture (*tahrif*) and the Islamic understanding of its status. The challenger of the debate in 1854 was the Muslim theologian al-Kairanawi, who intended to publicly demonstrate the inferiority of Christianity and make it clear once and for all that Muslims should not be shaken in their faith because of the proclamation of the Christian creed by Protestant missionaries in India in the past decades. India had been opened to Protestant Christian missionary activities by a decree of the British Parliament in 1813, and the first Anglican bishop was appointed in May 1814. In 1832-1833 non-British missionary agencies were allowed to follow and began to establish their network of Christian missions all over India, more or less officially supported by the British administration. It is interesting that Pfander was German, and that the Shi'a al-Kairanawi represented himself in 1854 as the defender of the Muslim religion and was accepted as such by the Muslim community. Although it was planned to extend the discussion to subjects of the Trinity (*tathlih*), the Qur'an being the Word of God and the sending of the prophet Muhammad, the debate did not proceed further than the authority of the Christian scriptures. The discussion centred on this point of controversy: al-Kairanawi insisted that the Christian scriptures had been abrogated and tried to prove this with examples taken out of the Bible itself, while the Christian missionaries persistently affirmed the integrity of the Old and New Testament. After two days the opponents separated and 'both sides claimed the victory'. Also a few conversations to Christianity took place following the debate. Besides the well-known Safdar 'Ali, who was baptized in 1864, perhaps the most famous Muslim convert to Christianity in India had been 'Imad ud-Din (ca.1830-1900), who was baptized in 1866, and ordained as an Anglican divine in 1872. He had been involved in mosque-preaching against Christian missionary work before and afterwards wrote several apologetical works against Islam such as the famous book 'Guidance for Muslims' (*hidayat al-muslimin*) or 'Inquiry into the Faith' (*tahqiq al-iman*).[41] One scholar of Muslim-Christian relations in India has assessed 'the public debates between him and Muslim scholars and the literature they produced set the tome for decades. These debates

---

[41] A A Powell, 'Maulaua Rahmat Allah Kairanawi and Muslim-Christian Controversy in India in the Mid-19th Century', *Journal of the Royal Asiatic Society*, Vol. 20 (1976), pp. 42-63.

sowed the seed of enmity and hatred in the hearts of Indian Muslims and they started to suspect the missionary efforts of the Christians as a plot to destroy Islam in India.'[42]

Similar debates continued after the mutiny in 1857, yet a real understanding of each others position was never really the objective. Genuine intellectual exchange was thus irrelevant to the purpose of the debates, each side could feel it had won because its imply judged its opponents by its own standards and did not explore a different intellectual or faith tradition framework. In participating in these debates, the Muslim community was largely reacting to the activities of Christian missionaries. However, as time passed a genuine intellectual attempt started to take shape as Muslims and Christians sort to grapple with each others faith.[43]

Some Indian Muslim views on Christianity

Much credit must go to the efforts Sir Sayyid Ahmad Khan (1817-1898), the Indian Muslim thinker, as the principal actor in the eventual transformation of Muslim self-understanding, hopes and social attitudes. The British suppression of the mutiny and rebellion in 1857-1858 convinced him that Muslims must accept a future shaped by British power. Sayyid Ahmad Khan, himself one of the Muslim aristocrats who had survived the destruction of Delhi, thought that Muslims must either adapt to their new rulers, while maintaining their faith, and to learn whatever new skills might be necessary for survival in the new condition or cease to be effective in the world.

If a rapprochement were to take place between Islam and Christianity, it would have to be established upon a firm basis, which was a complete knowledge of the scriptures. Therefore, Ahmad Khan employed a Jew to teach him Hebrew, and he had access to the Gospels through Persian translations. His research resulted in three volumes entitled *Tabyin al-Kalam*, a commentary on the Bible; he is recognised

---

[42] C W Troll, 'Christian-Muslim Relations in India: a critical survey', *op. cit*, p. 125.
[43] C W Troll, 'Islamic Thought in Modern India', *Islamochristiana*, Vol. 13 (1987), pp. 79-98; and 'Salvation of Non-Muslims: Views of Some Eminent Muslims Religious Thinkers', *Islam and the Modern Age*, Vol. 14, no. 20 (1983), pp. 104-114.

as the first Muslim to have undertaken such a work. The first volume focused upon the Bible as a whole, the second on Genesis up to chapter eleven and the third commented on Matthew 1-5.[44]

One aspect of this new program was to re-evaluate the basis for Muslim-Christian relationships. Sayyid Ahmad Khan established a journal, *Tahzib ul-Akhlaq*, with the aim of encouraging Muslims to distinguish between basic principles of their religion—which could not be changed—and their cultural practices—which could be revised. Since he believed that closer social relationships with Christians were desirable for Muslims, he urged re-examination of the attitudes and practices of his community. He believed that much Muslim behaviour was based on prejudice and custom. This meant, he thought, that the Indian Muslims should try to dissociate themselves from certain cultural attitudes and practices that they had acquired from their Indian environment, such as fears of pollution from foreigners and dislike of widow remarriages. Many Indian Muslims thought it wrong to eat with Christians, Sayyid Ahmad Khan insisted that there were *hadith* which affirmed the legitimacy of the practice. As part of this project of strengthening mutual knowledge and respect between Muslims and Christians, Ahmad Khan attempted to write a commentary on the Bible. He completed a commentary on Genesis 1-11 and Matthew 1-5. In his work it becomes clear that Sayyid Ahmad Khan considers the whole of the Old Testament Scriptures as a collection of books written by authentic prophets and therefore as genuinely revealed, he accepts only parts of the Gospels—which, after all have been written down only by *hawaris*—apostles, disciples of Jesus—as constituting what is designated by the Qur'anic term *ingil*. But by applying critical and proper exegetical methods, the genuine Evangel or *ingil* can be discerned within the four Gospels in the New Testament. Thus Sayyid Ahmad Khan assigns to the Bible a permanent and positive place in the life and teaching of Islam. The scriptures of Jews and Christians can and must be assessed positively as witnessing to the basic message of Islam, *Tawhid*. Even after the revelation of the Qur'an to Muhammad these scriptures continue to be relevant to Muslims, if only they read critically, that is, uninfluenced by the distortions of an

---

[44] Lloyd V J Ridgeon, *Crescents on the Cross: Islamic Visions of Christianity*, Oxford University Press, 2001, pp. 1-31.

erroneous Christian interpretation and in the light of the Qur'an's clear message of *Tawhid*. The Muslims as followers of Muhammad are, by the same token, followers of Jesus Christ who is their leader.[45] The pressure of his other activities prevented him from completing this work. His intention, however, remains clear, namely to encourage mutual understanding between Muslims and Christians based on scholarship. He did not think Muslims had anything to fear from such a process.[46]

In a later work Ahmad Khan elaborated on the reasons why Muslims could live in peace within British India. Rather than being *Dar al-Islam* or *Dar al-Harb*, India was *Dar al-Aman*—that is 'realm of security' in which Muslims could live according to the five pillars of Islam and also undertake Islamic preaching:

> ... as long as Muslmans [sic] can preach the unity of God in perfect peace, no Musulman can, according to his religion, wage war against the rulers of that country, of whatever creed they be ... Now we Mahomedans [sic] of India live in this country with every sort of religious liberty; we discharge the duties of our faith with perfect freedom; we can read our Azans (call to prayer) as loud as we wish; we can preach our faith on the public roads and thoroughfares as freely as Christian missionaries preach theirs; we fearlessly write and publish our answers to the charges laid against Islam by the Christian clergy; and even publish works against the Christian faith; and last, though not least, we make converts of Christians to Islam without fear or prohibition.[47]

Those who rejected Ahmad Khan's response to the Christian missionaries included Mirza Ghulam Ahmad, the founder of the

---

[45] Christian W Troll, 'Sayyid Ahmad Khan on Matthew 5, 17-20', *Islamochristiana* (Rome), Vol. 3 (1977), pp. 99-105.

[46] Christian W Troll, *Sayyid Ahmad Khan. A Reinterpretaion of Muslim Theology*, Vikas, New Delhi, 1978; and 'Sayyid Ahmad Khan et le renouveau de la théologie musulmane au XIXe siècle', *IBLA*, no. 2 (1976), no. 138, pp. 205-241.

[47] Quoted in L V J Ridgeon, *op cit.*, p. 12.

Ahmadi movement, and more significantly, the educated Muslims typified by the Deobandi clerics who despised Ahmad Khan and everything he stood for. The Mufti of Medina even issued a fatwa condemning him to death—Sayyid Ahmad Khan was called a heretic, a Christian, materialist, unbeliever 'the antichrist *(dajjal)*, and in every town and village *fatwas* were issued against him by the Mulawis, which declared him to be a kafir' (cited in L V J Ridgeon, *op cit.*, p. 13).

As one author has recently stated: 'It may not be too far from the truth to say that Ahmad Khan's understanding of Christianity and religion in general paved the way for future Indian Muslims to take the Muslim-Christian dialogue to its ultimate conclusion. For example, Amir Ali (d. 1928) believed that 'excepting for the conception of the sonship of Jesus, there is no fundamental difference between Christianity and Islam.' Professor Khuda Baksh viewed the new interpretation of Islam as indistinguishable from all true religions, especially Christianity, which he frequently praised. Ahmad Husayn went further and boldly declared: 'True Islam is but true Christianity writ short.' Such views either glossed over distinctive Islamic laws or re-interpreted the 'traditional' manner in which they had been understood.[48]

Another significant Indian Muslim thinker, was the poet-philosopher, Muhammad Iqbal.[49] Iqbal left India in 1905 and spent three years in Europe. He studied law in London and philosophy in Cambridge and in Germany. He received a doctorate from the University of Munich for a thesis on the metaphysics of the Persian mystical tradition. After his return to India, Iqbal exercised a major influence on his peoples self-awareness though his poetry, which stressed the need for a revitalized Islamic spirit. His poetry in Urdu and Persian has had a profound impact within his cultural *milieu*. He also advised many Muslim leaders, including Jinnah, on political issues. The statement he read to the Muslim League in 1930, which stressed

[48] *Idem.*, pp. 12-13.

[49] David A Kerr, 'Muhammad Iqbal's Thoughts on Religion: Reflections in the Spirit of Christian-Muslim Dialogue', *Islamochristiana*, Vol. 15 (1989), pp. 25-55; S Vahiduddin, 'Muhammad Iqbal's approach to Islam: Some critical reflections', *Recherches d'islamologie. Recueil d'articles offert à Georges C Anawati et Louis Gardet par leurs collègues et amis*, Éditions Peeters, Louvain 1977, pp. 321-332; and Annemarie Schimmel, *Gabriel's Wing: A Study into the Religious Ideas of Sir Muhammad Iqbal*, Brill, Leiden 1963.

the need for Muslims to retain control over the cultural development of their people, is generally considered to have played a significant role in guiding the movement that eventuated in establishment of Pakistan as an independent nation. His one published book on Islamic philosophy, *The Reconstruction of Religious Thought in Islam*, is unparalleled as an effort to restate Islamic principles in the light of philosophy, modern cosmology, and a new understanding of Islamic history. One thread which runs through many of these Indian Muslim thinkers reflections on Christianity, is a perception that Protestantism was closer to Islam than other forms of Christianity. Sayyid Ahmed Khan had observed that Luther in reinstating divorce was moving closer to Islam. The Protestant movement away from clerical celibacy, and away 'from legitimation of clerical authority by belief in the process of transubstantiation of the elements in the ritual of the mass', was perceived by Indian Muslim thinkers as steps toward what they understood as rationalism and freedom from superstition of Islam. The obvious charactering of Catholic Christianity (East and West) came on the whole from a lack of contact with the Catholic world and possibly a reflection of an outlook taken from many Protestant groups which operated in India, particularly in Muslim areas.[50] However, Iqbal arrived in a German philosophy department shortly after the death of Nietzsche (1900), and he was greatly fascinated by that German thinker's attack on the hypocrisies and spiritual mutilations of pietistic Lutheranism. Iqbal rated Nietzsche very highly as a prophetic critic of the modern West, but he felt that Muslims as critics could go even further and affirm ideals which could transcend the dilemma perceived by Nietzsche and other Western cultural critics. Iqbal, who died in 1938, perceived the First World War, the Russian Revolution, the Italian invasion of Ethiopia, and the Spanish Civil War as proofs of the failure of Christianity to provide rationale and practicable ideals. Iqbal thus viewed Christianity as a spiritual force which at its best had affirmed the spiritual dignity and freedom of individual human beings. As a tradition, however, he thought it had failed to affirm sufficiently the necessity of working to transform the

---

[50] We could note here also another Indian Muslim thinker's, Muhammad Ali's, enthusiastic responses to Harnack's criticism of patristic theology. Sheila McDonough, 'A Muslim Response to Harnack', *Islam and Christian-Muslim Relations*, Vol. 3, no. 2 (1992), pp. 292-303.

actual social, economic and political structures of the world in order that the perception of ideal values could be implemented by the creation of structures embodying justice. Most of his followers went to the new nation of Pakistan in order to work for these Islamic values.[51]

Some contemporary Christian approaches to Islam in India

The arrival of a the party of Jesuits at the court of the Mughal Emperor, Akbar (1556-1605), in Fatehpur Sikri, on the 28 February 1580, herald the first well-recorded Christian-Muslim encounter in India. Akbar specifically invited the priests to come and teach 'the Law'.[52] However, the modern history of Christian-Muslim relations in India, the Belgian Jesuit, Victor Courtois (1907-1960)[53] stands out as a pioneer and forerunner. He worked and published his appraisal of Muslim-Christian relations' years before the Second Vatican Council. Courtois saw as his foremost task making the Indian church aware of the Muslim dimension of its apostolic mission. From September 1946 until his death in December 1960, he almost single-handedly edited and wrote *Notes on Islam: A Bulletin of Information about Islam with Special Reference to India* whose subtitle was *A Help to Better Appraisement of Islamic Culture.* Courtois looked with admiration to the great Ramon Lull (1232-1315),[54] who, he said, studied Islam trying always to discover not what divides but what unites. This is the spirit that must be revived today, a spirit of intellectual fairness and charity.

---

[51] I owe much of my account of the thought of Muhammad Iqbal to S McDonough, 'The Muslims of South Asia (1857-1947)', *op. cit.*, 258.

[52] The work of Sir Edward Maclagan, whilst many decades old now can still be highly recommended: 'The Jesuit Missions to the Emperor Akbar', *Journal of the Asiatic Society of Bengal* (Calcutta), Vol. 65 (1896), pp. 38-113; *The Jesuits and the Great Mogul*, Burns, Oates and Washbourne, London, 1932; and Arnulf Camp, *Jerome Xavier SJ and the Muslims of the Mogul Empire: Controversial works and missionary activity*, Schöneck-Beckenried (Suisse): *Nouvelle Revue de Science Missionnaire, Supplementa VI*, 1957.

[53] C W Troll, 'A Pioneer in Christian-Muslim Relations: Victor Courtois, SJ (1907-1960)', *Vidyayoti*, Vol. 44 (1980), pp. 518-527.

[54] Dominique de Courcelles, *La parole risqée de Raymond Lull, entre le judaïsme, le christianisme et l'Islam*, Vrin, Paris, 1993; Dominique Urvoy, *Penser l'Islam: Les présupposés islamiques de l'"Art" de Lull*, Vrin, Paris, 1980); D Urvoy 'Ramon Lull et l'Islam', *Islamochristiana*, Vol. 7 (1981), pp. 127-146.

Insistence should always be made, not on what separates Christians from Muslims but on what may … bring them closer to each other and to the heart of Christ. We study them as enemies but as Brothers. To study we shall add much prayer.[55]

Courtois believed that what is needed is a sustained effort toward: '… friendly exchange of views with the idea of bringing about mutual understanding or concord,'[56] this however, must not be confused with 'the tendency of some well-intentioned speakers to slip over difficult problems: to ignore the differences between Islam and Christianity is not to solve them, nor is it a step towards better mutual understanding. These difficulties must be faced squarely in order to be understood and appreciated.'[57]

Interestingly he later said, 'The discrete fruit of mutual understanding and knowledge must needs be mutual friendship.'[58] This sentiment is echoed in the thought of the American Catholic writer David Burrell in his reflections on friendship and interreligious dialogue: *Friendship and the Ways to Truth,*

We may even say that history comes alive in and through friendships. Certainly what is most significant in the relationship between God and Abraham is its history; in this case, a history turned into a legacy inherited directly by two peoples, Jews and Arabs, and adopted by two religious families, Christian and Muslims. Scriptural reference to Abraham as a 'friend of God' (James 2: 23, citing Isaiah 41: 8) offers the ground for his descendants being called 'God's people' and becomes the cachet allowing Christians and Muslims to appropriate that title as well. Yet that proximity leads directly to the excoriation

---

[55] Victor Courtois' *Notes on Islam*, (May-June, 1949), p. 60. Quoted in Christian W Troll, 'Christian-Muslim Relations in India', *The Vatican, Islam and the Middle East*, (ed) Kail C Ellis, Syracuse University Press, 1987, pp. 295-307. I am deeply indebted to this article by Fr Troll for this section on Victor Courtois and the Islamic Studies Association.

[56] V Courtois: *Notes on Islam*, (June, 1957), p. 55.

[57] *Ibid.*

[58] V Courtois: *Notes on Islam*, (November, 1957), p. 113.

of Ezekiel 16; histories at one bind and empower, and friendships both require and acquire a history, if they are to live up to their promise.[59]

The recent history of Christian-Muslim dialogue in India, at least as far as the Catholic Church is concerned, is intimately bound up with the Islamic Studies Association (ISA). The ISA has its background in the debate within the Indian church regarding the need to come to a better understanding of Islam in India. The All-India Seminar on *The Church in India Today*, held in Bangalore, 1969, attempted to formulate a response to Vatican II. The Church expressed the need to set aside some people 'to study the Muslim religion, social life and culture in India, hoping by this means to come to a better understanding of this great people.' An overall effort by the Catholic Church in India to examine its response to the Second Vatican Council (which closed in 1965) and *Nostra Aeatae* culminated in the All-India Seminar in Bangalore. This seminar led to the Indian church's recognition of the need for large-scale dialogue on the great Indian religious traditions. Christian W Troll, identified a number of concerns articulated by the seminar: a) the change in the Church's attitude toward other religions, education toward this goal on various levels; b) a demand for a theology of dialogue; c) the need for experts in dialogue training and research, as well as for the promotion of dialogue on the scholastic level and for advising the Christian community at large; d) the setting up of centres to promote Christian-Muslim dialogue; e) the publication of suitable literature; f) development of the Christian ecumenical dimension of this work; g); and cooperation with non-Christians in the secular field.

At the *All-India Consultation on Evangelization*, held on Patna, 1973, a workshop was devoted to dialogue with Muslims. A detailed plan had been prepared by Fr. Wijngaards and sent to the *Consultation* but it was judged to be too elaborate.[60] However, the All-India

---

[59] David B Burrell, *Friendship and the Ways to Truth*, University of Notre Dame Press, Notre Dame, Indiana, 2000, pp. 2-3.

[60] Paul Jackson, 'Christian-Muslim dialogue in India', *Studia Missionalia* (Rome), Vol. 43 (1994), pp. 159-176. For an overall assessment of Christian study centres for Islam, see Jacques Levrat, 'En Inde. Le Henry Martyn Institute à Hyderabad le VIDIS a Delhi, une experience de dialogue', *Les Centres d' Etudes Chrétiennes en Monde Musulman*, Christlich-Islamisches Schriftum, Altenberge, 1987, pp. 120-158.

Consultation did publish concrete resolutions concerning Christian-Muslim relations. The need was stressed for courses, especially seminaries, on the pastoral approach to Muslims and Indian Islam, the founding of a Catholic Institute to study and engage with Islam and aid Christian-Muslim relations in India was recommend. Interestingly, it was also suggested that the Church should move cautiously in the 'Indianization' of the Church, 'that tended to be exclusively Hinduization.'[61]

The decisions taken at the *Consultation on Dialogue with Muslims,* held at Cathedral House, Agra, 28-30 March 1979, was the beginning of the ISA. As Paul Jackson, has record 'priorities in works to be undertaken were established; a Committee was set up to see to their implementation; and *JAMI Notes,* ('Jesuit Apostolate Among Muslims in India'—changed to *Salaam* in 1983), was taken over as a quarterly organ of communication. The quantum jump from ideals to implementation had occurred'. The *JAMI* group, which had been started by the German Jesuit scholar Christian Troll, had happily handed over its modest publication to fulfil the larger aims of ISA. It was also a symbolic action meant to underscore the Jesuit commitment to ISA. Three of the original five-elected committee members were Jesuits. In addition to supporting ISA, the Jesuits established VIDIS, Vidyajyoti, Department of Islamic Studies, which has published four important volumes in the series, *Islam in India: Studies and Commentaries.*[62] The objectives of the ISA include: 1) In the name of God and His ever greater service, to promote national integration of all Indian cultural, social, and religious groups; 2) To work toward harmonious relations among, Muslims, Christians and Hindus and other religions and social communities in India; 3) To promote study, socio-economic conditions and other aspects of Islam; 4) To promote the teaching and knowledge of languages, especially Urdu and 5) To give lectures

---

[61] Quoted in Christian W Troll, 'Christian-Muslim Relations in India', *The Vatican, Islam and the Middle East, op. cit,* p. 300.

[62] Christian W Troll, *Islam in India: Studies and commentaries: Vol. 1: The Akbar Mission and Miscellaneous Studies,* Vikas, New Delhi, 1982; C W Troll, *Islam in India: Studies and commentaries: Vol. 2: Religion and Religious Education,* Vikas, New Dehli, 1985; C W Troll, *Islam in India: Studies and commentaries: Vol. 3: Islamic Experience in Contemporary Thought by S V Vahiduddin,* Chanakaya, New Dehli, 1986; C W Troll, *Islam in India: Studies and commentaries: Vol. 4: Muslim Shrines in India: Their Character, History and Significance,* Oxford University Press, New Dehli, 1989.

and courses to students, colleges, seminaries and others on Islam and Muslim-Christian relations in India.NN The articulation of these goals underscores how far a Christian engagement with Islam as a religion has changed and how the future of Muslim-Christian relations in India have come to be symbolized by these frameworks of dialogue.[63]

Conclusion

Muslim-Christian relations in India, have been characterized by a variety of texture and context which is surprising in its richness. With the unfolding of a truly both dynamic and problematic engagement between Christianity and Islam as a global reality. The encounter between these two great monotheistic religions, as traditions of minorities within an Indian religious culture and society where Hinduism is dominant is unique for Christians and Muslims. It is still an unfolding event, which will continue to inform and enrich the meeting of Christians and Muslims worldwide.

---

[63] P Jackson, 'Association for Islamic Studies: Reflections on a Meeting', *Vidyajjoi: Journal of Theological Reflection*, vol. XLVI (1982), pp. 406-409.

MUSLIMS AND CHRISTIANS IN MALAYSIA, SINGAPORE AND BRUNEI: IN QUEST OF A COMMON VISION

Peter G Riddell

> By the year 2020, Malaysia can be a united nation, with a confident Malaysian society, infused by strong moral and ethical values, living in a society that is democratic, liberal and tolerant, caring, economically just and equitable, progressive and prosperous, and in full possession of an economy that is competitive, dynamic, robust and resilient.[1]

With the above words, Dr Mahatir Mohamad, Malaysian Prime Minister since 1981, announced his government's vision for the future in an address to the inaugural meeting of the Malaysian Business Council on 28 February 1991. This speech has come to represent the blueprint for the Mahatir government in its Vision 2020 project. This project aims for Malaysia to achieve developed country status by the year 2020, based on 'a correct balance between material and spiritual development'.[2] In this enterprise, Malaysia seeks to engage with the modern world, but in a way which consolidates, rather than sacrifices, the spiritual identity of the nation.

But given that Malaysia is a broadly pluralistic society, consisting of many faiths and ethnicities, we may well ask how fidelity to the dominant Islamic spiritual identity of the country is to be achieved without excluding the spiritual identities of religious

---

[1] Paragraph 5 from *Malaysia: The Way Forward*, working paper presented by Dr Mahatir Mohamad, Prime Minister of Malaysia, at the inaugural meeting of the Malaysian Business Council, 28 February 1991, in Shamsul, A B, *Malaysia's Vision 2020: Old Ideas in a New Package*, Development Studies Centre, Monash University, Melbourne, Working Paper 92-4, no date.

[2] Majid, Abu Bakar Abdul, 'Citizenry in 2020—The View From The 'Mahatir Window'', *Jurnal IKIM* 5/1, January/June 1997, p. 37.

minorities? Prime Minister Mahatir addresses such questions by stating that the overriding goal is to create '… a matured, liberal and tolerant society in which Malaysians of all colours and creeds are free to practice and profess their customs, cultures and religious beliefs and yet feeling that they belong to one nation.'[3]

In this task, Malaysia could be said to be at the very cutting edge of Islam's engagement with modern pluralist thinking. It would be valuable to explore Malaysia's progress along this path, with cross reference to the other regional Commonwealth states of Singapore and Brunei, and to seek to identify successes, pitfalls and remaining challenges to be surmounted in achieving the quest of 'a matured, liberal and tolerant society.'

A cross-section of religious adherence

Malaysia's population of around twenty-three million is divided among a kaleidoscopic variety of faiths. Government census figures suggest that 59 percent of the total population is Muslim, 18 percent Buddhist, 8 percent Christian, and 6 percent Hindu. The remainder of the population follows a variety of spiritualities, including traditional/primal religions among tribespeople in Sarawak and Sabah, and other religions originating in China, such as Confucianism and Taoism.

The distribution of these faiths is far from even, given Malaysia's diverse geography. Muslims are in a clear majority in peninsular Malaya, but in the states of Sarawak and Sabah the situation is different. In Sarawak, adherents of tribal religions constitute the largest group of the population at 35 percent, Buddhists and Confucianists represent 24 percent, while Muslims and Christians are represented by 20 percent and 16 percent of the population respectively. In Sabah Muslims are represented by 38 percent of the population, Christians 17 percent, and other faiths 45 percent.[4]

---

[3] Paragraph 11 from *Malaysia: The Way Forward, op. cit.*

[4] Statistics of religious adherence are drawn from the Adherents.com website. Statistical records vary to some degree according to which primary source is consulted. However, for our purposes the percentages cited for religious groups at both national and regional level can be considered as broadly accurate.

In this context, consideration of government policy is compelled to take account of contemporary ideas on pluralism, and this is a driving force behind the Malaysian government's Vision 2020 Project. But there are other forces at work as well, not least of which is the situation in Malaysia's neighbourhood.

Muslims and Christians similarly rub shoulders in most surrounding states. In Singapore and Brunei, religious plurality is also a fact. Singapore's population of just under three million is made up of 41 percent Buddhists, 18 percent Christians, 17 percent Muslims, 17 percent secularists, and 5 percent Hindus. Brunei, on the other hand, sees Muslims in a majority position at 63 percent, Buddhism at 14 percent, Christian at 8 percent, and other belief systems at 15 percent.

In the two other neighbouring states where the majority of the population is broadly of Malay stock, Indonesia's massive population of 220,000,000 is 88 percent Muslim, with Christians representing a minority of 8 percent, while in the Philippines the situation is almost a mirror image, with the principal religious statistics among the population of 81,000,000 being 91 percent Christian and 5 percent Muslim.

Thus Muslims and Christians cannot ignore each other's presence in the countries of the Southeast Asian region. However, of all the countries mentioned, the key is arguably Malaysia, as it is within its borders that religious minorities are most pronounced in terms of percentages. This situation forces the government of that country to engage with some of the most pressing and challenging areas of contemporary political and social thinking.

The coming of the world faiths to the region

Statistics provide a useful overview of particular communities, but they do not help us to see the human face of the communities concerned. In order for this to occur, we need to consider factors such as interaction between communities through trade, the clash of empires, and the movement of people groups through migration. We will therefore turn our attention to the factors which brought the world faiths to the Southeast Asian region, resulting in the multi-faith communities which exist today.

Traditional religion in that part of Southeast Asia which eventually played host to Islam and Christianity was focused upon tribal belief. These belief patterns, characteristic of traditional or primal religions, revolved around celebrations and rituals honouring spirits which were significant to the particular community. These traditional belief patterns predominated throughout the Malay world[5] until approximately the 1st century AD, and varieties can still be found today among certain tribal groups mentioned above in Sarawak and Sabah. But from that time on, dramatic changes were to affect the religious landscape of the Malay world with the arrival of the great world faiths. This occurred in three stages.

The first universalistic religion to reach the Southeast Asian region was Hinduism, brought from India via traders and cultural ambassadors. This route was to establish a pattern for future centuries and for the transmission of other religious traditions. The early centuries of the first millennium AD also witnessed the arrival of Buddhism in the Malay world, again originating in the Indian subcontinent and transmitted to Southeast Asia as part of the broader influx of Indian trade and culture to the region.

This development heralded the transition from small local power bases to the emergence of great Hindu and Buddhist kingdoms in the area. The greatest of these kingdoms during the first millennium AD was that of Srivijaya, centred in South Sumatra. Its power extended far beyond its immediate vicinity to encompass parts of the Malay peninsula and east Java, as well as islands located between Malaya, Sumatra and Java.

It is important to underline the complementary nature of Buddhism and Hinduism in the Malay world. The two religious traditions were gradually assimilated to the point where local courts drew on a synthesis of Buddhist and Hindu rituals. Once established, Hinduism and Buddhism, and indeed Islam at a later date, were to

---

[5] I use the term 'the Malay world' to refer to that area which is primarily populated by people of Malay stock and which comprises the modern-day countries of Malaysia, Singapore, Brunei, Indonesia and the Philippines. I distinguish this from 'Malaya', which is used to refer specifically to the Malay peninsular.

assume distinctly Southeast Asian characteristics which distinguished them from their South and West Asian counterparts.

Evidence of Islam's first arrival in the region is provided by archaeological, documentary and epigraphical data. The Malay state of Kedah was the site of the discovery of three coins minted during the rule of the 'Abbasid Caliph al-Mutawakkil (d. 861), one of which was dated to 848 AD.[6] Early Muslim contacts with the Far East referred to in Chinese court records provide us with an important point of reference for the Malay peninsula and its associated archipelago, which straddled the trade and travel routes between the Arab world and China. Travellers of necessity stopped off in Sumatra or the Malay peninsula en route to China.

The earliest Muslim monument in Southeast Asia is a gravestone at Leran (Gresik) in East Java, dating from 1082 AD. It may have been the grave of the wife of a merchant.[7] Such evidence is significant in pointing to the presence of Muslim individuals and groups in Southeast Asia, though it does not necessarily signal the establishment of whole Muslim communities as such.

The conversion of rulers marked the significant turning point in the history of Islam in the Malay world, and this represents the second stage in the changing religious landscape of the region. This development appears to have first occurred in the latter half of the 13th century in North Sumatra. Chinese court records of 1282 refer to envoys from the north Sumatran port city of Samudra-Pasai who bore Muslim names. Marco Polo touched on north Sumatra in his travels some ten years later and recorded that the state of Perlak was undergoing a process of Islamisation:

> We shall begin with the kingdom of Felech ... Its inhabitants are for the most part idolaters, but many of those who dwell in the seaport towns have been converted to the religion of Mahomet, by the Saracen merchants who constantly frequent them.[8]

---

[6] Awang, O B, 'The Trengganu Inscription as the Earliest Known Evidence of the Finalisation of the Jawi Script', *Federation Museums Journal*, 25, 1980, p. 44.

[7] Marrison, G E, 'The Coming of Islam to the East Indies', *Journal of the Malay Branch of the Royal Asiatic Society*, XXIV (1), 1951, p. 28.

[8] Wright, Thomas, *The Travels of Marco Polo The Venetian*, Henry G Bohn, London, 1854, p. 366.

The conversion of Malik al-Saleh, the Ruler of Samudra-Pasai, in 1297 is recorded by the great Malay classic *Hikayat Raja Pasai* ('Chronicles of the Kings of Pasai'). This conversion is supported by epigraphical data, in the form of a gravestone of this ruler dated to 1297. It is on the basis of such evidence that scholars now generally agree on a period of late 13th century for the initial establishment of Islam in the Malay world, with the port city of Samudra-Pasai being regarded as the cradle of Islam in that region.

The most significant archaeological discovery which provides persuasive evidence of the existence of Muslim communities in the Malay peninsula is represented by the Terengganu inscription, found on the north-east coast of the peninsula in the early 1920s. This is a four-sided stone inscription which carries a body of text with the date clearly written as Friday 4th Rajab 702 AH/Friday 22nd February 1303 AD. The text is devoted to the promulgation of certain Islamic legal provisions, suggesting that it was designed to be used by a local Islamic community. It is an important signpost pointing to the consolidation of Islam on the Malay peninsula around the same time that this was happening in the northern states of the island of Sumatra.

With the arrival and establishment of Islam in the Malay world, a series of powerful and regionally significant states developed throughout the island archipelago and the Malay peninsular. The first of these on the peninsula was Malacca, with the conversion of its ruler to Islam in the early 15th century being attributed to a dream which he had. This is described in the classic work of traditional Malay literature, *Sejarah Melayu* ('The Malay Annals'):

> ... a ship arrived from Juddah and proceeded to anchor. And from this ship a Makhdum disembarked, Saiyid 'Abdu'l- 'Aziz by name, and then prayed on the shore. And all who saw him were astonished at his behaviour and said, 'What means this bobbing up and down?' And there was a general scramble to see him, the people crowding together so thickly that there was not a space between one man and another and there was such a disturbance that the noise of it came to the ears of the Raja inside the royal apartments of the palace. And straightaway the Raja set forth on his elephant escorted

by his chiefs and he perceived that the Makhdum's behaviour in saying his prayers was exactly as in his dream. And he said to the Bendahara and the chiefs, 'That is exactly how it happened in my dream!'

And when Makhdum Saiyid 'Abdu'l-'Aziz had finished his prayers, the Raja made his elephant kneel and he mounted the Makhdum on the elephant and took him to the palace. And the Bendahara and the chiefs embraced Islam; and every citizen of Malaka, whether of high or low degree, was commanded by the Raja to do likewise. As for the Raja himself, he received instruction in the Faith from Makhdum Saiyid 'Abdu'l-'Aziz, and he took the title of Sultan Muhammad Shah.[9]

This account provides an important window into the nature of conversion to Islam by both the nobility and the masses in the Malay world during this period, even if the precise detail of this reported conversion might be open to question. The greatness of the Muslim Sultanate of Malacca, and that of its successor Johor, is the stuff of which legends are made, and provides fuel for a normative view among Malays today that Islam is the key component of their glorious past heritage.

What of the story of Christianity in the region? It represents the third stage in the coming of the great world religions to Malaya. The initial chapter in the account of Malayan Christianity goes back some considerable distance in time. Persian Christian traders established themselves in Barus, in western Sumatra, and on the west coast of Malaya, around the 7th century.[10] The role of traders in the initial introduction of Christianity to Malaya is a direct parallel of the Islamic case discussed previously. This community, which early Persian Christian documents record as established in Kalah (either modern day Klang or Kedah), merged over time with other local communities. In the process, the Christian faith brought by these traders disappeared.

[9] Brown, C C, '*Sejarah Melayu* or "Malay Annals"', *Journal of the Malay Branch of the Royal Asiatic Society*, XXV (2 and 3), 1952, pp. 53-54.

[10] Colless, Brian, 'The Traders of the Pearl. The Mercantile and Missionary Activities of Persian and Armenian Christians in South-East Asia. II: The Malay Peninsula', *Abr-Nahrain* IX, 1969-70, pp. 105ff.

For the next chapter in the local Christian story we must turn to the great state of Malacca, so crucial to the development of Malay Islam. The *Sejarah Melayu* not only describes the story of the Malaccan ruler's conversion to Islam, but also paints a detailed portrait of this most cosmopolitan of cities in the 15th century. With Malacca's strategic location on the trade routes between Europe, the Near East and China, Catholic emissaries travelled through the city en route to China in this early period.

The Christian presence in the city assumed a more permanent face with Malacca's fall to the Portuguese in 1511. The conquerors brought with them members of the Dominican and Franciscan orders who were committed to establishing a firm Christian presence in the city. Sixteenth century Malacca represented a real melting pot of faiths, with a Chinese temple dating from the Ming dynasty[11] cohabiting with mosques and churches established by the Portuguese. In 1641, the Catholic community stood at 20,000, with 20 churches having been established.[12] Nevertheless, at this time it was essentially expatriate, drawing on both European and some other non-Malay groups; owing to lack of personnel and other political and pastoral factors, the Portuguese did not achieve the same degree of success in evangelising the majority Malay community around them as did the Spanish in the adjacent Philippine islands.

In 1639, the European newcomers to the scene, the Dutch, drew up an agreement with the Sultan of Johor, under which each party agreed not to interfere in the faith of the other. Two years later, the Dutch captured Malacca from the Portuguese. During the period of Dutch control of Malacca, from 1641 to 1824, Christianity was consolidated to some degree, but the focus of the Protestant Dutch fell more on making inroads into the Catholic community and other non-Malay communities than in evangelising the Malays. With the departure of the Portuguese, the French were to become the most active missionaries for Catholic Christianity in Malaya.[13] But overall, Christianity remained an essentially expatriate faith during the Dutch

---

[11] C P Fitzgerald, *A Concise History of East Asia*, Heinemann, Melbourne, 1966, p. 249

[12] Ruck, Anne, *Sejarah Gereja Asia*, Gunung Mulia, Jakarta, 1997, p. 216.

[13] Roxborough, J, 'Early nineteenth century foundations of Christianity in Malaysia', *Asia Journal of Theology* 6/1, 1992, p. 54.

period, while Islam was firmly established as the faith of the majority Malay inhabitants of the peninsular.

The next chapter in the story of Malay Christianity occurs under the watchful eye of the British. Between 1786 and 1824 the British crown gained control over Penang, Singapore and Malacca, with these three locations becoming directly governed English colonies, known as the Straits Settlements. In 1841 the Sultan of Brunei ceded the territory of Sarawak to James Brooke, a British citizen, in return for his assistance with suppressing piracy in the region. In 1874 the Pangkor Treaty brought four peninsular Malay states into the British orbit, with British Residents advising the Sultans, but leaving matters pertaining to the Islamic faith of the Malays entirely under the jurisdiction of the Sultans. Between 1886-88 North Borneo, Sarawak and Brunei were placed under official British protection. By 1914 the remaining five peninsular Malay states were also within the British sphere of influence.

Missionary activities in Malaya flourished during this period. Catholic priests from Thailand established a Seminary in Penang in 1810, and the London Missionary Society established itself in Malacca and Penang from 1815. Though mission interest in the Malay peninsula fell away after the opening of China in 1842, a new surge in Christian activity accompanied the immigration of large numbers of Chinese and Indians.

An economic revolution took place in Malaya, especially in the period 1900-1920, as the region prospered from tin and rubber production. Chinese and Indian labourers were imported in large numbers. Between 1928-37 approximately 5,000,000 foreigners landed in the Malay peninsular,[14] a majority of whom were imported labourers. Although approximately 4,500,000 left in the same period, the massive turnover meant a rich field for harvest among Christian workers, who were not permitted to evangelise the local Malay population. But the growth of Christianity among expatriates during this period was not only due to mission outreach. Tamil migrants to Malaya included Catholics, Lutherans, Anglicans, and Methodists. Chinese Christians sometimes migrated as whole communities, as occurred in the case

---

[14] For detailed statistics on immigration to Malaya in this period, cf. Robequain, C, *Malaya, Indonesia, Borneo, and the Philippines*, Longmans, London, 2nd ed. 1958, pp. 119ff.

of the Methodist Foochows to Perak. This phenomenon repeated itself in the British Borneo territories, where there was substantial Chinese immigration, with Foochow Methodists establishing themselves in Sarawak and Basel Mission Hakkas migrating to British North Borneo (Sabah).

It should be noted in passing that the migration of large numbers of Chinese and Indians also brought about a significant increase in the numbers of people in Malaya, Singapore and the Borneo territories adhering to Hinduism and Buddhism. Thus in Singapore today, the majority faith of its predominantly Chinese population is Buddhism, as we have seen. This situation represents an echo of the past, as these were the very faiths which had preceded both Islam and Christianity to the region and which had been the predominant faiths in the area for over a millennium.

We have thus established a historical context for our study of the present day, which will form the focus of the remainder of this chapter. This historical survey has shown us that the region represented by modern Malaysia, Singapore and Brunei has a long social history of multi-faith pluralism, and that the quest of some community leaders today for interreligious partnership is merely another chapter in a lengthy search by the inhabitants of the area.

The early actors on the post-war
Muslim-Christian stage in Malaysia

Both Islamic and Christian communities have become increasingly organised in Malaysia since the Second World War. This is to be expected, given the transition from colonial status to full independence. In the process, there has been a distinct move away from local parochialism towards a greater focus on national issues, organisations and debates. This has been reflected in the establishment of national and ecumenical bodies.

On the Muslim side, a watershed event was the founding of the United Malay National Organisation (UMNO) on 11 May 1946. The formation of UMNO represented a reaction against the Malayan Union proposal put forward by the British colonial authority as a blueprint for a future independent Malaya. The Malayan Union proposal was scrapped under UMNO pressure, and the Federation of the Malay states which came into being in 1948 preserved a privileged position for the Malays in various ways. From this point on UMNO functioned as the catalyst of an increased sense of national identity, leading up to full independence for the Federation of Malaya on 31 August 1957. As it has evolved since its inception, UMNO has adopted modernist approaches to its primary Islamic identity, and it has been the senior partner in every government since independence.

Many would see the *Parti Islam SeMalaysia* (PAS—The Islamic Party of Malaysia) as being the antithesis of UMNO among Malay Muslims. It was formed on 24 November 1951, with the aim of lobbying for Islam to be made the official religion of an independent Malaya and for its government to be built upon Islamic structures and institutions. In the words of the Barisan Alternatif political alliance of which it is a member, 'PAS adopts a formal-legalistic approach to Islam'.[15] It is conservative and traditionalist in its ideological leanings, and has come to represent the principal opposition to the UMNO-led government.

Much more will be said about Muslim bodies in the following paragraphs. Let us now turn our attention to the Christian community, which has moved increasingly towards interdenominational and ecumenical co-operation since the Second World War.

The Malaysian denominational landscape is a mosaic, reflecting the multiple mission inputs by different Christian groups in previous periods. Catholicism represents the oldest surviving church, dating back to the arrival of the Portuguese in Malacca in 1511. It was joined by a variety of Protestant denominations in subsequent centuries, resulting in a diversity among Christian groups in Malaysia which can serve as both a weakness and a strength.

The most useful focus in exploring issues of Muslim-Christian interaction from a Christian perspective is at the ecumenical level, rather than the denominational level. This is because the most substantial contacts occur between Malaysian Islamic authorities and Christian umbrella groups, rather than individual churches or denominations.

---

[15] Barisan Alternatif Media Statement, 13 July 2000, http://www.barisanalternatif.org/archive/2000/biro/20000713_perpaduane.html

In January 1948 the Malayan Christian Council (MCC) was founded. It brought together local Anglicans, Methodists, Presbyterians, the Orthodox Syrian Church, the Lutheran Church, the Salvation Army, and the YMCA. From its inception it was presented with what it saw as an important opportunity, as the Communist Emergency which broke out in the same year led to the creation of over four hundred New Villages by the government to cut off communist insurgents from their base of support among local Chinese communities. Missionaries from various agencies under MCC auspices were very active in working among the New Villages, and they were supported by an influx of missionaries from other areas, especially China, with the expulsion of foreign missionaries after the Communist Chinese victory in 1949. These events provided a great stimulus to both the growth of the church and to denominational variety, with the missionaries involved coming from wide ranging denominations. Another phase of church growth occurred in the British Borneo territories in the post-war years, where there was a mass conversion movement among some of the animist tribespeople.

With the establishment of Malaysia in 1963, the MCC underwent a metamorphosis, becoming the Council of Churches of Malaysia and Singapore in 1967 and then the Council of Churches of Malaysia (CCM) in 1975. Both the CCM and its predecessors suffered from internal disunity. Problems of language worked against ecumenical effectiveness, as many churches were ethnically based and used the language of the main group in the particular church for worship purposes, thus tending to exclude Christians from other ethnic groups. Realising the problems inherent in this situation, the CCM has from the outset promoted the use of the national language in church life, with mixed success. But as Walters comments crucially, 'The real integration of ecumenism into the life of Malaysian churches had to wait until there were Malaysian issues which proved beyond doubt the value of this sort of co-operation.'[16]

---

[16] Walters, A. S. *Contemporary Presentations of the Trinity in an Islamic Context: A Malaysian Case Study,* Unpublished PhD thesis, University of Birmingham, 1999, p. 50.

Constitutional issues

The 1957 Constitution of the independent Federation of Malaya overtly equated Malay and Muslim in the following terms:

> Malay means a person who professes the Muslim religion, habitually speaks the Malay language, conforms to Malay customs.[17]

This inter-connectedness between Malay and Muslim is clearly explained by the prominent Malay scholar Chandra Muzaffar, who writes that '... Islam defines the Malay ... Islamic forms and rituals provide convenient channels for distinguishing the Malay from the non-Malay within the Malaysian milieu.'[18]

In order to cement the Malays, and their Islamic faith, at the very hub of the new state, the 1957 Constitution declared Islam to be the official religion of the State, though it accorded freedom of worship to other faiths. Only a Muslim could be Prime Minister, and while there was no restriction placed on Muslims propagating their beliefs to adherents of other faiths, the reverse was strictly prohibited under the Constitution. With the establishment of the Federation of Malaysia in August 1963, the above provisions were retained in the revised Constitution, as follows:

> 'Islam is the religion of the Federation; but other religions may be practised in peace and harmony in any part of the Federation ... State law and ... federal law may control or restrict the propagation of any religious doctrine or belief among persons professing the religion of Islam.'[19]

---

[17] Cited in Von Der Mehden, F, 'Malaysia: Islam and Multi-Ethnic Politics', J Esposito (ed), *Islam in Asia: Religion, Politics and Society*, OUP, 1987, p. 179.

[18] Muzaffar, C, 'Islam in Malaysia: Resurgence and Response', *Islamic Perspective*, 2 (1), 1985, p. 15.

[19] Schumann, Olaf, 'Christians and Muslims in Search of Common Ground in Malaysia', *Islam and Christian Muslim Relations*, 2/2, December 1991, pp. 244-245.

In spite of some inevitable inter-ethnic problems, the initial twelve years of independence for Malaya (and from 1963 the enlarged Malaysia) were remarkably stable politically. The country was ruled by the Alliance consisting of UMNO, the Malaysian Chinese Association (MCA) and the Malaysian Indian Congress (MIC). Matters relating to Islam were primarily the preserve of State authorities; the Federal government concerned itself with national affairs such as economic growth, political stability and internal security in the face of threats from a communist insurrection and a belligerent neighbour, Sukarno's Indonesia.

Race riots and Islamic revivalism

In the elections of 1969 the Alliance government retained power but with a significantly reduced majority, an event which triggered race riots in May of that year and led to a substantial reordering of the Malaysian political stage. A state of emergency was declared, and was only lifted in 1971. The elections had shown the critical danger posed by communal sectarianism if allowed to translate to the political arena.

A National Consultative Council was set up in 1969 in the aftermath of the riots, and it undertook a wide-ranging consultative process between the various ethnic groups, including Christian representation via the CCM. Output of this Consultative Council included the *Rukunegara* (Pillars of State), articulated as a measure to build national unity and to enunciate a common vision. The five pillars are belief in God; loyalty to the King and the country; upholding the constitution; rule of law; and good behaviour and morality.

In this way, the Malaysian government, as well as the representatives of the various ethnic communities, committed themselves to a framework for a common vision, based on the key ingredients of a civil society.

At the same time, the riots had demonstrated the necessity of Malay political unity, as far as it was achievable, and that Islam was a critical factor in maintaining this unity. Subsequent governments were to place much greater emphasis on developing Islamic institutions and consciousness, both to appeal to voters and to develop a more united Malay electorate.

The lifting of the state of emergency in 1971 led to the formulation of a new alliance, called the *Barisan Nasional* (the National Front), consisting of the three member organisations of the former Alliance (UMNO, MCA, MIC) as well as the Chinese opposition party, the Democratic Action Party (DAP), and the Islamic opposition party, PAS. This de facto government of national unity did not last, as PAS was forced to withdraw in 1977 owing to internal dissension in the National Front ranks. The DAP also later withdrew.

The social instability reflected in the events of 1969 occurred simultaneous to momentous events taking place on the world Muslim stage, reflected in a worldwide resurgence in Islamic identity. This resurgence translated itself to the Malaysian setting and was triggered by a number of factors. First, ethnicity played a significant part, with a rapid urbanisation of previously rural Malay communities placing the participants in largely non-Muslim environments such as west coast cities on peninsular Malaysia. This had the effect of encouraging the Malays concerned to seek traditional points of reference, such as their faith, in order to assert their identity in their new surroundings. Moreover, the ongoing influence of Western approaches and attitudes on the ruling elite in Malaysia encouraged an anti-Western Islamic resurgence amongst opponents of the government. This was in keeping with such developments in other parts of the Muslim world around the same time. Third, the increasing proficiency of non-Malays in the Malay language, resulting from the decision to promote Malay in the education system, forced Malays themselves to seek alternative symbols of affirmation of their ethnic identity to replace that of language which had hitherto served as an effective point of separation between the Malays and the non-Malays.[20] Finally, an important internal development which promoted an increase in resistance to authority in a religious guise was the passing of the Universities Act in 1971, which banned student political participation. The net result of this development was to encourage students to become active in religious rather than political groups, leading to an increasing politicisation of Islamic religious groups.

A range of external factors wielded a significant influence upon the rise and consolidation of *da'wa* resurgence in Malaysia. The

---

[20] Muzaffar, *op. cit.*, p. 14-17.

oil boom of the early 1970s proved to be a financial windfall for many Muslim nations. There was also the Iranian revolution of 1979 which represented a watershed in the rise of political Islam, and was accompanied by increasingly strident criticism by Muslims of the West and Western-influenced governments in the Third World.[21]

Many observers of Islamic events in post-independence Malaysia stress the unique aspects of Malaysia's Islamic resurgence, and discount any claims that it is merely a clone of Islamic revivals occurring in other parts of the Muslim world. The importance of the ethnic factor is one of the key elements to set the Malaysian resurgence apart. Schumann expresses this notion clearly in stating that '… the 'revivalist' camp … compares strangely with other Islamic revivalist movements which usually have a universal outlook, for here there is a strong feeling of Malay particularity.'[22]

The outward signs of Islamic resurgence within Malaysian society in the late 20th century were quite varied. Many were gender-related. They included more widespread use of the *hijab*, the modest female attire identified with Islamic consciousness. The PAS newspaper *Harakah* reported proudly in January 1999 that over 80 percent of women in Kelantan wore the *hijab*,[23] after almost a decade of PAS rule in the state. Furthermore, a limiting of intermingling between the sexes was noticeable, especially in PAS-dominated areas, where there was also a tendency for women to adopt less public roles.

In addition, an increased observance of Islamic dietary restrictions was quite pronounced, as was the rising popularity of literature and cassettes with Islamic themes, such as mosque sermons. Attention to content in the public media often translated to vocal opposition to elements considered unIslamic; for example, in early 2001 the national Conference of Muftis lobbied the government to limit broadcasting of Indian-made Hindi movies because they contained references to Hindu beliefs which could supposedly influence young Muslims in undesirable ways, and because they included passionate scenes between young men and women.[24]

---

[21] Nash, M, 'Islamic Resurgence in Malaysia and Indonesia', in Marty, M, *Fundamentalisms Observed*, Univ. of Chicago, 1991, pp. 706-707.

[22] Schumann, *op. cit.* p. 246.

[23] *Harakah Internet Edition*, 25 January 2001.

[24] 'Malaysian clerics rant against Bollywood', *The Times of India Online*, 16 February 2001.

The federal government response to Islamic revivalism

In responding to the rising mood of Islamic revivalism, the government sought to marginalise Islamic radicals by launching their own Islamisation drive. Political speeches became more embellished with Qur'anic quotations, and there was an observable increase in programs with Islamic content on the government-controlled television and radio stations during the 1980s.

Education was identified as a key target. The government undertook reforms to the educational system as part of its Islamization program. In 1975 the Ministry of Education under Education Minister Mahatir approved M$22 million for training of teachers of Islamic Studies. In the 1980s a compulsory course at university in 'Islamic civilisation' was introduced for all Muslim students, and on 24 June 1997 the Islamic Affairs Development Committee/Islamic Consultative Body joint meeting announced that this course was to be compulsory for all students of all religions.[25] In 1983 an International Islamic University was established; this was in part seen as a strategy to attract some of the thousands of Malaysian students who seek their Islamic education in Arabic-language institutions in the Middle East, principally Cairo.[26]

The government devoted considerable public expenditure to the establishment of various Islamic institutions. In 1974 *Pusat Islam* (The Centre for Islam) was established as the co-ordinating body for the government Islamisation programme. Further funding for its expansion was allocated ten years later. In 1983 the Bank Islam Malaysia and *Syarikat Takaful* were established as alternative Islamic banks and insurance bodies respectively.[27] Also established during the 1980s was an Islamic Economic Foundation and an Islamic foundation for social welfare.

A crucial part of the government-driven Islamisation program was the establishment on 3 July 1992 of the Institute of Islamic Understanding (IKIM), inaugurated by Prime Minister Mahatir.

---

[25] Hiebert, Murray, 'Required Lessons', *Far Eastern Economic Review*, 160/29, July 17, 1997, p. 22.

[26] *Asiaweek*, 19 July 1996.

[27] *Utusan Malaysia*, 20 June 1996.

The IKIM website states IKIM's mission in the following terms:

> Striving to uplift the understanding of Islam among
> Muslims and non-Muslims by highlighting its universal
> values and all-encompassing principles which are
> realistic and relevant to our daily lives … The Malaysian
> society which is fast changing in the economic, political,
> social and cultural domains demands a greater role of
> Islam as a source of inspiration, orientation and
> strength. The legitimacy of this is enshrined in the
> collective aspiration of Malaysia—to be a developed
> society in a holistic manner, a balanced quest for the
> material, socio-cultural and spiritual aspects. This is
> Malaysia's mould of development and Islam is central
> to this process of change. It is the role of IKIM to
> conceptualise, design and provide the required inputs
> of Islam in the process.[28]

State government responses to Islamic revivalism

It is important also to examine the responses of the governments in some of Malaysia's thirteen states to the Islamic resurgence. This level shows UMNO-PAS rivalry in some detail, and it also provides key insights into the dynamics of the relationship between Muslims and Christians in Malaysia.

PAS achieved a significant milestone in 1990 when it won the state elections in Kelantan, the northernmost state on the east coast of peninsular Malaysia. That victory gave it the opportunity to turn its Islamising rhetoric into active policy in the areas of state political jurisdiction.

The new government quickly moved to implement its policies. Manifestations of PAS Islamic legislation in Kelantan during the 1990s related to the banning of gambling, discotheques, karaoke lounges and unisex hair salons, as well as prohibiting the sale of alcohol

---

[28] http:/www.ikim.gov.my/s301-1.htm, copied June 2001.

to Muslims. Furthermore, the PAS government legislated that official permission should be obtained in order to organise carnivals, theatre performances, dances, beauty pageants and song festivals. In addition, the PAS state government legislated for gender-based checkout counters in supermarkets.[29]

With regard to punishments, the PAS government in Kelantan passed a bill in November 1993 instituting *Hudud,* or Islamic penal codes, in that state. It encountered strong opposition from UMNO-inclined Muslims, both within Kelantan and without. In response, the PAS Council of Theologians declared Muslims opposing the introduction of Islamic penal codes as apostates.[30] The government also ran into considerable opposition from non-Muslims, as it was committed to applying the Islamic penal codes to all residents of the state, regardless of faith. Here we see a clear example of non-Muslims being caught in the crossfire of intra-Muslim conflict, a feature which has repeated itself many times in Malaysia's recent history.

PAS success at the state level was repeated when it won the State of Terengganu for the first time in late 1999. In the same election PAS made major inroads into UMNO dominance in the states of Kedah and Perlis. Within days of the electoral victory, the new Chief Minister of Terengganu, Haji Abdul Hadi Awang, announced that his government would ban gambling outlets, the sale of alcoholic drinks, and entertainment centres.[31] From 1 January 2000 hotels in Terengganu were prohibited from selling alcohol. In addition, the new government introduced a dress code for Muslim women in the state, whereby they were to cover their heads 'and their dress should not reveal the 'aurat' or parts of the anatomy deemed alluring under Islam.'[32] Pressure was placed on local supermarkets by government officials to separate males and females into different queues at cash registers,[33] and the PAS authorities also announced soon after the

---

[29] *Asiaweek,* 6 June 1996.

[30] *Should Islamic Law Be Introduced in Malaysia?*, Kuala Lumpur, Malaysian Consultative Council of Buddhism, Christianity, Hinduism and Sikhism, no date, 1, citing *The Star,* 12 May 1992.

[31] *The Star Online,* 2 December 1999.

[32] *Bernama,* 20 March 2000. This requirement was not applied to non-Terengganu women visiting the state.

[33] Harrison, Francis, 'Malaysian state swaps tourism for morality', *The Guardian,* 21 April 2000.

elections that they would level the old Islamic tax of *kharaj* on non-Muslim run businesses, though it quickly adapted this announcement to the effect that these businesses could choose to pay a land tax in lieu of *kharaj*.[34] These moves represented an echo of policies tried and tested by the PAS state government over the northern border in Kelantan. In another parallel, Chief Minister Abdul Hadi Awang announced plans to introduce Islamic *hudud* punishments in Terengganu.[35]

These measures caused widespread concern among non-Muslims in Terengganu, as had occurred in Kelantan. In order to address this, and realising that minority support was vital if PAS was ever to displace UMNO and gain power at the national level, PAS simultaneously set out to woo non-Muslim minorities in the states it controlled. The new PAS government in Terengganu announced it would allow the rearing of pigs in designated locations by non-Muslims, a practice banned by the previous UMNO-led Terengganu state government. Furthermore, the PAS government in Terengganu offered over $260,000 to ten Chinese schools for development according to the schools' priorities, without state government strings attached. Similarly in Kelantan Malay reserve land was approved for the expansion of Chinese temples and schools.[36]

PAS policies in the states they controlled have pushed the stakes ever higher in the Islamisation contest between itself and UMNO. In response, UMNO governments at the state level have been pressured to adopt an increasing body of more overtly Islamic legislation in order to maintain its predominant position among the majority Malays. Several cases will suffice to illustrate this point.

In July 1997, three beauty contestants in the UMNO-dominated state of Selangor were charged with indecency for taking part in a swimsuit parade.[37] They were each fined $153. In Perlis, the UMNO state government passed a bill specifying that apostates from

---

[34] *The Australian*, 7 December 1999; *Utusan Malaysia*, 16 December 1999.

[35] *The Straits Times*, 14 January 2001.

[36] Cordingly, Peter, 'Mahatir's Dilemma', *Asiweek* 27/3, 26 January 2001.

[37] Matthew Chance, 'Islam's Grip Tightens as Malaysia's Boom Ends', *The Independent*, 22 September 1997; Ahmad Faiz bin Abdul Rahman, 'Islam's Grip Tightens as Malaysia's Boom Ends? How Ignorant Can Some People Get?', http://www.iol.ie/~afifi/BICNews/Afaiz/afaiz1.htm, copied June 2001.

Islam should be sent to rehabilitation centres.[38] Furthermore, the states of Penang, Selangor and Kedah gave consideration to amending the criminal code to forbid *khalwat* (a man and woman not married together being in 'close proximity') for non-Muslims.[39]

It would be wrong to suggest that such developments proceeded with unanimous support among the Malays. Voices of concern were heard from some quarters, including certain state Sultans. The Sultan of Selangor expressed a spirit of openness and compassion towards the rights of non-Muslims in commenting as follows after travelling through Selangor: 'I was very happy to see many mosques and suraus throughout the state, including Shah Alam. But I am very unhappy to see that there is not a single place of worship in Shah Alam for the non-Muslims ... I am also aware that portions of land have been identified for non-muslims' place of worship but its [*sic*] conversion has been stopped, perhaps by the state government or Selangor State Development Corporations (PKNS)'[40]

Nevertheless, the developments outlined above reflect what has been described as an 'escalating spiral of Islamization' resulting from UMNO-PAS rivalry to win over the Malay populace. As Roff states succinctly, '... UMNO-dominated governments have increasingly striven to match or outflank [PAS] rhetoric through national implementation of Islamizing policies.'[41] In the process, Christians and other non-Muslim groups have felt increasingly marginalised in terms of social policy and government priorities.

What is the situation in the states of East Malaysia? Both Sabah and Sarawak have retained a greater degree of regional autonomy since Malaysia's formation than the states in peninsular Malaysia. The environment in these states is quite different from that in peninsular Malaysia, as almost 90 percent of Malaysia's Christians live in the Borneo states, and constitute substantial populations in both areas.

Whereas in peninsular Malaysia the chief ministers of the various states are invariably Muslim, in East Malaysian states chief

---

[38] 'Creeping Radicalism', *Asiaweek* 27/3, 26 January 2001

[39] Batumalai, S, *Islamic Resurgence and Islamization in Malaysia*, Charles Grenier, Ipoh, 1996, p. 272.

[40] *Ibid.*, p. 273.

[41] Roff, W, 'Patterns of Islamization in Malaysia: 1890s-1990s: Exemplars, Institutions, and Vectors', *Journal of Islamic Studies* 9/2, 1998, p. 218.

ministers have at times been non-Muslim. This is particularly the case in Sabah, where the first Chief Minister, Donald Stephens, was a Christian during his first tenure of this post, though he later converted to Islam, which opened the way for him to serve as Malaysian Ambassador to Australia. Furthermore, Dato' Joseph Pairin Kittingan, the Catholic leader of Parti Bersatu Sabah (United Sabah Party), served as Chief Minister of Sabah from 1985 for almost a decade. Since its formulation the state constitution of Sabah has stipulated that when the Chief Minister was from the majority Kadazan (non-Muslim) ethnic group, the ceremonial Head of State would be a Muslim. Thus inbuilt within the political power structures of Sabah is an interreligious balance which is quite unique for Malaysia.

This has not prevented the drive towards Islamisation from influencing events in Sabah. The second chief minister, Mustapha Harun, introduced a number of measures designed to Islamise the state. Under his leadership, the Sabah State Constitution was amended to make Islam the official religion reflecting the situation federally. Furthermore Mustapha sought to extend his base of support to include the large communities of South Filipino Moro refugees and Indonesian immigrants in Sabah, and even targeted the large Muslim population in the southern Philippines.[42]

When UMNO entered the Sabah political scene to contest elections in the early 1990s, a revolutionary step was taken, which again sets Sabah apart from its west Malaysian state counterparts. Membership of UMNO, and the definition of Malayness, in Sabah was extended to include non-Muslim indigenous *bumiputeras* ('sons of the land'), such as the large Kadazan community.

Over the years, state governments in Sabah have provided financial assistance from public funds to both Christian and Muslim activities, whereas at federal level such funding support has only been provided for Muslim activities. For example, public funds in Sabah have been given to support the construction of a state mosque, a Catholic cathedral, an Anglican cathedral, and a range of other churches.[43]

Thus the responses of state governments to the Islamic

---

[42] Puthucheary, Mavis, 'Sabah electoral history', *Saksi*, 4, March 1999.

[43] Goddard, Hugh, 'Christian-Muslim Relations in Nigeria and Malaysia', Ridgeon, Lloyd, (ed.) *Islamic Interpretations of Christianity*, Curzon, Richmond, 2001, p. 240.

revival have varied from state to state, according to which party was in power.

The Christian response to Islamisation

One aspect of this Islamization drive, which was to have a significant impact on race relations, was the central and state governments' attempts to bring their administrations in line with religious requirements ... [Non-Muslims] entered the fray by activating their own organizations, mobilizing their members, or forming their own societies in order the champion the cause of their co-religionists in the face of the Islamists' challenge.[44]

The response of the diverse Christian community of Malaysia to the increasing Islamisation around it can be summarised in terms of seeking safety in numbers. The decade of the 1980s witnessed the formation of several new umbrella groups designed to strengthen the Christian voice in its discussions with the predominantly Muslim authorities of Malaysia.

In May 1983 the National Evangelical Christian Fellowship (NECF) was formed. This brought together a large group of Protestant evangelical churches, including the Assemblies of God, Baptist churches, Brethren groups, Full Gospel Churches, the Evangelical Free Church, the Full Gospel Assembly, Lutheran, Methodist and Presbyterian evangelical churches, the Sidang Injil Borneo churches in Sarawak and Sabah, and a number of other groups. The NECF joined the World Evangelical Fellowship, the worldwide grouping of evangelical churches.

Three years later the two largest umbrella groupings of Christian churches, the NECF and the previously mentioned Council of Churches of Malaysia, came together with the oldest church in the

---

[44] Bakar, M A, 'Islam, Civil Society, and Ethnic Relations in Malaysia' Mitsuo, N, Siddique, S, and Bajunid, O F (eds), *Islam & Civil Society in Southeast Asia*, Institute of Southeast Asian Studies, Singapore, 2001, pp. 69-70.

region, the Catholic Church of Malaysia, to found the Christian Federation of Malaysia (CFM). Its establishment in 1986 occurred as the federal government-driven Islamisation programme was picking up steam. The CFM is a broad-based Christian alliance, including almost all Christian denominations and representing approximately 90 percent of the Christian population of Malaysia, thus demonstrating a commitment to broad ecumenism which can serve as a model for other Christian communities elsewhere. The third of the stated aims and objectives of the CFM constitution strikes loud bells in terms of the dynamics of Christian-Muslim relations in Malaysia. It commits the CFM 'to look after the interests of the Christian community as a whole with particular reference to religious freedom and rights enshrined in the Federal Constitution.'[45]

Furthermore, reflecting the commitment of Malaysian Christians to joining with like-minded groups to address the challenges posed by Islamisation, the CFM, and its constituent groups joined an even larger umbrella body, the Malaysian Consultative Council of Buddhism, Christianity, Hinduism and Sikhism (MCCBCHS), which was founded in 1983. This body has been at the forefront in advocating for the rights of religious minorities when they have felt pressured or threatened by the Islamisation process taking place at federal and state levels.

Malaysian voices on Muslim-Christian relations

The UMNO-led Malaysian government has long been intractably opposed to any 'throwback' approach of returning to an ancient pristine society. It accuses PAS of having this as its core goal. UMNO has thus vigorously resisted the frequent calls by PAS leaders for the institution of Islamic Law at both federal and state levels. But in expressing its opposition to PAS policies, UMNO employs Islamic terminology wherever possible, in order to avoid any semblance of being opposed to Islam *per se*. The anti-PAS vitriol by UMNO is strong, as is the reverse. Prime Minister Mahatir has accused PAS of being a

---

[45] http://www.ccmalaysia.org/ie/images/together.htm, copied July 2001.

traitor to the Malay heritage and to Islam because of its downgrading of academic excellence, commenting 'Such people are the reason why Muslim countries are always left behind in development.'[46]

The stakes rose dramatically in late 1999 when the UMNO-led Barisan Nasional Coalition government lost ground in federal and state elections. The principal opposition parties—PAS, the Chinese-based Democratic Action Party, and two small reformist parties, the Parti Keadilan and Parti Rakyat Malaysia, formed a multi-ethnic alliance, calling themselves the Barisan Alternatif, to oppose Barisan Nasional. A little over half of all Malay voters in peninsular Malaysia supported the governing alliance, compared with over 70 percent in previous elections.[47] Much, if not most of the loss of support, is attributable to the campaign of the government against the popular former Deputy Prime Minister, Anwar Ibrahim, who was dismissed from his post in 1998, arrested, tried and found guilty on charges of indecent behaviour.

Lim Kit Siang, the former head of the Democratic Action Party, the principal Chinese opposition, said after the 1999 elections there was a danger that 'parliament in the next five years will principally become the battleground between UMNO and PAS for the hearts and minds of the Malays in the Malay heartland, resulting in a spiral of Islamisation policies.'[48]

This takes us back to the starting point of this chapter, with Prime Minister Mahatir's Vision 2020 Project which aims to create '… a matured, liberal and tolerant society in which Malaysians of all colours and creeds are free to practice and profess their customs, cultures and religious beliefs and yet feeling that they belong to one nation.'

There would seem to be an in-built tension between striving for a 'matured, liberal and tolerant' society on the one hand, and pursuing policies which entrench advantage and empower one religious group over other religious groups within that same society. It would be useful to listen to the voices of some of the main actors on the Malaysian Muslim-Christian stage to see if they can help resolve this tension.

---

[46] *The Star*, 24 June 2001.

[47] Jayasankaran, S, 'Mahatir Reaches Out', *Far Eastern Economic Review*, 1 February 2001.

[48] Reuters, 2 December, 1999.

Prime Minister Mahatir, who has for so long pondered on the dilemma posed by Malaysia's multi-ethnic society, accounted for the emergence of this multi-ethnicity in the following terms in one of his public speeches: 'the last two centuries of the country's history saw the arrival of Chinese and Indians who were recruited into the economic enclaves created by the colonial government. Then in 1957 Chinese and Indians were bestowed citizenship. This transformed Malaya, and later Malaysia, into a multi-ethnic, multi-cultural and multi-religious society. The reason for such magnanimity on the part of the indigenous Malay-Muslim population is that their value system is inclined towards tolerance and accommodation.'[49]

Here the key words are 'tolerance and accommodation': tolerance of the presence of other ethnicities and other faiths, and accommodation to the extent that they are free to pursue their own cultural conventions and to practice their own faiths. This is indeed tolerant and accommodating, but it is not sharing a common vision to the extent that all contribute on equal terms to the formulation of such a vision. To do the latter would be to run the risk of alienating some of Malaysia's majority Muslim population and to drive it into the arms of PAS, which adopts policies *vis-à-vis* religious minorities reminiscent of the classical Islamic concept of dhimmitude.

Criticism of the PAS approach was implicit in an interview given by Anwar Ibrahim in happier days, prior to his eviction from government and jailing. He justified government policies in the following way in 1993: 'There cannot be an Islamic agenda devoid of and oblivious to the realities of a multi-racial society … you cannot afford to be unjust to Muslims and non-Muslims. You should allow for freedom of worship for Muslims and non-Muslims. You should allow for the development of other language and culture. It is affirmative action in a constructive sense. To my mind it is a very Islamic position.'[50]

The successor to Anwar Ibrahim in the position of Deputy Prime Minister, Abdullah Ahmad Badawi, also expressed concern at the possible damage resulting from a spiral of Islamisation resulting from competition between the government and PAS: 'We must check the tendency towards any kind of extremism. And we should not

---

[49] http://www.ikim.gov.my/s301-civilization.htm, copied June 2001.
[50] Jamal, M (Prod.). 'Islam and Pluralism', *Islamic Conversations*. Epicflow, London, 1993.

play a game of one-upmanship with the Islamic Party. There will be no end to that game.'[51]

Nevertheless, when writers and politicians in Malaysia speak of striving for a correct balance between material and spiritual priorities, the understanding of the term 'spiritual' at the level of policy-making rarely allows for alternative spiritualities to that of the predominant Islamic faith. Indeed, leading figures accept that a reinforcement of spiritual values will of necessity be equated with dissemination of Islam through different media. This is articulated by Dr Ismail Bin Ibrahim, Director General of IKIM, as follows: 'The government is also making a concerted attempt to introduce Islamic values of honesty and integrity, of justice and compassion, of diligence and discipline into the public services. Indeed, the Malaysian government's oft-repeated commitment to a fully moral and ethical society—as envisaged in its vision of the future, Vision 2020—is infused by an Islamic worldview.'[52]

As for PAS concerns, they typically resonate with issues drawn from Islamic jurisprudence. A key concern has been lobbying by PAS spokespeople for legislation relating to apostasy from Islam. After there were a number of reports of Muslims renouncing Islam in the mid-1990s, a bill was brought before federal parliament in 1998 prescribing punishment for apostasy of up to three years' imprisonment or a maximum fine equivalent to about £900 or both.[53] This bill was proposed on two occasions by then PAS member for Marang Abdul Hadi Awang, who later became Chief Minister of Terengganu.[54] The UMNO-led government voted the bill down both times, stating on 4 August 1998 that apostates (*murtad*) would not face government punishment so long as they did not defame Islam after their conversion.[55] The PAS newspaper *Harakah* justified the PAS approach in the following terms:

[51] Vatikiotis, Michael, 'Umno Suffering Isn't Over', *Far Eastern Economic Review*, 14 December 2000.

[52] Ibrahim, Ismail Hj. 'The Image of Islam: An Insight', *Jurnal IKIM* 4/1, 1996, pp. 64-65.

[53] *Straits Times*, 17 April 1998.

[54] *Harakah Internet Edition*, 10 August 1998.

[55] 'US Department of State Annual Report on International Religious Freedom for 1999: Malaysia', Bureau for Democracy, Human Rights and Labour, Washington DC, 9 September 1999; 'Country Profile: Malaysia', Christian Solidarity Worldwide, http://www.csw.org.uk/malaysia.html.

The Anti-*Murtad* law introduced by PAS is meant to create better understanding between Muslims and non-Muslims as the Non-Muslims might not be aware how sensitive the case of a *murtad* is for a Muslim. It is a well-known fact that nobody renounced Islam for finding another religion better than Islam, but only because they do not believe any religion and therefore it does not matter what their religion is. They change religion to suite [sic] their convenience and this is to make mockery of religion. This Islam takes seriously. The fight is against irreligion and sacrilege and not against the non-Muslims.[56]

What of Christian voices? They articulate a range of perspectives and issues regarding Muslim-Christian relations. A common message is one of concern with the Islamisation process, both federal-government driven and that of state governments.

Many Christians do not accept that inculcation of Islamic values should be the only mechanism for bringing about the spiritual reinforcement of Malaysian society. Paul Tan, Director of the Catholic Research Centre, argues as follows: 'If the intention of introducing the subject of Islamic Civilization [in universities] was that the non-Muslims would come to understand Muslims better through it, then for the same noble reason the government should introduce a subject of other major religious civilizations so as to help the Muslims to understand the non-Muslims.'[57]

Christian voices are often most clearly articulated within the framework of lobbying by the umbrella groups described earlier. The MCCBCHS has regularly lobbied the federal government about the religious rights of non-Muslims, in a range of issues including establishment of new burial grounds, obstacles to construction of places of worship, banning of Christian symbols, banning of the teaching of non-Muslim faiths in schools, exclusion of non-Muslim

---

[56] Roslan, S M S, ' Islam phobia and the Extremist Preachers', *Harakah Internet Edition*, 17 August 1998.

[57] Basri, Ghazali *Christian Mission and Islamic Dakwah in Malaysia*, Nurin Enterprise, Kuala Lumpur, 1990, p. 32.

programming from the public media, and restriction imposed on the distribution of Bibles in hotels.

On a particularly sensitive matter, government legislation was drawn up forbidding non-Muslim faiths from making use of four terms (*Allah*, *Kaabah*, *Baitullah*, *Solat*) in any non-Islamic literature.[58] As the first of these terms was commonly used by Christians in Malaysia and Indonesia to refer to God, this legislation has left a lasting legacy of resentment.

The Malaysian Christian academic Albert Walters sees two main problems facing the Malaysian church. He points out that 'the challenge remains for the churches to relate themselves more fully to the soil of [Southeast Asia]—to get down to the rice-roots level of Asian civilisation.'[59] In making this observation, Walters is reminding us that Christianity, though it has had a presence in the Malay peninsula for 500 years, has essentially remained a non-indigenous phenomenon, projecting a profile of a foreign faith to Malaysian Muslims. This no doubt explains the observation by Ng that '... Muslim scholars are only interested in pursuing a dialogue with Western Christians rather than local Christians. After all, dialogue confers legitimacy and this is what Islamic scholars want *vis-à-vis* the West. However, dialogue with local Christians is avoided since it confers legitimacy on local movements.'[60]

The second problem identified by Walters relates to the mindset of Malaysian Christians. He asserts that they have tended to retreat into a ghetto mentality, resulting in a lack of commitment to engaging through their faith with the world around them. Walters calls on the church to strive to understand other religions around it, through study and contact of various forms.

The situation in neighbouring Commonwealth states

Malaysia is the key reference point for its smaller Commonwealth

---

58 Batumalai, *op. cit.*, pp. 262, 270.

59 Walters, *op. cit.*, p. 71.

60 Ng, K W, 'Dialogue and Constructive Social Engagement: Problems and Prospects for the Malaysian Church', *Trinity Theological Journal*, vol. 4 (1995), p. 32.

neighbours, Brunei and Singapore. It would be useful at this juncture to turn our attention briefly to these two states, to see how Christian-Muslims relations have been played out in the context of developments taking place across the border in Malaysia.

The 1959 Constitution of Brunei echoes that of Malaysia in stating 'The religion of Brunei Darussalam shall be the Muslim religion according to the Shafeite sect of that religion: ... all other religions may be practised in peace and harmony by the person professing them in any part of Brunei Darussalam.'[61]

In support of the Constitution, the Sultanate of Brunei proclaimed at independence in 1984 the National Philosophy of *Melayu Islam Beraja*, (MIB—Malay Islamic Monarchy), which gives clear priority to Islamic institutions and values. Special days in the Islamic calendar, such as the great feast days and the birthday of the prophet Muhammad, are observed publicly. During the fasting month of Ramadan working hours for government employees are reduced and sporting and entertainment activities are suspended. The Sultan publicly endorses daily Qur'an recitation prior to the commencement of the work day. The Brunei government website explains the purpose of the national philosophy in the following terms: 'The nation hopes that through the true adoption and practice of the MIB philosophy, the purity of Islam, the purity of the Malay race and the institution [of] Monarchy can be maintained and preserved as a lasting legacy for future generations.'[62]

A key instrument for the implementation of the MIB philosophy is the department of the State Mufti. On 1 April 1962, the first State Mufti was appointed by the Sultan of Brunei. With the crystallization of the national philosophy in 1984, steps were taken to more effectively empower the Mufti, and in November 1994 the State Mufti's Office was established separately under the Prime Minister's department. Its functions were threefold: to produce *fatwa*; to provide Muslims with *irshad* or guidance on Islamic laws; and to serve as a key reference centre for Islamic knowledge. In justifying

---

[61] 'US Department of State Annual Report on International Religious Freedom for 1999: Brunei', Bureau for Democracy, Human Rights and Labour, Washington DC, 9 September 1999.

[62] Cf. the official Brunei government website, http://www.brunei.gov.bn/government/mib.htm.

the establishment of the State Mufti's Office with funding from the public purse, the Sultan of Brunei issued the following statement on 24 January 1996: 'Experience taught us that when problems concerning Islam arise, it is very difficult if an Islamic nation, which has made the pure religion of Islam the official religion, does not have a scholar who is appointed strictly to be responsible for or concerned with the issuing of *fatwa*, the expounding of laws and injunctions (of Islam) for the betterment of the Brunei ummah and the country.'[63]

Thus while endorsing freedom of religion for the 37 percent non-Muslim minority of Brunei, the weight of government resources and support is given to the Islamic faith of the majority, with structures set in place to perpetuate this official support for the predominant position of Islam.

In terms of practical outworkings of these policies, friction between some among the Christian minority and the Islamic authorities has occurred. The Undesirable Publications Act has been used by the government to ban the importation of non-Muslim religious teaching materials or scriptures such as the Bible, and to censor magazine articles on other faiths, blacking out photographs of crucifixes and other Christian religious symbols. Government offices have also blocked requests to expand, repair, or build new churches, as well as places of worship of other non-Muslim faiths. The Brunei government has frequently clamped down on Christian ministry among Muslims.[64] However, it would be unfair to focus only upon such measures. Demonstrating openness to certain church activities, in February 1998, the Brunei government approved the establishment of the first Catholic apostolic prefecture in the country and the installation of Brunei's first apostolic prefect.

Singapore represents something of a contrast, which is not surprising given the vastly different religious structure of the island state. Its Constitution acknowledges ethnic Malays as the indigenous people of Singapore, which belies their minority status. The Constitution charges the government to give support to the political, educational, religious, and other interests of the Malay minority.

---

[63] http://www.brunet.bn/gov/mufti/p_ingsrc.htm, copied July 2001.

[64] 'US Department of State Annual Report on International Religious Freedom for 1999: Brunei', *op. cit.*

The Constitution of Singapore provides for freedom of religion, as do those of Malaysia and Brunei. However, unlike these latter two, in Singapore there is no official religion. All religious groups are free to preach their faith to adherents of their own and other faiths. Religions are required to register legally under the Societies Act. The Maintenance of Religious Harmony Act of 1990 bans inappropriate involvement of religious groups and officials in political ' affairs.[65]

The government of Singapore gives support to a special category of ethnic/communal organisations, in order to promote national goals and cohesion among the various communities. These bodies 'are monitored to ensure that their activities are not perceived to jeopardize the harmonious multi-ethnic, multi-religious model of tolerance, the perimeters of which are set by the state.'[66] The government provides some funding support, and insists upon strict accountability.

One of the key Muslim organisations in this context is MENDAKI (Council for the Development of Singapore Muslim Community), established in 1982 with the original purpose being 'to uplift the educational performance of the Muslim Community.'[67] Since then its activities have expanded to include social, cultural and economic development, though the primary focus still falls on educational development. It is registered in Singapore under the Charities Act.

In 1991, the Association of Muslim Professionals (AMP) was established by a group of young professionals 'who felt that MENDAKI had not been sufficiently proactive in tackling the community problems.'[68] It too came into existence with the blessing and financial support of the Singapore government. The AMP has wide-ranging activities, covering early childhood programmes, operation of a student centre for older youth, family education and

---

[65] 'US Department of State Annual Report on International Religious Freedom for 1999: Singpapore', Bureau for Democracy, Human Rights and Labour, Washington DC, 9 September 1999.

[66] Siddique, S, 'Islam and Civil Society: A Case Study from Singapore', Mitsuo, Siddique and Bajunid, *op. cit.*, p. 136.

[67] http://mendaki.org.sg/mendakiNew/about.htm, copied July 2001.

[68] Siddique, *op. cit.* 136.

support programmes, training of workers and research activities.[69] In the words of one of its most prominent members, 'The AMP views *Malay/Muslim Singaporeans* as a *dynamic community* within a *larger Singaporean society*—in other words, as a component of a multi-ethnic, multi-religious society.' [70]

The Singaporean government also maintains links with the Muslim community via the Islamic Religious Council (MUIS) which was established as a government statutory body under the Administration of Muslim Law Act in 1968.[71] The body defines its vision on the government-hosted website as 'To fulfil its roles as the supreme Islamic authority of Singapore and to guide in the building of an exemplary Muslim community.'[72] The MUIS has an important advisory function, giving counsel to the government when appropriate on matters pertaining to the Muslim community. MUIS administers the Islamic Centre of Singapore (ICS) which hosts the offices of the Secretariat staff, meeting and conference rooms, a library, an audio-visual room, and a Syariah Court of Appeal.

In 1998, the Singapore Parliament passed the Administration of Muslim Law (Amendment) Bill, which amended the 1968 Act 'to confer concurrent jurisdiction on the civil courts and the Syariah Court in certain matters, to extend the functions of the Majlis Ugama Islam, Singapura, [MUIS] and to extend the powers of the Syariah Courts.'[73]

Furthermore, the government of Singapore provides some financial assistance for the construction and maintenance of mosques. Singapore's community of 372,000 Muslims has over 70 mosques. The MUIS prepares a standard sermon every week, which is distributed to all mosques in electronic form.[74]

One cannot fail but be impressed by the way that organisations such as MENDAKI, AMP and MUIS have facilitated the emergence of a new, dynamic, educated class among Singaporean Muslims, a community which had long been one of the most

---

[69] http://www.amp.org.sg/about_us/index.html, copied July 2001.

[70] Siddique, *op. cit.* p. 138.

[71] A Hindu Advisory Board also functions as a statutory body under government auspices, providing further evidence of the government's determination not to privilege any particular faith community over others.

[72] http://www.muis.gov.sg/about/index.asp, copied July 2001.

[73] *Al-Mahjar*, 3/2, December 1998, p. 3.

[74] 'Singapore mosques wire up to stay relevant', *Utusan Express*, 5 January 2001.

disadvantaged groups in Singapore in socio-economic terms. Government-supported efforts to improve the economic well-being of the Muslim Malay minority paid great dividends in the first 10 years following the launch of a range of new policies in the early 1980s. The 1990 Singapore Census recorded an increase in the average household income of Singaporean Malays from S$896 in 1980 to S$2246, 'a 150 percent improvement in 10 years'.[75] Thus much credit must go to the pluralistic, flexible policies of the government of Singapore, policies which promote a sense of shared formulation and ownership of national goals among the diverse ethnic and religious communities resident in the island state.

Conclusion

There is no doubt that the Vision 2020 project is an important pioneering experiment. Malaysia is at the cutting edge of thinking on pluralism within a majority Islamic context. As is succinctly stated by Dr Ismail Bin Ibrahim, 'Muslims in Southeast Asia ... have shown how Islam can be a positive force in building just, harmonious, compassionate societies ... [They] have a unique opportunity to blaze a new trail into the future—a trail which will light the skies for the whole of humanity.'[76]

In the process, an uneven playing field needs to be levelled. This situation can be traced right back in history, as although both Islam and Christianity have been established in the region of modern Malaysia for centuries, the paths they followed have been somewhat different. From the outset Islam threw down roots into indigenous Malay communities whereas Christianity has tended to focus largely on expatriate groups. The results are, first, that religion is often identified with ethnicity, which can be a volatile mix, and second that Christianity still tends to be regarded as a foreign faith, despite its 500-year presence in the region.

The articulation of the *Rukunegara* in 1969, after a national consultative process, provided key ingredients for the development

---

[75] http://mendaki.org.sg/mendakiNew/about.htm, copied July 2001.

[76] Ibrahim, *op. cit.*, pp. 65-66.

of a common vision. But this has been somewhat undercut by the Islamisation process within Malaysian institutions and society which has been fuelled by rivalry between the two main political groups among the Malays.

The priority allocation of public resources to the establishment and support of Islamic institutions has led to a feeling of marginalisation among Malaysian Christians and other non-Muslim groups. This has been expressed in various forums. Malaysian governments have been very open to the expression of such views, which is consistent with the core principles of Vision 2020. This augurs well for Christian-Muslim relations in the future.

Malaysia's challenge is to take the exciting initiative which Vision 2020 represents and to forge a genuinely 'democratic, liberal and tolerant society' based on a common vision which is both articulated and owned by all faith communities. The infusion in society of wide-ranging faith values, including Islamic and Christian perspectives, will go a long way towards the development of such a common vision. In this the models of Singapore and Sabah can provide useful points of reference. If this is done, there is no reason that both Christianity and Islam, as well as the other faiths, could not jointly 'blaze a new trail into the future.'

THE NEED TO REDISCOVER COMPASSION:
SOUTH-EAST ASIA AND SOUTH ASIA
Dato' Ismail bin Haji Ibrahim

Introduction

I am gratified that the theme for this session concerns 'rediscovering compassion', rather than just 'discovering' it. The need for 'rediscovery' suggests that something of it had been lost along the way, but not entirely. There is no need to reinvent the whole wheel.

The world's great religions share many universal values. The quest to rediscover compassion today should therefore be a joint effort. It is complementary and mutually enhancing across the different faiths, not a zero-sum game.

The need to undertake this quest is obvious—sometimes, painfully so. Even in the age of space exploration, so much of human suffering and misery on Earth is the results of human failings. This quest to rediscover compassion serves not only to realise more of our respective religious truths. It is also essential to ensure the continued survival and success of our civilisation.

How then does this universal quest translate into a fact of everyday life? Much will depend on how we allow human relations within and between societies, as nations, to develop.

South-East Asia (re-)visited

Allow me at this point to refer to the experience of South-East Asia. As this conference has taken Indonesia out of South-East Asia and placed it in Australasia, I have a choice of speaking about the rest of South-East Asia and South Asia as designated, or about Indonesia's experience with Muslim-Christian tension, but that would now seem to be outside my regional scope.

I have chosen to speak on South-East Asia, which happens to be my home region. In abiding by my given remit, my remarks will address some bilateral relations in South-East Asia, as well as relations in South Asia and within Malaysia.

The historical links between South Asia and South-East Asia are clear. Many believe about six centuries ago, Islam was brought by traders from the Indian sub-continent, mainly Gujarat and the Coromandel Coast, to the west coast of the Malay Peninsula. From the early Malay states, Islam spread rapidly to the rest of the Malay archipelago in South-East Asia.

Migration from South Asia especially during the colonial period has also helped to configure the demographic landscape of parts of South-East Asia, in particular Malaysia. But since the era of decolonisation and national independence half a century ago, links between these two regions have become less pronounced.

To visitors from afar, it is astonishing how a group of small countries clustered so closely together in South-East Asia can have such diverse cultures and histories. Much the same can be said of the different regions of Asia, which is after all the world's largest and most diverse continent.

It is important to note these differences, as well as the similarities. But diversities are not divergences. It is also important to be mindful of the differences and similarities that are real, as distinct from those which are merely perceived.

Locally, the classic text of the *Sejarah Melayu* or 'Malay Chronicles' provides insights into political development and social custom. But this text is as much an account of fable and legend as it is a work of history.

On the other hand, distant observers tend to presume that Islam was spread everywhere through conquest and force, thereby encountering local resistance and reaction. But this experience of it in parts of Central and West Asia was not replicated in East Asia, in particular South-East Asia.

Unlike certain other regions of the world, religious affiliation and inter-faith relations in South-East Asia have long been placid and liberal. This is partly because of the easy temperament of the peoples, and partly because of the great and long-established mixes of culture and ethnicity: of race, custom and belief.

Between the Malays of Malaysia and Indonesia, those in Malaysia are more cosmopolitan. Anthropologically speaking they are 'Deutero-Malay,' being mixes from antecedents of Indian, Arab, Thai, Chinese and European extraction.

The story of Islam in South-East Asia is perhaps typical of this particular character of this region. The history of Islam in early Malaya further exemplifies this nature.

Islam arrived on the shores of the early Malay kingdoms on the Malay Peninsula, in particular the Malacca Sultanate. It came principally with Muslim Indian traders and merchants. The philosophical mysticism, its aspects of metaphysics or mysticism *(tasawwuf),* the religion practicality and universality have attracted the native population who embraced Islam. The process is through acceptance and cultural assimilation rather than through force or decree.

Thus through this cultural and gradualistic process, Islam in Malaya won adherents. Then from the Malay Peninsula, it spread outwards similarly to the rest of the Malay Archipelago.

This 'regional tradition' of organic assimilation had been established earlier in the spread of Buddhism and Hinduism in South-East Asia. These great religions then grew to their respective zeniths in the Buddhist empire of Sri Vijaya in Sumatra, and the Hindu empire of Majapahit in Java. Elements of the latter survive to this day on the Hindu island of Bali.

Even where the spread of Islam was accompanied by the founding of dynasties and empires in South-East Asia, the native population was never coerced into adopting the faith. Until today, this liberal mode of diffusion has also characterised the spread of the other major religions in the region—Buddhism, Christianity, Hinduism and Taoism.

Given this somewhat harmonious background, the prospect of rediscovering compassion in this region should not be so remote. It might be said that in South-East Asia, compassion in the various faiths has not really been lost, but just concealed for a time by layers of 'modern' imperatives.

Among the most interesting countries in this region for our consideration is Malaysia. Malaysia is an Islamic country—having a majority of Muslim populations and Islam has been integral in its socio-cultural changes since the early time. However, Malaysia also is a showcase of a pluralistic society where major race, ethnics, religions and sizeable minority communities co-exist in harmonious and productive manners.

Malaya attained independence from the British in 1957, when the country had already become exposed to both Catholic and Protestant Christianity from its European colonisers—the Portuguese, the Dutch and the British. This was centuries after the arrival of Buddhism, Hinduism and Islam.

Then in 1963, Singapore, Sarawak and Sabah joined the 11 states of the Federation of Malaya to form Malaysia. All these states had also been under the British. Singapore however left two years later.

Sabah, or the former British North Borneo, is a highly cosmopolitan state in itself. Its previous experience of the Sulu Sultanate and its proximity to the southern Philippine island of Mindanao had exposed it to Islam. At the same time, its experience of British rule and exposure to the Philippines as a whole, which is predominantly Christian, made Christianity a permanent feature of its cultural landscape.

None of this has created any problems within Sabah society, with its three-dozen native ethnic groups. Sabah today is host to Filipino migrants, numbering some twenty per cent of its population. Such demographics might destabilise many countries in other regions, both developed and developing. But Sabah remains self-assured, and it is because rather than in spite of this heterogeneity that Sabah has felt so comfortable within a very multi-ethnic Malaysia.

Problems that occasionally arise tend to originate externally. There was the decades-long Philippine claim to Sabah, a political position that Manila has now effectively abandoned. More lately, there is the much-publicised kidnap of twenty-one hostages on Sabah's Sipadan Island, by the Abu Sayyaf Islamic group from the Philippines. Nearly half of the hostages are Malaysian and one of them was a Muslim.

Apart from the fear, distress and risks to life posed by the kidnapping, the question that might be asked quite legitimately is: 'If a Muslim group like the Abu Sayyaf can kidnap even innocent

Muslims in staking their demands, what compassion can they have for anyone, in particular the non-Muslims?'

The answer is, first, Islam does not sanction the kidnapping of innocent people, whether Muslim or non-Muslim. This is regardless of how strongly the perpetrators may feel about their cause. Second, it is doubtful if the Abu Sayyaf is itself a legitimate Islamic group advancing a political struggle as it claims.

It is not simply because the Abu Sayyaf has become an embarrassment that its religious credentials are to be rejected. Besides their dubious and criminal methods, their obvious confusion and inconsistency cannot but make them out to be erratic outlaws.[1]

Most Muslim Filipinos in Mindanao, or Moros, pledged to a political struggle as a people are represented by either the MNLF (Moro National Liberation Front) or the MILF (Moro Islamic Liberation Front). Although the latter continues its armed struggle against Manila to this day, neither the Abu Sayyaf nor the MILF identifies with each other.

No doubt the MILF would argue that it does not lack compassion any more than the largely Christian forces of the Philippine military. For its part, the Abu Sayyaf enjoys little legitimacy, both among fellow Moros and within the international Islamic community. However, regardless of the precise nature of the grievances, armed struggle continues in the Philippines. But this remains only a minority option in ways to resolve political differences in the region.

When Singapore left the Malaysian Federation in 1965, the occasion was not without some bitterness. For Malaysia, Singapore had walked out. But for Singapore, it had been ejected. That was about the extent of the disagreement between the two countries, which was essentially over the political direction of Malaysia. Although occasional differences-as-irritants emerge over a range of issues, these are minor in significance.

---

[1] Confusion over their leaders' remarks, the vagueness of their demands, and the outright criminality of their methods have posed serious questions about the genuine religious convictions of the Abu Sayyaf. Such doubts are shared by Muslim and non-Muslim governments, agencies and observers. These problems have also hampered attempts by governments to negotiate in the kidnapping.

Singapore and Malaysia are not only next-door neighbours, but also trade extensively, with strong mutual investments, share historical roots, have close kin among their respective peoples, and are fellow members of ASEAN (Association of South-East Asian Nations),[2] the Commonwealth, and the Five-Power Defence Arrangement.

Singapore's predominantly ethnic Chinese community, which is mostly Buddhist, Taoist or Christian, works well with other communities in Singapore and Malaysia—including Malaysia's predominant Muslim Malay community. It is here that religious and other societal differences do not pose a significant or noticeable obstacle to normal, healthy inter-state relations.

The occasional differences that arise tend to be for reasons of history and national sentiment. That is to say, they emerge principally from political causes.

Consider the most serious external conflict ever suffered by Malaysia—the Indonesian *Konfrontasi* (Confrontation) in the 1960s. President Sukarno's Indonesia had taken offence at the formation of Malaysia, and launched a very political campaign against Kuala Lumpur, including sporadic acts of subversion.

The world's largest Muslim nation, peopled mostly by Malays, had all but declared war on its neighbour, another nation led and peopled mostly by Muslim Malays. Once again, a political dispute between states had arisen for political reasons. And once these very political considerations had emerged, the very non-religious world of *Realpolitik* takes over. Notions of a shared religious identity and other commonalities then become secondary. In a political world, political criteria naturally take precedence.

If further confirmation of this is needed, consider the decades-long skirmishes undertaken by Malaysia against several insurgent groups on its border with Thailand. For a whole generation, in the jungle areas along their common border, a largely Muslim Malaysia and a predominantly Buddhist Thailand have joined forces

---

[2]   ASEAN is widely considered one of the world's most successful regional groupings. The equivalent organisation for South Asia is SAARC (South Asia Association for Regional Cooperation), which has not been as successful. How might SAARC benefit from ASEAN's experience?

to root out not just atheist communist guerrillas but also separatist groups that are either Buddhist or Muslim.

Insurgent groups share the threat potential of destabilising the politics of the state, even if they also happen to share the religion of the state. The security of the state, which is a political consideration, comes before any other consideration.

Malaysia

In political disputes and conflicts, political differences are more significant than religious ones both within a country and between countries. Malaysia's worst domestic conflict, the violent rioting of May 1969, had been over economic disparities and racial identities. Despite the horrors of the time, religious differences were not a problem.

Since the mid-1980s, domestic political disputes were between different groups of Muslim Malays, among the Chinese, Indian and a small ethnic group of Kadazan in Sabah. The ruling UMNO (United Malays national Organization) party has since seen three splits, with disgruntled members leaving the party to set up three opposition parties. Among the three only PAS (Pan Malaysia Islamic Party) became the main opposition party in the parliament.

Malaysia, due to its heterogeneous nature is alive politically. Perhaps by looking at the Malaysia's political democracy model which is working well with the difference communities and religious traditions, one could gauge the degree of compassion which has been internalised and put into practice.

Malaysia model exhibits the following attributes:

- The importance of power-sharing among the different ethnic groups;
- The importance of democratic processes in accommodating ethnicity provided there is also regulation and effective control on the destructive tendency;
- The role of the economic growth which does not

ignore the economic redistribution and keep in mind the needs and aspiration of the different communities;
• The willingness to accept cultural and religious diversities as a source of strength (the resilience and stability of the nation state);
• The importance of a commitment to balance and accommodation at the attitudinal level.

Much the same can be said of South-East Asia in general. Where religious differences appear to be a cause of conflict, they are often found to be only a 'distress multiplier', or a convenient excuse for an intrinsically political or economic disjuncture. This region today does not see the kind of communal, Christian-Other conflict that South Asia is lately experiencing. After the Khmer Rouge experiment with genocide in Cambodia a generation ago, there has not been the kind of mayhem and killings as seen recently in Gujerat and Orissa. Malaysia's own tragic experience is now more than three decades ago.

The universal condition that gives vent to ugly racism is a public disposition to crude and demeaning caricature of certain groups in society. It is easy to stereotype certain people, particularly when their professed identity such as religion clearly distinguishes them from others. And it is just as easy to scapegoat a group of people once they are suitably condemned as an undesirable stereotype.

Stereotyping and scapegoating are the basic ingredients for prejudice, encouraging all manner of communal hatred including the vilest pogroms and genocides. Throughout history, we seem to allow the lowest elements of humanity to corrupt and destroy the rest. Where will it end? Will there even be an end?

It is here that an appeal must be made for a return to compassion, at least among intellectuals as influential individuals in society. A society's intelligentsia must no longer stay silent or turn away in the face of horrific absurdities. Scholars have a duty to society, and they perform this best when they do their work well. They have to be more analytical, more professional, more honest and generally more critical in their work.

They should not unquestioningly accept such given notions

as religious differences necessarily being the causes of political conflict. They must rise above simple media portrayals of complex historical or political relationships that may or may not have religious implications. They need to resist the popular prejudices in society. They must question any seeming justification for a so-called 'clash of civilisations.' To fail to do so would be to commit a grave injustice on all religions, and against their own professional reputations.

Worse still, in an imperfect world of human frailties, unthinking presumptions by supposed scholars encourage political leaders to compromise on their humanity, exchanging compassion for expediency. 'Scholarly sanction' for inhumane policy only jeopardises human civilisation. Chauvinistic leaders then emerge to perpetrate gross barbarities on the human race.

With the proper attitude and approach, scholars can expose popular mythologies for what they are—however widespread they may be. This will not only dispel common prejudices and their tragic consequences, but also help to resolve the real problems, now demystified and clearly identified.

However, this does not mean that we should underrate, ignore or deny the dangers of religious animosities where they actually exist. What is needed is a properly balanced perspective on these matters—and then perhaps a more compassionate position can be found for public policy issues.

South Asia

At this point, let us consider briefly the situation in South Asia. The differences and similarities between this region and South-East Asia are interesting and instructive, particularly for an 'interested near-outsider'.

The Partition of British India seemed only like wishful thinking to its proponents at the time. Then circumstances prevailed to turn that passing possibility into an immutable fact. In time, its consequences came in a series of events that made independent Pakistan a reality that everyone had to live with. The eloquence of Jinnah won against the force of Indian nationalism. Although the prospect of an independent Pakistan had not been perceived as inevitable, its proponents might want to trace its historical legitimacy back at least to Alexander of Macedonia and Darius of Persia.[3]

The pain of Partition and of its continuing aftermath has to be balanced against the perceived injury of non-Partition, had a brave new India emerged whole. However, such value judgements are highly subjective, hypothetical, and therefore of academic interest only. Partition became a fact of history. After Pakistan, Bangladesh emerged. The rest of India remains heterogeneous—but for how much longer?

Based on the logic of separation, heterogeneous states have no hope or right of surviving. Similar pressures have wracked the former Yugoslavia, and to some degree today in Russia. On the Indian sub-continent, the Punjab has already twitched its nerves if not flexed its muscles. Assam, Mizoram and Nagaland have likewise tasted the separatist sentiment.

And yet, populations of nation states are generally becoming more heterogeneous. Britain today is just one such example. There are also successful experiments in multiculturalism, among them the United States and Malaysia. One might also add here the once-happy city of Sarajevo, before it fell to uncompassionate politics. Do separatists then argue that all successful multicultural states today are doomed to fail? Or that the ideals of multiculturalism and multiracialism can exist only in the spiritual sphere?

There have been dire predictions of breakdown, leading to the break-up, of multicultural societies. Selig Harrison[4] had predicted this fate for India four decades ago. But today, India has still not been dismembered as catastrophically as was forewarned. The prophets of secessionist doom however could still argue that such monumental changes work in larger historical cycles, as the pressures tending towards balkanisation continue to prevail.

---

[3] In 522 BC Darius became Emperor of Persia, and proceeded to build the largest empire in the world. This stretched from southern Europe through West, Central and South Asia to include latterday Armenia, Palestine, Afghanistan, Uzbekistan and western Pakistan. In the 4th century BC, Alexander the Great spent six years conquering the present Afghanistan, Uzbekistan, Khazakstan and Pakistan before marching down the Indus Valley and across southern Persia to Babylon, just before his death in 323 BC.

[4] Harrison, Selig; *India: The Most Dangerous Decades*; Princeton University Press, Princeton; 1960.

Upon Partition, India-Pakistan tensions focussed on Kashmir, then grew to encompass a nuclear arms race. Not only is there little prospect of resolving current tensions permanently, there is also no guarantee that new tensions would not arise between them. Nor is there any assurance that cross-border tensions would never arise involving Bangladesh.

This is where South Asia parts company with South-East Asia. The most pressing conflicts in this region lately have been residual tension from Cambodia's civil war, the remains of localised insurgencies in Myanmar, and skirmishes in the southern Philippines. All of these are domestic conflicts, well contained by government forces, and have no prospect of triggering an arms race or regional war. They are also being scaled down progressively as each country's *status quo* asserts itself to marginalise violent opposition.

The supposed flashpoint in the South China Sea, over rival national claims to island territories, has seen more speculation than sober analysis. Neither China nor any of the other claimant states seeks to declare war over limited territory of uncertain value. But where such disputes or occasional conflicts present themselves, they arise from strategic or economic concerns rather than religious, political or even ideological differences.

As the MNLF in Mindanao has shown, the overriding problem stems from a lack of equitable access to the fruits of development, not questions of theology. Other groups like the MILF may employ the language of religion for reasons of identity, legitimacy and popular appeal, but their concerns and aspirations are nonetheless economic, making use of means that are political. The Moro people feel the pangs of economic deprivation most acutely.

There is unlikely to be serious separatism in South-East Asia. And even where separatist sentiment exists, it is not founded on religious differentiation as such. The slow pace of economic development in the Autonomous Region of Muslim Mindanao, governed by the more moderate MNLF, has only presented the rival MILF with ready ammunition to promote their militant cause further. But the politico-economic failure of the MNLF need not be synonymous with the politico-religious promise of the MILF. To the destitute, however, the temptation to think in such hopeful terms may be too great to resist.

In South Asia, recent years have seen the subject of reunification being considered by people in both India and Pakistan. Inevitably, there is a diversity of views on such a subject. Among Indians and Pakistanis who generally agree on the merits of reunification, some regard it as feasible only when national prejudices of one country against the other are overcome. Others think the prospect is unfeasible because such prejudices are unassailable. It is intriguing to find that even where such disagreement exists, there is at least agreement that mutual prejudices are an obstacle to improved relations.

Observers might note that disagreements over the prospect of India-Pakistan reunification are divided along lines of practicality, or what the commentators on both sides regard as the realm of possibility. It is hardly divided over national or religious identity. Optimists could consider this as already being a hopeful sign of progress in bilateral relations.

Along the way, however, there are occasional bumps on the road like Kargill. Such tragedies are generally seen as setbacks to improving relations, or worse. But if the tragedies of conflict have to happen at all, as they must for as long as conflict continues, they can serve as costly reminders of their own futility. Mutual hostility invites only mutual injury. Devoid of compassion, there are only net losses all-round.

The successful reunification of Germany has encouraged reunification of the Koreas, and perhaps even in Ireland. Political impediments to closer ties and reunification between states are not immutable. Where such aspirations exist and are believed to be for the common good, compassion acts as a catalyst to produce the political will to make them possible.

Conclusion

In South-East Asia, Senior Minister Lee Kuan Yew of Singapore had mooted the prospect of reunification between Malaysia and Singapore. This drew a range of responses in the two countries, most of it unreceptive. Soon afterwards, there was widespread speculation and suspicion of the intended purpose of his statement.

This ranged from an attempt to test the accommodation of Malaysia to provoking a renewed sense of nationalism among Singaporeans.

But whatever the rationale for such statements, they help encourage people in both countries to assess the importance of their mutual relationship, to ponder the challenges their countries face as separate entities, and to consider the value of improving ties. Weighing these prospects can help to nurture a more sensitive and compassionate consideration for the other across the border.

Reunification today is not any more inevitable, or even desirable, than separation or Partition had been in their day. The direction that nations choose to take requires the emotional preparedness of the people and the political will of their leaders. Even more important than the formation of nation states and the policies they adopt, which are secondary or reactionary, is the primary disposition of their peoples. Historically, the people's outlook of life and needs have ultimately determined their aspirations and destinies. Beyond those public needs are popular perceptions, with the shaping and management of these perceptions being the task of politics.

In a similar vein to Lee's announcement, Malaysian Prime Minister Datuk Seri Dr Mahathir Mohamad recently reflected publicly that Malaysia might one day have a non-Malay prime minister. Although Malaysia has always been a very multiracial country, ever since independent Malaya it had accorded special rights to the indigenous and majority Malays. Mahathir's statement again prompted a variety of responses and speculation over its motive. They included feelings of Malay defensiveness, and a reassurance to the non-Malay electorate that the multiracial, ruling Barisan Nasional coalition was able to dispense fair opportunities to all the races. In both Lee's and Mahathir's cases, the public statements consisted of floating political 'weather balloons' as feelers to test the progress of public sentiment in a particular direction. Differences between Malaysia and Singapore, or between different perceptions of rights of the Malays and non-Malays in Malaysia, were held up for passing scrutiny to help in closing ranks among Singaporeans, or among Malays in Malaysia. With both Lee and Mahathir, considerations for the Other—Malaysia, and non-Malays—were not questioned or compromised, but subordinated to the concerns of temporal politics.

Islam requires that the complete person fulfil his responsibilities in both spheres, the temporal world (horizontal integration between man and man and man and environment) and the spiritual realm (vertical integration between man and God). Such a holistic approach regards a person's competence in one sphere (ability to internalise divine guidances) as facilitating his competence in the other (with understanding, skills and right approach). The example of the Prophet Muhammad in governing Madina is a good example of it. We can find it also in some Muslim government, Malaysia as one of the example, who took a directed pragmatic approach (pragmatic with divine guidance) in governing the state.

Compassion in societal governance thus requires a more inclusive and equitable approach in today's heterogeneous societies. This is not only for compassion in its own right, but also for greater social harmony, political stability, public welfare and national integrity. It is also to remain true to the universal values at the heart of all the best religious and philosophical traditions, as well as to our common humanity.

Compassion itself is a quality that belongs in the normative sphere of mortal men. It arises in the real world of lived experience, the world of human interaction, the world of daily sentiment and exchanges. Compassion is virtue that is not only felt but also done. It is nothing if not the performance of kindness and virtue. And these need to be performed in the present and physical world.

One universal plane upon which the spiritual and temporal spheres converge is politics, that is public policy and administration. Political movements may begin with certain values and aspirations. These movements might then produce parties that crystallise these values and aspirations into platforms and policies to make them more comprehensible. When in power, these parties in government then transform platforms and policies into workable plans and programmes that are more practicable.

Besides maintaining the essence of their original values and aspirations, ensuring the popular appeal of platforms and policies, and certifying the effectiveness of plans and programmes, political parties in government have the responsibility of doing all these for the greater public good. This principle applies regardless of the political system or national culture in place. Ideology, ambition and organisation do not in themselves contribute in any way to public welfare.

This responsibility of government constitutes a demonstration of compassion for the people and the institutions of the state. The journey from values and aspirations to plans and programmes can often encounter roadblocks, detours and U-turns, and even hijackings. Laudable beginnings do not always result in admirable destinations. Once again, this applies regardless of political system or national culture.

Hindutva, or Hindu nationalism, might have begun innocently enough in India. But its exclusivism has tended towards chauvinism, which being antisocial then needs to be checked. Political parties with such proclivities need to assure a settled status quo of continued harmony, and work to fulfil that pledge.[5] The sad alternative would be such tragedies as the destruction of the Babri Mosque in Ayodha. This clearly demonstrates a painful lack of compassion for the Other, and ultimately also to Oneself, since the common society incorporates both.[6]

As responsible individuals and thoughtful opinion leaders, a nation's intelligentsia ought to consider five pertinent questions at this point:

1.   How far are seemingly religious disputes really over religious incompatibilities? Many disputes that appear or claim to be religious are essentially nothing of the kind.

2.   How can disputes that are political, economic or social in origin avoid being considered religious? Once cloaked in religious garb, they can inflame passions further. There is a need to contain if not resolve disputes at source, without complicating the original problems.

---

[5] The rise of the Hindu nationalist Bharatiya Janata Party (BJP) in India in recent years has been a cause for concern about escalating communal tension and conflict. If the BJP itself is mindful of such dangers, the onus is on the party to avoid and resolve them.

[6] See for example, Pratap Bhanu Mihta; 'VHP's Version of Hinduism Is Seen As Unappealing,' *India Abroad*; 4 September 1998

3.   Since conflicts are physical and therefore political, rather than spiritual or esoteric, how might they be resolved politically? Failure to do so can compound problems in both religious and profane worlds.

4.   How to identify and overcome human failings causing religious disunity, both within and between religions? Unity is vital for religious identity and national integrity.

5.   How to develop the basic, universal values common to all religious traditions to promote greater human compassion and welfare? In the world today, much can and should be done to avoid and alleviate unnecessary pain.

There may not be easy or immediate answers to these questions. One is nonetheless tempted to think that the solutions were perhaps more evident, or the problems less prevalent, in certain periods of history. That might or might not be so—that sensation could only be an illusion. What is more important is that greater effort, both constant and concerted, be brought to bear in a rediscovery of the answers.

We must remain confident that whatever the obstacles today, if the kind of energy, commitment, resources and sacrifice used in religious conflict and in-fighting had been employed in securing the answers we seek, we would see a better world by now. The quest of rediscovery is not necessarily easier or more difficult than that of original discovery. But like all urgent quests, it has to begin somewhere—and there is seldom a better alternative to acting in the here and now.

*A DYNAMIC ROLE
IN THE FUTURE*

COMMONWEAL AHEAD?

Kenneth Cragg

'No one ever wished it longer than it is,' remarked Samuel Johnson in his wry way of John Milton's *Paradise Lost*. 'We read Milton,' he went on, 'for instruction, retire harassed and look elsewhere for relaxation.'

It would be churlish for any who attended the 'Christians and Muslims in the Commonwealth' Conference in July, 2000 at St Catharine's Foundation, Windsor, to say they found it over long, nor hopefully for readers of these pages now to 'retire from them harassed'. 'No one ever wished it longer' would be doing no justice to the elegant surroundings and the generous hospitality they enjoyed. Some seventy hours were all too few.

But there have been multitudes who would never have wished the British Empire longer than it was, whether in longitudes and latitudes of redness painted on the map, nor lengthening decades of imperial rule 'over pine and palm'. Yet, in measure, 'wishing it longer than it was' lay behind both the initiative for, and the concept of, 'the Commonwealth'. Oxford, which in the 19th century had done so much to man the Empire with 'Viceroys' and 'administrators', also presided over the dreaming of 'the Commonwealth' as, somehow, hopefully, perpetuating ideals of democracy as the legacy of the old order, whose legatees in turn would cherish and assume them so that its passing might rescind its wrongs and conserve its high intent.[1]

The 'Commonwealth' concept since the mid 20th century has had a chequered history, its founders puzzled to discern how it could be more satisfactory than it has availed to be. Into that equation the religious faiths are obviously drawn. For, in their diversity both

---

[1] Some discussion of this intriguing Oxford sequence from Empire to Commonwealth may be had in Richard Symonds: *Oxford and Empire*, London, 1986: A Rumbold: *Watershed in India*, London, 1979, and in the careers of Reginald Coupland and Margery Perham. Cf. also my *Islam among the Spires*, Melisende, London, 2000, pp. 69-89.

between and inside themselves they bear directly on the tasks the Commonwealth ideology confronts. How religious faiths read and interpret the human situation and what moral resources they can deploy to serve and guide its perplexities—these are vital dimensions of both hope and despair concerning a global, human future.

There is a certain irony in the term 'the British Commonwealth of Nations', in case the adjective somehow compromises or limits the 'common-ness'. For all its sundry dimensions and elements would be needed to achieve the goal of 'common-wealth'. And there is a further, and related, irony in the fortunes of the word that has the hyphen. 'Wealth' has come to mean material products and the money that transacts them, as opposed to literal (rather than metaphorical) 'poverty'. 'Weal', however, by definition, was much more. Just as 'health' stems from what 'heals', so originally 'wealth' is the fruit of 'weal', and 'weal' is very close to the Islamic term *falah* which comes in the *Adhan*, or 'call to prayer' by the muezzin: 'Come ye to well-being.'[2] 'In weal and woe,' said Queen Victoria, 'I have ever had the sympathy of all my people.'

So it is urgent that we relate 'commonwealth' to 'commonwoe'. Honesty and realism in taking the true measure of the latter, penitence in knowing their massive contributions to it and genuine compassion in redeeming it—these will be the obligations of religious faiths. They are clearly obligations which require them to search their own histories and bring their witness concerning God and their verdicts about humankind to bear patiently on the conflicts and tragedies of this 21st, this 15th, century.

The Editors wanted this 'epilogue' to deal with that sense of things as the future might test both the wisdom and the will that Muslims and Christian might have to bring to it. 'Futurology' is always a risky pursuit but it would seem fair to pursue the purpose of 'commonweal ahead' in three areas of obvious urgency that present themselves from all the foregoing Papers and the discussions they aroused. The three are:

(1)   Our faith about divine magnanimity and the secular mind accompanying today's technology.

---

[2] *Hayya 'ala-l-falah. Falah* is 'prosperity', 'satisfaction', 'well-being'.

(2)   Our faiths and the issues of civic society, democracy, conscience and the rule of law.

(3)   Our faiths and the burdens of a global humankind.

That there has been, in the West—and elsewhere—a long recession in the sense of God, in the readiness for worship, is evident enough. 'Secularisation' has gone far in eroding the major institutions of religion and the authority of their claim on allegiance.

The reasons have been manifold. The conclusion of much modern philosophy, in the words of Iris Murdoch, is that 'we (humans) are on our own.' 'I can see no evidence to suggest that human life is not something self-contained.'[3] The competences we reach in techniques *seem* to many to confirm that conclusion. What we trust in travel is the 'jumbo', a marvel of expertise: what we rely on in surgery (key-hole or otherwise) is incredible human skill, and so on through all the empire of our sciences. Where should prayer come in? People ask. Is the old order of worship quite obsolete?

Many, at least in their habits, so conclude. Islam has not yet suffered so markedly from this phenomenon. But there are many signs that it is not exempt. Moreover, the factors inducing it are everywhere for export. Muslims in Riyadh or Timbuctoo may not say: 'We will unload the crates that bring the machinery and sterilise them against the mind-set that produced it.' The lust born of luxury is no less liable to be contagious in Saudi Arabia than in Los Angeles.

Faiths have large duties *vis-à-vis* the secular mind in its seemingly viable attitude of living *min duni-Llahi*—'to the exclusion of God'. Among those duties is a right witness to the magnanimity of Allah. 'The God with whom we have to do' is One who has 'let us be' and deputed the 'trust of the world and its economy', to our human hands as trustees. Such is the Christian and the Quranic understanding of divine 'omnipotence'. But there has been a tendency in Islam to read 'almightiness' in often tyrannical and all-disposing terms that ignore the Qur'an's own doctrine of the human *amanah*

---

[3]   Iris Murdoch, *The Sovereignty of Good*, London, 1970, p. 79.

and *khilafah*. A God who pre-determines, enjoins and dictates all things is not the Allah of Surah 2.30 and 7.172, conferring on us the dignity of 'management' and 'authority', and asking: 'Am I not your Lord?' and awaiting the answer—'We (freely) so acknowledge.'

Not to see this and tell of some utterly arbitrary deity plays into the hands of those who point to how, evidently, there is a genuine power in our technology. It only confirms the illusion which dismisses God entirely. Sheer arbitrary power-girt-ness contradicts the guesthood we know ourselves enjoying in the world. Then the God we must reject contravenes the One we must acknowledge. Nuclear physicists and genetic engineers must not be left to be like 'little gods' replacing the all-controlling One whom their sense of power can never recognise, when all the time that very power tells them of the magnanimous One whom they should obey.

We must, therefore, reach for a theology which understands that the most ultimate power is not the sort that can never delegate, never give room for participants. It is rather the power that is so self-sufficing in love that it can risk delegating and endowing and be all 'the greater' *(akbar)* for being 'powerfully generous'—as, indeed, all understanding of creation must concede to be the case.

The Qur'an says: 'Make Him greatly great'—*kabbirhu takbiran* (17.111). This must mean a theology that—far from being ousted or daunted by what human techniques demonstrate as powers in our human hands—claims those very powers as granted to us by the Lord to whom they engage us in gratitude and submission—submission, not by renouncing our powers but by their true consecration to His will—a consecration He awaits from our liberty to bring it.

This wiser theology belongs, of course, with the clear Quranic understanding of our human entrustment to be 'over nature under God'—i.e. 'in the middle state', obligated to subdue our 'exploits' in due 'exploitation' (under our given mandate) to the will and design of God—the God who has granted precisely that 'governance' of the natural order to our creaturehood. Far, then, from disengaging us, our secular technologies make us ever more liable for gratitude, reverence and the will to consecrate. The world should be no less a place of wonder for a technician in a laboratory than for a shepherd in a pasture.

This truth of a right theology, where the scientists research and explore and the poets celebrate and sing, and all 'seek the face of their Lord,' is of course confirmed by the role of prophethood, as the corollary of creaturehood. If we were puppets, pulled on arbitrary strings, there would be no point in messengers summoning us to acts of will. It is clear that the divine 'sending' of prophets is the supreme tribute to our human status as 'delegates for Allah' in the natural order and in the whole realm of economics and politics that stems from it. So our faiths have to make good the entire significance of our human-ness and not surrender to those who would have us read our privilege as exempting us from a right *islam*, i.e. a full and genuine response, from mind and heart and will, to that ever patient question: 'Am I not your Lord?' For an entire theology is in the question and the answer.

This brings us to 'issues of civic society', the second dimension of 'commonweal' and its future. For life is political and humans are political animals. Islam, indeed, has long been, thanks to the Hijrah, the most politicised of all the major faiths. But there are enormous problems around that post-imperial ideal of 'government by the people for the people'. Empire itself had failed to realise it. But the theme of 'independence', with India and Pakistan the great Asian exemplars and Ghana the first in Africa, brought with it, through the Commonwealth idea, the ambition for democratic elections, a free judiciary and popular suffrage, and the legitimacy of political parties and open debate.

This 'Westminster' model idea was fraught with almost overwhelming obstacles. It was sometimes forgotten that it presupposed general literacy, standards of education, concepts of personal integrity, often hard to realise where poverty abounded. But these social factors apart, there were enormous issues of doctrine and tradition for Muslims in agreeing and fulfilling these ideas. There is a deep and tragic irony in words used by Liaquat Ali Khan in 1950 at the National Press Club in Washington.

> 'In a world of conflicting ideologies, nations that have recently achieved full sovereignty are likely to be the victims of mental confusion and consequent instability. Is it not, therefore, a matter of supreme satisfaction

that at least one nation ... should not suffer from confusion and should, as a matter of tradition and belief, be pledged to clear international principles of democracy and social and economic justice.'[4]

He spoke entirely sincerely but he had not foreseen General Zia al-Haqq and he was himself murdered within some fifteen months of the speech by one of his own religion. Pakistan celebrated its half century with a dark, unhappy retrospect of constitutional and social frustration and indecision.

Doubtless the odds against its first Prime Minister's vision were heavy and cumulative. But they are also deeply-grounded in the classic traditions of Islam—these that belong with *Dar al-Islam* and the concept of *Jihad*. In the light of these, there is a question whether Muslims are not in theory subversive of any regime under which they live which is not Islamic. If so, it must be of great significance for the quarter of the world's Muslims now domiciled outside *Dar al-Islam*.[5]

In *Dar al-Islam* the realms of faith and of power are co-extensive. Thus any Muslim who would leave the faith must emigrate into *Dar al-Harb*. 'Islam is not like any other religion because it lays clear and unambiguous claim to government.'[6] Muslims ought only to be ruled by Muslims who will tolerate in their statehoods as *dhimmis* those of other faiths in minority status. They should not—by these lights—meekly accede in permanence to non-Muslim rule but, ideally, will for its being islamicised. Certainly the Shi'ah tradition of *taqiyyah*

---

[4] Liaquat Ali Khan, *Muslim Educational Problems*, Lahore, No. 7, 1952, p. 235. He saw Pakistanis as 'free from disintegrating doubts' with 'the surest safeguards against disruption'.

[5] According to a recent reckoning one quarter of Muslims are in e.g. India, Europe, and the Americas, where it seems near to impossible that their (Meccan) situation as 'just a religion' is likely to give way to a Medinan order of power. There are no more Pakistans to be contrived—certainly not inside India—to meet the demand for separate statehood. Oddly, too, that 'success' doomed the Muslims of India (as partition made it to be) to the abiding impossibility of that solution which Pakistan's logic said was essential to any Islamic survival.

[6] See Zakaria Bashier, *Hijrah: Story and Significance*, Leicester, 1983, p. 103. He adds that 'to be accepted as a full Muslim in a non-Muslim society' is 'a false hope'. Any such hope should 'be shed and exposed as mere fantasies.' P.104.

conformed to non-Shi'ah authority only until there was occasion to make it Shi'ah.[7]

There is, therefore, a serious conceptual question about (a) the ready viability of open-to-all democracy in Muslim societies with any minority elements and (b) the sincere readiness of Muslims, lacking *Dar al-Islam*, to participate genuinely in a mixed society whose politics they will never dominate in *Dar al-Islam* terms.

This is not to say that Muslim thought is not capable of wrestling with this long tradition or of amending its precepts. There are clear resources for its doing so. It is to say that the task calls for sustained self-scrutiny, and for creative leadership. The compatibility of religious pluralism with Islamic order sets exacting questions for its corporate mind.

But how far can mind be corporate? There is the vexed question, encountered painfully by Pakistan, as to a scrutiny of legislation—and possible veto—on the part of a non-elected body of 'Ulama' thus potentially frustrating the normal working of democracy. Who is capable of *Ijtihad*? Can an elected Muslim 'parliament' be trusted to be 'Islamic' without the supervisory veto of the pundits with turbans? Can there be a legitimate 'laicisation' of *Ijtihad* so that conscientious loyal Muslim surgeons, engineers and the like can share in it—the more so in that so many of the new problems for conscience and Shari'ah arise in their spheres of genetics and cybernation and the rest?

An attendant question for all faiths has now to be how far can/should/may conscience enter into the minding of Shari'ah law? Is the divine will (and perceiving of it) lodged for ever, unchangingly, in a fixed corpus of law? Or can it be argued that this holds for our loyalty principles and precedents which we in our time are called to apply, if need be, beyond their 'letter' in quest of their 'spirit'?

Such matters, in turn, lead back into the exegesis of the Qur'an as 'a mercy to the worlds' on the part of God 'who is not overtaken.'[8] For internal reasons of Scriptural concepts and usages, Christians have

---

[7] Often translated 'dissimulation', *taqiyyah* is only that, out of a more primary hope, one day, to change the régime, to which, in one's heart, one has not been reconciled. To maintain a will to change is crucial to any hope of attaining it. Hence the interim quietism hiding its heart and biding its time.

[8] The phrase comes twice in Surahs 56.60 and 70.11. The meaning is obscure but certainly no one will be able to 'get in front of God', or find Him 'out of date'.

found and pursued more probing initiatives than have, normally, been reached among Muslims. What, for example, when a sense of conscience about e.g. human rights or women's claims, or social oppression or so-called 'shame murders', pleads against long established prescripts of authority? Can reforms be read as the eternal Shari'ah in its renewed task of justice 'in the Name of God'?

That faiths should be capable of self-amendings and vigorous in the pursuit of them, is crucial to their ministry to their society, not to say also their credibility and relevance in a world they have too long ill-served. The willingness to co-exist with others and to make honest common cause in the interests of society in civic matters makes sharp demands on old attitudes of mind, used to instincts of separatism sanctioned by doctrines as to finality and truth-claim. It makes for a difficult but potentially fruitful tension between *both* holding one's interior faith and holding open the reality others find in theirs. There is no place for the kind of nonchalance that implies nothing differs much or that convictions may be fluid— and flaccid. Rather it requires a fidelity that is also hospitable and eager to identify what, in either, can speak tellingly to the other.

For Muslims outside their age-long *Dar* there is the fascinating fact that they are virtually 'back in Mecca' having only the *Balagh*, the 'message' to which Muhammad, in that city, was insistently held as his 'sole duty'.[9] Will a return there conceptually inspire a right response to lack of Islamic power to buttress their faith? But what of the post-Hijrah Medinan dimension fully enshrined in the ongoing Qur'an? Some have suggested that the Hijrah quest for a political shape of Islam was entirely valid then in the real circumstances of a politicised paganism among the dominant Quraish, requiring to be forcefully overcome. But if the fifteenth Muslim century situates Muslims in a quite contrasted world, will it be loyal to argue that what was once valid is no longer so in the old terms? There is already the doctrine of abrogation inside the Qur'an and there is the time-honoured invocation of *asbab al-nuzul*, ('occasions of the Qur'an's *tanzil*') which require reference to the

---

[9] This directive holding Muhammad to an exclusively verbal mission is clearly of great importance. For it is so often repeated—Surahs 6.164, 17.15, 39.7. 42.48 and 53.38—all of them Meccan Surahs.

where and when if interpreting the text is to be sound. Is there a 'where and when' that can translate into centuries?

These are issues for the Islamic mind into which outsiders should not venture. They bear strongly on the self-assessments which must go with the need to be open-hearted *(sharh al-sadr)* in the will for constructive co-existence. Christian faith, too, has had to wrestle with passages in its Scriptures it has needed to re-assess.[10] All such interior matters of intellectual and spiritual integrity, for any one faith, are a large part of its task in relating to any other faith. Should not this include a capacity to listen to the reckonings others make, whether hostile or well-considered, so that response to them is not sheer, perhaps angry, rebuttal but mature reflection? The latter is more likely to give pause to what is merely contentious from the other side.

Western 'Islamophobia' is a vexed case in point. There is no doubt that many in the USA and elsewhere have developed a fixation about Islam, perhaps as 'a great Satan' to replace the former bogey of Communism. It is then grossly negligent of broad qualities of Islamic culture, its sages and poets, its architects and saints. It needs vigorous and sustained rejection. Yet such rejection could be aided by open Muslim reckoning with the image in fact presented from many sides which has kindled the phobia—not to condone, still less to accept, it but rather to gain an angle of self-study which might not otherwise be had.

Aside from the 'image' in sundry 'mirrors' political, a case in point is the usage *hizb-allah*, in contrast to *hizb al-shaitan* in the Qur'an.[11] It could be unexceptionable in respect of spiritual militancy and a lively awareness of evil, but it conceals a potential idolatry which the mandatory Muslim detection of, and veto on, *shirk* would

---

[10] Notably the sharp ethnicism of the Pentateuchal literature, the mandate for displacing peoples in the Book of Joshua and the imprecatory character of certain psalms—all of them incompatible with the Christian openness of grace equally and unpreferentially to all peoples. There are various ways in which, it is argued, a Scriptural loyalty can handle incompatibles within its pages. They may have 'ministries' in measuring the growth of wisdom.

[11] The terms of course, were in the Qur'an long before the first was adopted by a 'political' faction, making it the more sad and—indeed—profane, that Allah should ever be conjoined with a political party. See Surahs 5.56 and 58.19 and 22. The hidden moral question in all such language is: Who is possessing who? To be God's 'partisans' may be a high ambition but it can never mean that we have God in our power—as it may well be thought to mean by every kind of zealotry or bigotry. All such are not 'letting God be God' and to do that leads into idolatry, in that God is 'falsified'.

have to take in hand. There could be an element of *shaitan* in the pride taken in being Allah's champions. But more, if we mean that God is exclusively on our side, then we have made him an 'idol' as solely the 'patron' of our own cause. We have presumed to 'privatise' 'the Lord of the heavens and the earth', no longer Lord of those *we* have assigned to Satan. Perhaps unwittingly, we have forfeited the supreme truth of the divine Unity, albeit—in our intention—on God's own behalf. We can only be on His behalf in terms of His own inclusive sovereignty which will never be in our exclusive hands. Why not?—because He alone is Lord.

Due Islamic care for this theme may be 'a hard thing'. But such are the reckonings that go with genuine co-existence. There is a difficult hurdle also for the Christian mind in the long concern to enquire: 'Was Muhammad a Prophet, the final Prophet of God?' and, frequently, assume a negative answer. The reasons are obvious— coming from a legitimate concern for the finality of Christ, not to mention the bitter experiences of Christian tribulation in and after the expansion of Islam. The emotional and doctrinal frontiers of incompatibility had to be sharply drawn and guarded.

It has been hard for Christians to come round to realising that that burning question was not the one rightly to ask. In any event, there was at least the abiding fact of Muhammad's prophethood on the stage of world history. It could hardly be intelligent to relate to it only by willing it away or regretting that it did exist. Such a self-shielding Christian attitude would be neither 'the love of Christ' for fellow creatures nor the positive wisdom of relating to Islam's actuality. Facts of belief are facts of our situations and call for intelligent cognisance.

Moreover, the bare question as to status as 'prophet' ignored or obscured far more important issues that could only be registered once the fact of Muslim belief as to Muhammad had been acknowledged genuine and actual. Those issues had to do with how prophetic truth 'succeeded' in the world, and, more importantly, whether being 'educated, informed, guided and exhorted' by 'message' and 'messengers' was all we needed and should anticipate from God.[12]

---

[12] The question of what, boldly, we might think of as divine 'obligation' towards humankind has long been difficult where the theme of total divine 'unconditionedness' has prevailed.

That question would turn on what we could realistically conclude about ourselves as humans. If we proved such as to be rebellious, perverse, self-willed under laws in hand and heaven-given, then prophethoods, however final, might not suffice as Allah's response to our condition.

If 'to know is to do' then 'knowing' is all but if we can know and not do—so that 'ignorance' is not our problem then what informs and instructs and enjoins will seem to fall short of all that those ministries of word and counsel had in mind to achieve. The ultimate theme, then, would not be whether as to prophethoods but whether even with them the human problem was resolved. Islam, of course, in its 'pillars', its structure, its patterns of habituation and its unsurpassed genius for concerting solidarity has its response to these needs that go beyond what *huda*, *wahy* and *tanzil* can ultimately meet.[13]

Thus it is vital for co-existing faiths to be radical with their own role in mutual engagement and receptive to uncommon handling of common issues. If the foregoing seems to some readers over-theological it is only the necessity of being duly alert and realist *vis-à-vis* the third task earlier described as 'the burdens of a global humankind'.

Muslim/Christian relationships within the Commonwealth are only relevant as part of a far wider globalism in which the Commonwealth must sometimes seem no more than a wistful gesture to a past of nostalgia and a future of fond hopes. With China a rising world power and with the shift of 'superpower' leadership to America alone, any Commonwealth 'dynamism'—to quote the Conference agenda—can at best be ancillary. It can, however, if only symbolically, help to move discourse away from Euro-centrism and

---

But a God who 'had no need of humans,' hardly tallies with the actuality of creation. Nor does it fit the giving of revelation that expected human heeding. Any notion of divine unconcern makes an end of theology and religion alike. Significantly, Surah 4.165 itself makes the point. Noting how 'apostles, good-news-bringers and messengers' have been sent it goes on: 'in order that men would have no case *(hujjah)* against Allah after' their coming. Clearly, had 'messengers' *not* been 'sent', God would have failed to fulfil what it was due from Him to do. Their being sent has fulfilled His 'obligation'. Clearly, then, it is right to 'anticipate' what God might do—need to do—in being Himself.

[13] This is the theme of 'the originality of sin'—the proneness of human structures and institutions to corruption, arrogance and contention and, with the 'powers,' the evil-bent in individuals caught up in them.

away from 'white' aegis. It needs to be remembered that the populational weight of Christianity in the world is moving away from the West, with its significant growth centring on non-white races, notably in Africa.

It seems clear that the vision and energy either faith can reach and apply will be tested by the burdens of globalism in ways far exceeding the scope of past traditions and attitudes. Where, for example, are debates about *Ijtihad* and any closing of its 'door' in the onset of WWW and the internet and the ever proliferating confusion of instant media?[14] Sadly, these agencies do nothing to diminish the prejudices and passions that go with the pride of cultures. They can, however, serve to diminish the bias of 'imaging', whether of 'the East' or of 'the West' that has been a long-running mutual reproach.[15] Academic scholarship could no doubt be indulged in the 19th and 20th centuries, to denigrate 'natives' in the interests of empire or commerce, just as assessments in reverse could take revenge. Religions played a large part in the traffic of depreciation and the ledger historically is a hard one to calculate honestly. They should now serve to the utmost of their power in reckoning with a world increasingly inter-aware and inter-exposed.

It is, moreover, a world in which familiar cultural spheres and continental preserves will find themselves increasingly pressured, if not invaded, by mass migrations challenging the immunities long assumed and cherished. The Commonwealth, from its British 'spring-board' to the ends of the earth, is peculiarly positioned in respect of this prospect. For what the Statute of Westminster called 'Dominions'—a term drawn from the Book of Psalms—were thought of, outside Asia, as territories for mainly 'white' settlement and some have carefully guarded that perception. The term 'Commonwealth' did not alter it , if also, in its way, ignoring it.

Finding habitats, however, is going to become a far more

---

[14] Gary Bunt, *Virtually Islamic: Computer-mediated Communication and Cyber Islamic Environments*, The University of Wales Press, Cardiff, 1996.

[15] A notable instance of 'eastern' umbrage about 'western' 'orientalism' was Edward Said's volume of that name in 1978, which had some loaded judgements against scholars who, none the less, had contributed largely and expertly to research into Islam and its history. There may have been more point to Said's strictures on western fascination with Muslim sexuality and the Ottoman harem.

urgent, notably less romantic, enterprise in the present century. The chronic imbalance of livelihoods under world capitalism apart, the March, 2001, United Nations Report on world population foresees an annual increase of some seventy-seven millions, most of the flow coming from six nations, namely China, India, Pakistan, Nigeria, Bangladesh and Indonesia. Islam is thus contributing more massively to human numbers than any other religio-cultural world community.

The incidence of growth is heavily in economies least able to sustain it economically. Near fifty of the world's least developed countries are destined to triple their populations. It grimly follows that human pressure on food and water is set to aggravate already enormous problems of disadvantage, poverty and deprivation, with the further hobbling of educational efforts and hopes of combating illiteracy, that perennial enemy of human betterment.

Somewhere round the middle of the present century, with the most sober of hopes as to fertility levels, the Report warns that nine out of every ten people will be living in the burdened economies of the least developed states, while population levels are steadily falling in Europe. Africans will outnumber Europeans by 2050 three times over, whereas in 1950 Europe had around a quarter of the world's humans and Africa a mere eight percent.

These projected statistics give an ironical turn to the old gibe about 'Eurocentrism'. It is, however, an irony sharpened by another, namely that with the workings—as they are—of global capitalism, the multinationals and world debt patterns massively enshrine the West in general as arbiter of the economics of 'uncommon wealth'. Short of siding madly with the anarchists, it is hard to discern what decisive role faiths can play, other than being unresting guardians of conscience and the claims of human compassion, holding the powers, financial and political,[16] to moral judgement in their global reach.

Thanks to the world's appetite for fossil fuels and the incidence of their location, Islam also wields much wealth that might alleviate its own vast poverties elsewhere, were there a more efficient

---

[16] 'Financial and political' in that order. It seems clear that the organs of international trade and finance have drawn off from governments some of the control they once had over policies and ends.

inter-Muslim organ of 'common weal'. It is, however, difficult to see how the deep potential of Islamic economic doctrine can avail in relation to capital investment on the scale of contemporary development. The principle of fair profit legitimated by personal stake in the enterprise—as against the sort of remote 'interest' that 'gambles' with a concern only for yields that 'justify'—has an excellent ethical edge but a norm hardly viable in the complexity of the ever bartering world.

The ultimate relevance of both faiths returns us to the dignity and liability of the human creature as the duly mandated 'agent' and 'trustee' of the divine will in the natural world. All the issues of a right ecology belong in that theology. That truth of the human order, enjoined in both Scriptures, has to be known as itself in trust. The ever-present temptation of religions is to want to 'be master', to dominate and 'rule', to seek to be 'awesome' for their own sake. It is a temptation all the more subtle and perilous because they can invoke the alibi that all is 'for the sake of God'.[17] They read their right to claim allegiance as warranted by their 'mission' in His Name. Thus the arrogance is where the humility ought to be, seeing how 'they who serve the greater cause may make the cause serve them.'[18] There is no realm where 'letting God be God' is, more urgent than among the religionaries whom, by their lights and in their Scriptures, He has 'let be' as servants—no less, no more. Even in the ultimacy of revelation God remains 'the only Lord'. Thus the supreme vocation of religious faith is to be always in 'submission', never usurpers of the rights of God.[19]

The foregoing does scant justice to how a memorable Conference might review itself, still less to the theme of 'compassion' which, in its ample comfort, it set itself, still less again to 'the burdens of a global humanity'. Will it not be right to conclude that the heart duty of religious faith is to bear with suffering in both senses—to

---

[17] It is clear that this was the ground on which the Qur'an reproached Jewry, i.e. that of pleading their vocation to be 'the people of God' as somehow making themselves 'necessary' to God, retaining their exceptionality as their sufficient exoneration from any charge of pretension.

[18] T S Eliot, *Murder in the Cathedral*, London, 1968 ed., p. 48.

[19] 'Servant of God has chance of greater sin than the man who serves a king.' *Ibid*, p. 48. This is the more a danger when 'the cause' becomes political.

enter vicariously into, as well as to probe, its meaning and find a theology of its relation to human sin and wrong. If faiths must forego arrogance, they must also accept vulnerability, not merely in their status and their doctrine at the hands of sceptics, but further in their personal experience.

For, on so many counts, the human scene is a tragic panorama, a daunting spectacle of pain and grief, of weariness and 'common woe'. It is only pretence—perhaps successfully contrived for some by dint of good fortune or a will for ignorance—that pretends it otherwise. Too many live and die beyond the effective reach of any neighbour's compassion, made victim by imponderables over which they have no control and which escape all censure. Ills and sorrows abide beyond the reach of either palliative or comfort or relief. It falls to all agencies of compassion, Muslim or Christian, to say, of their utmost benediction: 'When we had done all, we were unprofitable servants.'

Is there, then, not room among the faiths of the world for one that sets this 'burden' in the human scene at the heart of God? Buddhism, we might say, undertakes the load and the puzzle but only by setting an untroubled serenity in the ultimate place, 'questioning nothing, answering nothing'. A compassion humanly avails but for no transcendent reason discernibly supreme. It was finally out of a garden called Gethsamane, its place in the experience of Christ and in the quality of 'God in Christ', that the Christian faith emerged, via the teaching of Jesus, into its role among the faiths of humankind. In a contemporary ecumene of religious diversity, its inner loyalty requires it to be present in those terms, the terms it learned in the Passion of Jesus as the Christ. They are ready to co-exist. They want to reckon patiently with all the reasons why Islam must disallow where the corporate heart beats. But they are responsive, with them and in them, to a human realism that—all other reading apart—has to be the burden of us all.

REFLECTION: 9 JULY 2000
Christopher Lamb

I speak with all the limitations and all the benefits of an English Christian with some 30 years of exposure to Islam and Muslims, for whom Islam began as something exotic and now seems a friend—though, like some friends, not one I always understand. My experience over that time has been the slow growth of trust, initially during six years' residence in Pakistan, and subsequently through many friendships with Muslims in Britain. Friendship, I find, does not demand that one approves of everything the other does or says, or even fully grasps the reasons behind their actions. None of us are entirely consistent in what we do or entirely explicable, which all makes for a richer life. My trust in Muslims and Islam has grown by observing that the things I find most abhorrent in human behaviour are equally abhorred by the Muslims I know personally, while the Islamic sense of dependence on divine initiative and providence both supports and challenges my own. My prayer is that you may be stimulated, even provoked by what I have to say, to hear what God is saying to you. I once picked up a book of English translations from the Urdu poet Ghalib in a bookshop in Lahore, entitled *Reverberations*. What I offer are some reverberations from our conference.

Plural societies, and that means all the societies we now live in, desperately need peace and harmony if they are not to break up into warring factions or separated communities like Cyprus or Bosnia. Personal and communal relationships are critical, yet so many of our politicians seem obsessed with economic issues, presumably because these are what can be measured and built up into statistics. This is not to claim that poverty is anything but real. It is however the gap between rich and poor, and the sense of being deprived in relation to others which hurts. It is this which leads to fractured relationships—something far harder to measure. I watch with dismay as a new group of houses are built in Coventry surrounded by high walls and electronic gates for protection. Such developments make neighbourly relationship impossible, and engender resentment and fear. When this rich/poor non-relationship is compounded by factors of ethnicity, culture and faith the walls of ignorance become too high to scale. Our media encourage us to judge by extremes, so that as non-Muslims we are led to believe that Saudi Arabia is the paradigm of Muslim culture and practice. At the same time we are ignorant of how it feels to be a Muslim minority in the West, with being constantly made to feel that you do not belong.

Personal worth is bound up with a secure sense of identity. Observers note that children in British schools have often found that the Muslim, Hindu and Sikh children have a keen sense of who they themselves are and what their cultural heritage is, while the white children are left asking 'Well, who are we?'—'You're Christians,' they are told. And the response is 'Oh.' Because they can't give any real content to that word, and have no idea what it means to be a Christian apart from a vague notion of Christmas. Sometime you hear the complaint that 'They're even bringing religion into Christmas!' This is part of what the Bishop of London described as the crisis in the faith tradition of Western Europe, where for decades religion has been consistently edited out of public life and policy-making. It is a sign of hope that this attempt to treat religion as a merely private thing is beginning to be re-thought in the UK, not least because of Muslim insistence that faith matters, and British Muslims' conviction that their own sense of identity has its basis in a faith commitment and not merely a particular ethnic origin.

Community relationships are central to social stability and people's sense of identity has to be taken seriously, but these are complex matters and particularly difficult to assess from a distance, outside of the situation concerned. Each of us has spoken from a very particular situation. Symbols and social cues matter and can be seriously misunderstood. I recall my own embarrassment on being introduced to the female librarian at the Sociology Department of the Punjab University in Lahore. I automatically stuck out my hand, only to be firmly told—as I should have known - that in that society Muslim women did not shake hands with men. Trust and mutual respect has meant—I think—that we have not experienced problems here, principally because here we have been able to give each other the precious gift of time. But we need to remember that what is merely cultural for some, a matter of taste even, is for others a religious issue. Such complexity means that the natural instinct to look for reciprocal gestures and actions is liable to come unstuck when people are having to relate across national boundaries.

The European Churches, Catholic, Orthodox and Protestant, have a joint consultative committee on Islam in Europe. In my time serving on it we attempted to write a paper about Reciprocity. The initial idea was to urge that Christian minorities in Muslim lands be treated with the same fairness and consideration as we attempt to treat Muslim minorities in Europe and the West. This is an idea often discussed in non-Muslim circles in this country when Islam is in focus, and widely regarded as a minimum requirement for good international relations. It quickly became evident, however, that this appeal to Reciprocity, intended to produce positive results, was contentious and ill-considered, liable to back-fire quite seriously. When we consulted Middle-Eastern Christians, we found that they were very conscious of historic injustices against themselves from Western Christians, and had no desire to be held hostage to perceived and real current injustices against Muslims in Europe. In any case, said both Christian and Muslim friends, reciprocity smacked of a commercial, bargaining spirit. It would be only too easy to allow double standards to persist in such an arrangement. So that first paper and the term Reciprocity itself had to be scrapped and replaced by an expression of our determination to maintain human rights for all, without consideration of how others behaved.

Religious people claim a prior relationship with God which *in principle* (because we recognise that human beings are at best a disappointment) must override all other relationships. So we do good even if it is not reciprocated, because our behaviour and identity must not be controlled by the behaviour of others, but determined by our faith and the conviction that we are one humanity under God. We are not simply pleasure-seekers ('Consumer Unbeliever International' in the Bishop of London's phrase), but have a sense of the capacity and obligation to do God's will. And so we can also work with people of good will, even if they have no faith.

This freedom in principle from the common human pattern of behaviour gives religion the power and energy of deep conviction, and so makes it potentially very dangerous. Governments will always want to control religion, as will groups who are determined to maintain their own grip on power, wealth or security. Such groups will often manipulate the fear of the Other—the unknown, misrepresented and demonised—held by 'the folks at home', the fear of perceived threats to basic values, and even perhaps the fear of a true peace/*salam*/*shalom*. The media reflect, dramatise and often exacerbate these fears. Meetings such as this dispel them. Fear often feeds on a particular interpretation of the past. It is often necessary to remember the past differently—we were grateful for Matthew's generous humour over African history. It is better to see our forebears as absurd and fallible beings rather than as two-headed monsters.

The power in religion is most evident in the radicals who attempt—however wrong-headedly—to put God first. Can we make relationships with our own radicals, Christian and Muslim, to begin to harness that energy and commitment for long-term, realistic aims? Some of the radicals hold utopian convictions, believing like Franz Fanon that violence can have a kind of cleansing, purgative effect. In that respect they are like the political extremists of right and left. Many, however, eventually become disillusioned with that nihilistic path. Can we help them to humanise the religious instinct which reaches out for absolute solutions, and invite them to work with us on practical models and intermediate goals? Can we harness the anger? Can we engage with them instead of simply berating them or demonising them?

This practical, humanising, non-theoretical context may be where women operate particularly well—which is why those who do not want change or only violent change scorn women and oppress them. There is nothing like looking after small children to teach you the value of compromise and compassion. In the family we learn to be just, compassionate and endlessly flexible. We need the skills of both sexes to develop the civilising institutions which many nations lack and which in others only benefit certain sections of society. We need also the tempered optimism, the hope, offered by the belief that our God is for us, and that all that is good in our aims and objectives finds its origin in him.

It is that conviction which ultimately must sustain us, and therefore we have a fundamental task of maintaining and refining our own theological discourse. We should avoid the temptation to exchange our basic theological convictions for a set of ethical values which may be shared with believers of other confessions only in appearance, and which may mean different things to different people. The formulations of Global Ethics cannot take the place of our theological work. For only by that will we carry our fellow-believers with us and nourish the roots of our faith. We need to go on wrestling with our scriptures and our 'God-talk', or we shall find that our values are no more than impressive-sounding words. In this spirit I offer you a mini-sermon on John 6: 12; 'Gather up the fragments that nothing may be lost.' This is the final instruction of Jesus to his followers after a miraculous multiplication of five loaves and two fishes offered to feed 5,000 people. What do we understand from this story—the subject of thousands of sermons? It must be that God takes our gifts and energies, limited and inadequate as they are, when they are offered in faith, generosity and hope. He multiplies them and uses them to do the job and sees it through to completion, 'that nothing may be lost.' Our work, like our human relationships, is necessarily fragmentary and incomplete, at best a mere sign pointing towards what is good, but we can rest in the confidence that God who is the Perfect One will bring it to completion.

A QUILT OF FAITH[*]

John Ovenden

My plan of action was, I thought, pretty foolproof and straightforward—I knew well in advance that a high powered conference at Cumberland Lodge was taking place this weekend entitled 'Christians and Muslims in the Commonwealth: a Dynamic Role in the Future'. In preparation I duly consulted from my own library, one or two of the well known books on the subject, thinking that I might use some of their ideas and thoughts and present them as my own. No one, I thought naively, would be any the wiser. In any case everyone who comes to the Royal Chapel requires a pass so I was 100 percent certain that my plan would succeed. On Thursday pushed through my letterbox was a list of participants, and blow me down, of the two books that I had selected, the names of those two authors were attending the conference and had ticked their names for coming to Matins this morning. A very warm welcome to you all.

I had to take a different tack. I could fall back on the other theme for today 'Sea Sunday', but that did not help much because for the last 48 hours I have been equally at sea struggling with an ocean of ideas and thoughts which just would not come together into any comprehensible shape. However, just when the going got really tough, and I felt submerged beneath a wave of preacher despair, a small beacon of light shone unexpectedly. Driving through Ascot on Friday, no, not to go the races again, but to see someone in hospital, I noticed a rather large sign at the Heatherwood roundabout. It read 'National Quilt Championship'. This intrigued me. Was it a competition to find out who could make the quilt in the fastest time? I phoned up to

---

[*] Before leaving Cumberland Lodge many participants—both Christian and Muslim— attended the service of Matins on Sunday 9 July. The sermon reproduced here (and adapted for the printed page) was preached by the Revd Canon John Ovenden, a Canon of Windsor and Chaplain in the Great Park.

find out. No, I was told, it was a display at the Ascot Racecourse of quilts from all over the country and the idea was find the most original and colourful. Anyone who has ever made a quilt will know how long it takes, and how patient you must be, and how you have to piece all the different sections together. The finished article is a patchwork of colour and variety with each square contributing to the beauty of the whole. It is indeed a commonwealth of colour and design. Any conference therefore entitled 'Christians and Muslims in the Commonwealth' must take as its starter two basic points. First that compromise for the sake of compromise is not the name of the game—like making a quilt you cannot force the pace—it has to be gradual and patient work and secondly the common tenet of both faiths is humanity—starting where people are, not where you expect them to be and using the offering at your disposal. Such a conference will focus on what it is to be human, what it is to live in God's world and to draw upon life in all its fullness, richness, colour and variety. It must manifest a deep reverence for God as creator, and humanity made in the image of God, with each person unique and valued. It must realise in the words of Gerard Manlcy Hopkins that the world is charged with the grandeur of God and the things of God are everywhere if we but look. 'Angelic Mayonnaise' is spread throughout creation and we must be alive to its flavour and taste. A common wealth and colour will always unite rather than divide. As Rosie Clayton, one of the six women to walk to the South Pole recently, told us here in the Royal Chapel on Friday night in her excellent slide show and talk: we are dependent on one another and for the wellbeing of the whole, we have to acknowledge strengths and weaknesses. They would assess if they were to progress. Accordingly at the end of each day they reviewed good things and bad, the clear and the obscure, the tidy and the untidy. Like the quilt, the bold colours stand side by side with the lighter colours. All is held under God, nothing is rejected or wasted. We cannot then put limits under God; the bold and the outrageous have their place, nothing is thrown out as worthless, we cannot moreover confine peoples' thoughts and fears and box them in where they have no freedom for expression.

So it is with faith. No one faith system has the monopoly; no one is emperor of truth; there is no package tour of the absolute. Truth is shared and celebrated, and as we listen to others and relate stories, so we learn a little more and are ourselves enriched. This conference has not, I hope, ignored difference or pushed it under the table. It will not, I hope, have appealed to syncretism where anything goes and all is a mish-mash. It is only when you hear the difference that you know what you are and who you are. The trouble is that we have for too long now domesticated our faith and religion and played safe within the known boundaries and structures. We have for too long seen things from a small perspective. The word 'parochial' has become too confined. Parochial actually comes from a Greek word *paroika* which means open ended and unfettered. Our borders must not be within our own perimeter: if they are, we get fenced in and become like a bird in a cage which cannot escape and dies. Faith perishes if it is enclosed. We do not want a faith with too many closures and answers. Christians, said Archbishop Michael Ramsey, are going to be tested more by questions received from outside the Church than from within. Creative life, when the real questions and issues are raised, takes place at the edge and the margin where there is not necessarily congenial agreement but strenuous honest encounter.

A group I formed in my previous London parish of multi-faith and multi-culture underlined this point. It came together with no fixed agenda where business so often obstructs reality, but where people were free to be themselves and speak from whatever tradition or faith they came from. It celebrated, like the patchwork quilt, diversity and richness. It affirmed the value of every human life as best it could, but above all it tried to express a deep concern for truthfulness. It wanted to express spirituality with a common wealth of people and faith and indeed with many of no faith. It tried to express a deep reverence for the things of God and encourage the development of a spirituality innate in everyone. As a result, we were all, I think, the richer for it.

The gospel, as Archbishop Robert Runcie says in the foreword to Bishop Kenneth Cragg's excellent book *The Christ and the Faiths*, can only be gospel when it is involved in the process of life and faith through which each religion brings forth from its treasures things both old and new. We all need to look beyond to that wider vision of God. Theology is an interactive discipline, not just a set of propositions and dogma; but a place where people meet, where imagination, emotion, energy and passion are set free and released. It is a movement from the care of the heart as much as of the mind. It is dynamic and of the Spirit. That is our common wealth of spirituality, to know its wealth and to share it. May we go forward together, each one of us, brushed with the flames of eternity with the treasure at our feet, before our very eyes. R S Thomas, in his poem *The Cry to Elisha*, talks about the negative aspect of going our own way, doing our own thing. There is a wealth of activity if we but look.

> 'I yield since no wisdom lies
> In seeking to go his way.
> A man without knowledge am I
> of the quality of his joy;
> yet living souls, a prodigious number,
> Bright-faced as dawn
> Invest God's chamber.'

Post Scriptum

Among the prayers on the day, Sunday 9 July, Canon John Ovenden included a quotation from the Holy Qur'an, which may be translated into English:

> God is our Lord and your Lord.
> We have our Ways and you have yours.
> There are no differences between us,
> and unto Him is the Homecoming.
>
> Sura 42 (Counsel), verse 14

PARTICIPANTS

Aziz Abdul-Nour, Secretary, Council of Oriental Orthodox Churches, UK

Dickson Adeyanju, Religious Affairs Correspondent, *The Guardian*, Lagos

Yousif al-Khoei, Director, Al-Khoei Foundation, London

Dr Saeed Al Shehabi, Trustee, Dar al Hekma Trust, London

Majeed Alawi-Shehab, Researcher and writer, based in London

Professor Dr Azyumardi Azra, Rektor, Institut Agama Islam Negeri Syarif Hidayatullah, Jakarta, Indonesia

Revd Dr John Azumah, Presbyterian Church of Ghana, currently at the Henry Martyn Institute, Hyderabad, India

Mavis Badawi, Chartered Psychologist and writer on Muslim and multifaith issues

Shaikh Dr M A Zaki Badawi, Director of The Muslim College, London, and Chairman of the Council of Imams and Mosques

Revd Dr Michael Barnes, Lecturer in Theology and Religion, Centre for Christianity and Interreligious Dialogue, Heythrop College, University of London

Revd Eric Beresford, Ethics and Interfaith Consultant, Anglican Church of Canada

Imam Ebrahim Bham, Hamidia Masjid, Newtown, Johannesburg and Secretary-General, Jamiatul Ulama Transvaal, South Africa

David Bone, Teacher, Morgan Academy, Dundee, representative of the Church of Scotland

Professor Gary Bouma, Department of Political and Social Inquiry, Monash University, Melbourne, Australia

Barbara Butler, Executive Secretary, Christians Aware

Rt Revd and Rt Hon Richard Chartres, Bishop of London

Very Revd Knolly Clarke, Dean of the Cathedral Church of The Holy Trinity, Port of Spain, Trinidad

Dr Barry Collett, Senior Lecturer in History, University of Melbourne, Australia

Rt Revd Kenneth Cragg, Retired Hon Assistant Bishop, Oxford

Alistair Charteris Duncan, Director, Altajir World of Islam Trust

Mrs Mariana Duncan

Dr Andreas D'Souza, Director, Henry Martyn Institute, Hyderabad, India

HRH Prince El-Hassan bin Talal of Jordan

Aser El-Saqqa, Freelance Arts Manager

Fatimah Ghani, sometime lecturer in Arabic, National University of Malaysia

Dr Ida Glaser, Tutor, Crowther Hall (CMS), Birmingham

Dr Elizabeth Harris, Secretary for Inter-faith Relations, The Methodist Church of Britain

Revd Canon David Hamid, Director of Ecumenical Affairs, Anglican Communion

Colleen Hamid, Department of Haematology, St Thomas's Hospital, London

Dato' Dr Ismail Bin Haji Ibrahim, Director General, Institut Kefahaman Islam Malaysia, Kuala Lumpur

Rt Revd Josiah Idowa-Fearon, Bishop of Kaduna, Nigeria

Revd Canon Michael Ipgrave, Inter-faith Adviser, Archbishop's Council of the Church of England

Professor Anthony H Johns, Research School of Pacific and Asian Studies, Australian National University, Canberra

Yohanni Johns, sometime Senior Lecturer, School of Asian Studies, Australian National University

Professor Ian Jones, Visiting Principal, St Catharine's Foundation, Windsor

Revd Dr Matthew Hassan Kukah, Secretary General, Catholic Secretariat of Nigeria, Lagos

Revd Canon Dr Christopher Lamb, Rector in Warwickshire and Canon Theologian of Coventry Cathedral

Tina Lamb, former teacher now involved in spiritual direction and retreat leading

Dr Philip Lewis, Interfaith Advisor to Bishop of Bradford

Peter Luff, Former Secretary-General of the Royal Commonwealth Society and Steering Committee Member

Dr Shaikh Abdul Mabud, Director-General, The Islamic Academy, Cambridge

Dr Aminah McCloud, Associate Professor of Islamic Studies, Depaul University, Chicago, USA

Nadeem Malik, Research Consultant, South Asia Partnership, Pakistan

Sir Peter Marshall, Trustee of St Catharine's Foundation, Windsor

Sir John Moberly, Chairman of the Trustees, Altajir World of Islam Trust

Lady Moberly

Dominic Moghal, Director, Christian Study Centre, Rawalpindi, Pakistan

Michael Mortimore, partner, Drylands Research, formerly of Bayero University, Kano, Nigeria

Revd Colin Morton, Focal Person, Churches Together in Britain and Ireland, Middle East Forum, Edinburgh

Carol Morton, Secretary-Treasurer, Scottish Palestinian Forum

H E Hossain Mousavian, Senior Diplomat, Ministry of Foreign Affairs, Tehran, Iran

Ghazi Musharbash, Businessman and Anglican Consultative Council Standing Committee member, Amman, Jordan

Professor Jørgen Nielson, Centre for the Study of Islam and Christian-Muslim Relations, Selly Oak Colleges, University of Birmingham

Anthony O'Mahony, Centre for Christianity and Interreligious Dialogue, Heythrop College, University of London

Revd Canon John Ovenden, Canon of Windsor, Chaplain to the Great Park and to St Catharine's

Roger Peacock, Vice President, University Development, University of Melbourne, Australia

Mahmoud Kebbeh Phoday, Executive Director, Islamic Relief Association, Gambia

Susannah Pickering-Saqqa, Senior Executive Officer, The Commonwealth Foundation

Mary Pring, Foreign and Commonwealth Office, London

Professor Merle Ricklefs, Head, Melbourne Institute of Asian Languages and Societies, Australia

Dr Peter Riddell, Director, Centre for Islamic Studies, London Bible College

Professor Neal Robinson, Director, Centre of Islamic Studies, University of Wales, Lampeter

Dr Bernard Sabella, Associate Professor of Sociology, University of Bethlehem and Executive Secretary, Department of Service to Palestinian Refugees, Middle East Council of Churches, Palestine

Dr Abdullah Saeed, Head, Arabic and Islamic Studies Program, University of Melbourne, Australia

Imam Dr Abduljalil Sajid JP, The Brighton Islamic Mission

Jamila Sajid, Chair, Sussex Muslim Ladies Circle

Mohammad Abdul Karim Saqib, Chairman, Al-Hijrah Trust, Birmingham

Dr Ataullah Siddiqui, Research Fellow, The Islamic Foundation, Markfield, Leicestershire

Dr Azzam Tamimi, Director, Institute of Islamic Political Thought, London

Revd Professor Michael Taylor, President and Chief Executive, Selly Oak Colleges, University of Birmingham

Revd Dr William Taylor, Anglican Dean of Portsmouth and former Chaplain in Amman

Dr David Thomas, Senior Lecturer, Centre for the Study of Islam and Christian-Muslim Relations, Selly Oak Colleges, University of Birmingham

Revd Albert Sundararaj Walters, Lecturer in World Religions, Seminari Theoloji Malaysia, Negeri Sembilan DK, Malaysia

Peter Willey, Interfaith Officer, Diocese of Salisbury

Dr Geoffrey Williams, Director of Studies, St Catharine's

Sandra Willson, Conference Organiser, St Catharine's

Revd Canon Dr Andrew Wingate, Director of Ministry and Training, Diocese of Leicester

Alhaji Kabiru Yusuf, Editor, *Weekly Trust*, Kaduna, Nigeria

Hajiya Bilkisu Yusuf, Vice President, Federation of Muslim Women in Nigeria and Citizens' Communications, Kaduna, Nigeria

Professor Sani Zahradeen, Bayero University, Kano, Nigeria.